Little Oxford Dictionary of **Word Origins**

Little Oxford Dictionary of
Word Origins

Julia Cresswell

OXFORD

UNIVERSITY PRESS

OXFORD
UNIVERSITY PRESS

Great Clarendon Street, Oxford, OX2 6DP,
United Kingdom

Oxford University Press is a department of the University of Oxford.
It furthers the University's objective of excellence in research, scholarship,
and education by publishing worldwide. Oxford is a registered trade mark of
Oxford University Press in the UK and in certain other countries

First Edition Published 2014

Impression: 1

Published in the United States of America by Oxford University Press
198 Madison Avenue, New York, NY 10016, United States of America

British Library Cataloguing in Publication Data

Data available

Library of Congress Control Number: 2014946126

ISBN 978–0–19–968363–5

Printed in Italy by L.E.G.O. S.p.A.

Contents

Introduction

English has always been a habitual borrower of words from other languages, unashamedly picking up anything that looks as if it might be useful and making it its own. When the Anglo-Saxons settled in Britain, around the time the Romans left, they had already borrowed a few words, such as *linen* and *pear*, from the Latin their Continental Roman neighbours spoke, but mostly they spoke a language we now call Old English. This was a Germanic language; in other words one that shared the same ancestor as German, Dutch, and the Scandinavian languages. In fact, Old English was never one unified language, for the Anglo-Saxons were a collection of different tribes from the north Atlantic seaboard, stretching from modern Denmark down to what is now Belgium. This is one of the reasons English has such a variety of dialects in a comparatively small land mass. The words we inherited from Old English form the bones of modern English, with most of the commonest words in the language—*to be*, *to get*, *and*, *of*, *this*, and *that*—as well as many everyday objects, inherited from it. Once a word has been identified as Old English, there is not usually much to say about its earlier history, except for cases where there is an interesting connection with other languages from the same root (origin) in Indo-European, the ancestral language behind most of Europe's languages. Which is not to say there is not

Introduction

plenty of interest in these words' later development, either in the Middle English of the Middle Ages, or in Modern English.

In the later Anglo-Saxon period came the Scandinavians, both as Viking raiders and as settlers, and for some time the northern part of England spoke their language, Old Norse, blended to a greater or lesser degree with Old English. Everything was then disrupted by the Norman invasion of 1066, bringing with it a new ruling elite who spoke first of all the Anglo-Norman dialect of French, and later the more fashionable Old French. At the same time the language of religion and learning was Latin. Many religious words from both Latin and Greek entered the language early on, but from the later Middle Ages onward people began to translate Latin works into English, adopting and adapting Latin and later Greek words into the language when they could find nothing suitable to use. This debt to the classics has continued to this day, with many scientific terms still being formed from classical roots.

Other Romance languages (those descended from Latin) made their contributions, but comparatively few words were adopted from Welsh and Irish and Scottish Gaelic, the other languages spoken in Britain. As British contacts expanded through the world, first through exploration, then through Empire, the language collected words from innumerable sources, including Polynesian (*tattoo*) and Hindi (*cot, chintz*). Also influential are the many Englishes now spoken outside the British Isles. Of these the most obvious is USA English, which has a significant Spanish element (*lasso, cinch*), but Canadian English and Australian (*plonk, bush telegraph*) have also made their contribution.

List of Entries

List of Entries

List of Entries

Horses
canter
jade
mare
palfrey
palomino
pillion
pony
ride
stable
steeplechase

Insults
gormless
lackadaisical
loon
ludicrous
po-faced
prude
scruff
toady
twit
wimp

Language
Babel
bombastic
cockney
gossip
idiom
jargon
laconic
palaver
syllable
waffle

Hygiene
bath
bidet
detergent
fastidious
fumigate
hygiene
lather
launder
scald
swab

Jewellery
amber
amethyst
aquamarine
brilliant
carat
emerald
ivory
jet
pearl
ruby

Law
affidavit
affray
arson
bequeath
copper
curfew
jeopardy
libel
ombudsman
reprieve

Insects
antenna
butterfly
caterpillar
cockroach
earwig
fly
insect
larva
mite
wasp

Jobs
abbot
charwoman
chauffeur
detective
guard
henchman
navvy
pundit
tailor
valet

Light
blaze
halo
incandescent
inferno
limelight
luminous
minaret
neon
tinsel
twinkle

List of Entries

Literature

anecdote
bathos
epilogue
lampoon
plagiarism
poet
rhyme
romance
story
verse

Machines

crank
damper
engine
gadget
gasket
ignition
piston
technology
valve
widget

Magic

charm
conjure
enchant
glamour
magic
sorcerer
wand
warlock
whammy
witch

Mammals

badger
deer
gopher
mammal
porcupine
rodent
shrew
squirrel
weasel
wolf

Marriage

alimony
annul
bachelor
conjugal
divorce
engage
husband
trousseau
widow
wife

Mathematics

algebra
average
calculate
computer
count
cylinder
data
digit
fraction

Medicine

cataract
disease
germ
influenza
inoculate
malaria
measles
rheumatism
surgeon
virus

Military

admiral
amok
berserk
camouflage
detonation
manoeuvre
rifle
sabotage
strafe
torpedo

Mind and Mental Health

delirium
gaga
hallucination
hysteria
melancholy
migraine
obsess
paranoia

List of Entries

List of Entries

Adventure see also CHANCE

adventure

Adventure came from Latin *advenire* 'to arrive'. In the
Middle Ages it meant 'anything that happens by chance'
or 'chance, fortune, or luck'. Gradually the idea of 'risk
or danger' became a stronger element and later evolved
into 'a dangerous or hazardous undertaking', and still
later into 'an exciting incident that happens to someone'.
Related words are **advent** 'coming, arrival' and
adventitious originally describing something happening
by chance.

audacious

Today audacious means 'willing to take surprisingly bold
risks' and 'showing a lack of respect, impudent', but it
originally had a more direct sense of 'bold, confident,
daring'. The root is Latin *audax* 'bold'.

caper

Caper was adapted from **capriole**, a movement
performed in riding in which the horse leaps from the
ground and kicks out with its hind legs. Its origin was
Italian *capriola* 'leap', based on Latin *caper* 'goat'.
Members of the Victorian underworld seem to have
been the first to use the word in the sense 'an illicit or
ridiculous activity'. In an 1867 edition of the *London
Herald* a policeman is quoted as saying: 'He'll get five

years penal for this little caper.' Edible **capers** are
something quite different—the word comes from Greek
kapparis.

challenge

Challenge was first recorded in the senses 'an accusation'
and 'to accuse'. The Latin base is *calumnia* 'false
accusation', which also gave **calumny** 'a false statement
damaging someone's reputation' in late Middle English.

chance

The ultimate source of chance is Latin *cadere* 'to fall'. In
medieval times chance meant 'an accident' as well as
'the way things happen, fortune'. There are several
stories associated with **chance your arm**, meaning 'take
a risk'. One suggests that it was used by tailors who, in
rushing the job of sewing in a sleeve, risked the stitches
coming loose. Another refers to the rank-based stripes
on the sleeve of a military uniform. Something that
broke military regulations might risk your losing your
stripes. The most colourful explanation tells of a feud
between the Irish Ormond and Kildare families in 1492.
The Earl of Ormond is said to have taken refuge in
St Patrick's cathedral in Dublin. The Earl of Kildare,
wishing to end the feud, cut a hole in the cathedral door
and put his arm through. The Earl of Ormond accepted
his offer of reconciliation and shook his hand rather than
cutting it off.

danger

From the Middle Ages into the 19th century danger meant 'jurisdiction, power', originally 'the power of a master, power to harm'. This reflects its origin, Latin *dominus* 'lord', the root which also gave us **dame**, **predominant** and **dungeon**. In the later Middle Ages danger also developed its main modern sense.

dare

Dare has deep roots, related to forms in Greek and in Sanskrit, the ancient language of India. Originally meaning 'to have the courage to do something', by the late 16th century there also existed the sense 'to challenge or defy someone', which is behind **daredevil**, a contraction of 'someone ready to dare the devil'. This sort of formation is also seen in **cut-throat** and **scarecrow**.

escape

This is from Old French *eschaper*, based on medieval Latin *ex-* 'out' and *cappa* 'cloak', with the idea of leaving your pursuer just clutching your cloak. **Escapade** comes from the same source and originally had the same meaning.

explore

This comes via French from Latin *explorare* 'search out', from *ex-* 'out' and *plorare* 'utter a cry'.

Waltzing Matilda

Australian bushmen used various women's names for
a bundle or 'swag' of personal belongings, but Matilda
is the one whose name stuck, especially after 1893
when A. B. 'Banjo' Paterson (1864–1941) wrote his
famous song 'Waltzing Matilda'. To waltz (or walk)
Matilda is to travel the roads carrying your swag. The
other woman's name forever associated with Australia
is Sheila, an Irish name that has meant 'a girl or
woman' since the 1820s.

 Anger see also EMOTION

blame

Blame is from the Old French *blamer, blasmer*, from a
popular Latin variant of ecclesiastical Latin *blasphemare*
'reproach, revile, blaspheme', from Greek *blasphēmein*,
source also of **blaspheme**.

curt

'In more temperate climes, hair is curt', wrote Sir
Thomas Herbert in his 1665 account of his travels in
Africa and Asia, reflecting curt's original meaning, 'short
or shortened'. The word comes from Latin *curtus* 'cut
short, abridged', source also of **curtail**. By the 19th
century you could use curt to describe people who were
not only brief in what they were saying, but rudely so.

grouch

The words grouch and **grudge** are variants of obsolete *grutch*, from Old French *grouchier* 'to grumble, murmur', of unknown origin. **Grouse** may be related.

peremptory

This was first used as a legal term meaning 'admitting no refusal' when used of an order or decree. It came via Anglo-Norman French from Latin *peremptorius* 'deadly, decisive', from *perimere* 'destroy, cut off'. The base elements are Latin *per-* 'completely' and *emere* 'take'.

rage

In medieval times rage could also mean 'madness'. It goes back ultimately to Latin *rabere* 'to rave', which is also the source of **rabies**, and **rabid**, of which the early sense was 'furious, madly violent'. The sense 'affected with rabies' arose in the early 19th century. Since the late 18th century something that is very popular or fashionable has been **the rage** or **all the rage**. In 1811 the poet Lord Byron wrote that he was to hear his fellow poet Samuel Taylor Coleridge, 'who is a kind of rage at present'. **Road rage** is first recorded in 1988, since when many other kinds of rage have been reported, among them **air rage**, **trolley rage** in a supermarket, and even **golf rage**.

rile

Rile 'to anger' and **roil** 'to anger or to churn' are both the same word, probably from Old French *ruiler* 'mix mortar'.

Anger

sarcasm

The words of a sarcastic person are 'biting', the idea that is behind sarcasm. It came into English in the mid 16th century from French, and is based on Greek *sarkazein* 'to tear flesh', and also 'to gnash the teeth, speak bitterly'. **Sarcophagus** has a similar history. The original Greek meant 'flesh-eating', formed from *sarx* 'flesh', the root also of **sarcoma**, and *-phagos* 'eating'. Sarcophagi were originally made of a type of stone that the ancient Greeks believed consumed the flesh of any dead body in contact with it.

sardonic

The Greek epic poet Homer, of the 8th century BC, used the word *sardanios* to describe bitter, scornful laughter. Later Greeks and Romans did not really understand the reason for this word and decided it must be *sardonios* 'Sardinian' and refer to a 'Sardinian plant' which produced facial convulsions resembling horrible laughter, usually followed by death. English adopted sardonic in the mid 17th century to refer to grimly mocking or cynical smiles, grins, and looks, as well as to laughter. The island of Sardinia also gave us the name of the **sardine**, the small fish which was once common off its shores—the Latin source of the word, *sarda*, is probably from the Greek name for the island, *Sardō*.

savage

According to the origin of the name, savages live in woods. Savage derives from Latin *silva* 'a wood', the source also of **sylvan** and perhaps of **sylph**, an imaginary spirit of the air. In the later 18th century the French writer and philosopher Jean-Jacques Rousseau (1712–78) conceived the idea of the **noble savage**, an idealized being uncorrupted by civilization and showing the natural goodness of humankind.

scold

This is probably from Old Norse *skáld* 'poet'; there may have been an intermediate sense 'lampooner'. In early use scold often referred to a woman using ribald language. The verb had gained the sense 'chide' by the early 18th century.

Appearance
see also CHARACTERISTICS, FASHION, INSULTS

chic

Adopted from French, chic, 'elegantly fashionable', is probably from German *Schick* 'skill'.

dishevelled

In the past, when no respectable person would dream of going out without a hat or similar head covering, anyone

Appearance

bare-headed would be regarded as scruffy and
dishevelled. The word comes from Old French *chevel*
'hair', from Latin *capillus*, the source also of **capillary**.
It originally meant 'having the hair uncovered', then, of
hair, 'hanging loose', before becoming 'disordered,
untidy'.

elegant

These days, someone elegant is well dressed, but the
basic idea behind the word is being discerning and
making careful choices. It comes from Old French
élégant or Latin *elegans*, from *eligere* 'to choose or select',
which was the origin of **elect**, **eligible**, and **elite**.

frump

This is probably a contraction of late Middle English
frumple 'wrinkle', from Middle Dutch *verrompelen*.
Frump originally referred to a mocking speech or action;
later as *frumps* it meant 'the sulks'; this led to the word's
use for a bad-tempered, and eventually dowdy woman.

handsome

The original sense, showing that the root word is **hand**,
was 'easy to handle or use'. In the 16th century this
developed to 'suitable' and 'apt, clever'. The current
senses 'good-looking' and 'striking, of fine quality'
followed soon after. In the proverb **handsome is as
handsome does** the original reference was to chivalrous
behaviour.

pretty

In his diary entry for 11 May 1660, Samuel Pepys
mentions 'Dr Clerke, who I found to be a very pretty
man and very knowing', meaning that the doctor was
admirable, 'a fine fellow'. This is merely one of the
many senses that pretty, which comes from a root
meaning 'trick', has had over the centuries. The earliest
was 'cunning, crafty', followed by 'clever, skilful', 'brave',
and 'admirable, pleasing', before the main modern
sense, 'attractive' appeared in the 15th century, each
individual step easily followed, even if the modern sense
is a long way from the original. Around that time the
meaning 'considerable, great' also developed, now only
found in **a pretty penny**. **Sitting pretty**, 'comfortably
placed', originally American, is first recorded in 1915.

sturdy

'Reckless, violent, rebellious, obstinate' were early
meanings of sturdy, which comes from Old French
esturdi 'stunned, dazed'. Sturdy may be based on
Latin *turdus* 'a thrush', a bird once associated with
drunkenness, probably because it was once common to
see thrushes intoxicated after eating partly fermented
grapes—a French expression *soûl comme une grive*,
means 'drunk as a thrush'.

tawdry

Tawdry was originally **tawdry lace**, a fine silk lace or
ribbon worn as a necklace in the 16th and 17th centuries,

Appearance

a contraction **St Audrey's lace**. Audrey was a
Latinized form of Etheldreda, the 7th-century patron
saint of Ely, said to have worn showy necklaces in her
youth, before she became a nun. When she became
terminally ill with a throat tumour she saw her illness
as retribution for her vanity. Tawdry laces, along with
other finery, were traditionally sold at St Etheldreda's
Fair in Ely, and their cheap quality led to the modern
use of tawdry.

ugly

Ugly came into English in the 13th century from Old
Norse *uggligr* 'to be dreaded', with a stronger meaning
than now, 'frightful, horrible'. In Hans Christian
Andersen's fairy tale the '**ugly duckling**' is a cygnet
hatched by a duck that is rejected until it turns into a
graceful swan. The tale appeared in English in a
translation of 1846, and ugly duckling was soon in use
for people. About the same time Cinderella's **ugly
sisters** came to be used for an unattractive person or
thing or an undesirable counterpart.

unkempt

People have only combed their hair since around 1400;
before that they *kembed* it and their hair would have
been **kempt**. These forms were replaced by the related
word comb, a word which may have the underlying
sense of 'tooth'. They have survived, though, sometimes
in the form kempt but especially in **unkempt**, which

has come to mean 'untidy or dishevelled' rather than 'uncombed'.

Architecture see also ART, HOME

aisle

The early spellings *ele, ile* are from Old French *ele*, from Latin *ala* 'wing'. The spelling change in the 17th century was due to confusion with **isle**; the word was also influenced by French *aile* 'wing'.

balcony

Balcony is from Italian *balcone*, based on *balco* 'a scaffold' from a Germanic root meaning 'beam'. The English word was pronounced with the stress on the second syllable until about 1825, reflecting the Italian source.

belfry

Although you will find bells (as well as bats) in a belfry, the Old English word bell is not related to belfry. A belfry was originally a movable wooden tower used in the Middle Ages by armies besieging a fortification. The word originally had an 'r' not an 'l' in the middle, and came from Old French *berfrei*. The first part probably meant 'to protect' and the second 'peace, protection'. The first belfry associated with a church was a separate bell tower: the word began to be used for a place where

the bells were hung in the middle of the 16th century.
Bell is a Germanic word. **Saved by the bell** comes
from the bell marking the end of a boxing round. **Bells
and whistles** for attractive but unnecessary extras,
particularly on computers, is an allusion to the bells and
whistles of old fairground organs.

bracket

This meaning has apparently developed via French
braguette from Spanish *bragueta* 'codpiece, bracket,
corbel'. The base is Latin *brāca*, singular of *brācae*
'breeches'; the architectural bracket may get its name
from a resemblance to the codpiece of a pair of
breeches. An erroneous connection with Latin
bracchium 'arm', because of the notion of 'support',
seems to have affected the sense development.

canopy

Conopeum, the Latin word from which canopy derives,
referred to a mosquito net over a bed. The ultimate
source is the Greek *kōnōps* 'mosquito'.

ceiling

The reason ceiling has the *-ing* ending usually associated
with action is that it was originally an action, from to
ceil meaning 'line (a room) with plaster or panelling',
perhaps from Latin *celare*, 'conceal'. The sense 'the
upper interior surface of a room', is 16th century.

garret

'Watchtower' was the first meaning recorded for garret. It comes from Old French *garite*, which (like **garrison**) is from *garir* 'to defend, provide'. The sense of a room on the top floor of a house arose early in its history, in the late 15th century.

palace

The Roman emperors had their imperial residence on the Palatine hill, one of the seven hills of Rome. The Latin name was *Palatium*, which came to refer to the emperor's home and then to any vast and luxurious building housing the powerful. Palace derives from this, as does Italian *palazzo*, a large mansion of an Italian noble family. From the 1830s lavish places of entertainment were also called palaces, as in **gin palace** for a gaudily decorated pub. **Paladin**, for a noble knight, comes from the same source: Latin *palatinus* 'palace official' became Old French *paladin* 'warrior', and was adopted into English in the late 16th century.

penthouse

A penthouse now suggests a luxurious apartment with extensive views, but originally was much more humble—a shed, outhouse, or lean-to on the outside of a building, called a *pentis*. Penthouse came from a shortening of French *apentis*, from Latin *pendere* 'to hang', the source of **appendage**, **appendix**, and

pendant. In the 16th century people began to forget its origins and associated it with French *pente* 'slope' and house. The modern sense, the top floor of a tall building, began during the 1890s in the USA. Initially these were not necessarily exclusive—the first reference to one describes it as accommodation for a janitor and his family.

spire

Old English *spīr* was a 'tall slender stem of a plant', related to German *Spier* 'tip of a blade of grass'. The word came to be used in the late 16th century for a slender structure such as a spire of rock or a church spire. **Dreaming spires** comes from Matthew Arnold, writing of Oxford in *Thyrsis* (1865) 'And that sweet city with her dreaming spires...Lovely all times she lies, lovely to-night'. Spire is unconnected with **spiral** which comes from Latin *spira* 'coil'.

 # Army see also MILITARY

adjutant

An adjutant was originally an 'assistant, helper'; the origin is Latin *adjutant-* 'being of service to', from *adjuvare* 'assist'. Adjutant now usually describes an officer assisting a senior officer with administrative matters.

battle

Along with **battalion**, **batter**, and **battery**, battle goes
back through French to Latin *battuere* 'to strike, beat',
also found in **combat** 'fight together'. Battle appears in
many phrases. We **fight a losing battle** when a struggle
is bound to end in failure; something that contributes to
success is **half the battle**.

bayonet

A bayonet first described a kind of short dagger. The
word is based on Bayonne, a town in south-west France
where these daggers were first made.

billet

A billet (from Anglo-Norman French *billette*, a little bill)
was once a short written document. In the mid 17th
century, it became a 'written order requiring a
householder to lodge the bearer of the billet'; this was
usually a soldier, hence the current meaning 'temporary
lodging for a soldier'. The early sense is preserved in the
old-fashioned **billet-doux**, French for 'sweet letter'.

bivouac

'A night watch by the whole army' was the original
meaning of bivouac. The origin is French, probably
from Swiss German *Bîwacht* 'additional guard at night',
apparently referring to a citizens' patrol giving support
to the ordinary town watch. It is said to have been

introduced into English during the Thirty Years War
(1618–48). The abbreviation **bivvy** is early 20th century.

brigadier

The no doubt respectable brigadier and the lawless
brigand are related. Both words go back to Italian *brigare*
'to contend, strive'. This gave *brigata* 'a troop, company',
which, via French, English adopted as **brigade** in the
17th century. French *brigade* also gave us brigadier.
Brigand has been around since the late Middle Ages. It
came through French from Italian *brigante* 'foot soldier',
also formed from *brigare*. Originally a brigand could be
a lightly armed irregular foot soldier.

commando

Commando was originally a word for an armed unit of
Boer horsemen in South Africa. During the Second
World War the name was adopted to describe troops
specially trained to repel the threatened German
invasion of England. The word came into English from
Portuguese, based on Latin *commandare* 'to command'
from *com-* (giving emphasis) and *mandare* 'commit,
command, entrust'. To **go commando**, to wear no
underpants, said to be common among commandos,
dates back to the 1980s and probably originated as
American college slang. It was popularized by its use in
an episode of the 1990s TV comedy *Friends*. Also from
South Africa and the same period is **commandeer** from

Afrikaans. **Command** itself came into use in Middle English, taken from the Latin via French.

major

Latin *major* means 'greater' from *magnus* 'great', a sense still found in old-fashioned schools where 'Smith major' might be used to label the older of two brothers. The military rank is found from the late 16th century, while the sense 'serious, excessive' as in a **major foul-up** dates only from the 1950s. The **mayor** of a place, the title **majesty**, and the **majority** all get their names from the same source.

sergeant

Sergeant came from Old French *sergent,* from Latin *servire* 'serve', initially meaning 'attendant, servant' and 'common soldier'. The term was later applied to specific official roles. The Middle English word **serjeant** is a variant used in legal contexts.

soldier

Soldiers get their name not because they are trained to fight but because they are paid to do so. The word entered English in the 13th century, from Old French *soldier*, from *soulde* 'pay, especially army pay'. The ultimate source is Latin *solidus*, the name of a gold coin that the Romans used. You might say **don't come** (or **play**) **the old soldier** to a person trying to use their

greater age or experience to deceive you or shirk a duty.
An old soldier, who has been around and knows all the
tricks, has been proverbial since the 1720s.

 Art see also ARCHITECTURE

art
Originally art was simply 'skill at doing something'. Its
modern sense is early 17th century. It comes from Latin
ars, from a base which meant 'to put together, join, or
fit'. Related words, showing its practical roots, include
artefact and **artifice** from Latin *arte factum* 'something
made by art'; and **artisan** from the Latin for 'instructed
in the arts'. **Art for art's sake** was the slogan of the
Aesthetic Movement, which flourished in England
during the 1880s. The Latin version, *ars gratia artis*, is the
motto of the film company MGM, and appears around
its roaring lion logo. **Art deco** was shortened from
French *art décoratif* 'decorative art', from the 1925
Exhibition title *Exposition des Arts décoratifs* in Paris.

baroque
A baroque was originally the name for an irregularly
shaped pearl, its shape reminiscent of the elaborate
detail of the architectural style. It came via French from
Portuguese *barroco*, Spanish *barrueco*, or Italian *barocco*
but the ultimate origin is unknown.

canvas

You can smoke **cannabis**, or, more legally, make canvas out of its fibre. This versatile plant, also known as **hemp** (ultimately from the same root), gives its name to the fabric, both coming from Latin *cannabis*. In the early 16th century to **canvass** meant 'toss someone in a canvas sheet', as a punishment or as part of a game. Other early meanings included 'to beat' and 'criticize severely'. This led to the idea of discussing an issue, and then proposing something for discussion. Finally, the word acquired the meaning 'to seek support, to canvass for votes' at an election.

cartoon

Cartoons were not originally meant to be funny, but were full-size drawings made on paper as a design for a painting, fresco, or tapestry. The word seems to have developed its modern sense in the 19th century; the first recorded use comes from the magazine *Punch* in 1843. Cartoon was applied to animated films in the early 20th century. The word is from Italian *cartone*, literally 'big card', from Latin *carta* or *charta*, the source of **card**. **Carton** comes from the same source, via French, as does **cartridge**, both typically made of light cardboard.

doodle

If you are a **doodler**, you may not be pleased to know that doodle's original meaning was 'a fool, a simpleton',

Art

from German *dudeltopf* or *dudeldopp*. The modern senses, 'scribble absent-mindedly' and 'a rough drawing', date from the 1930s. The Second World War **doodlebug**, or German V-1 flying bomb, may have got its name from the 1930s slang sense 'a small car or railway locomotive', or from English dialect for 'cockchafer', a large beetle which flies around slowly at dusk, making a deep hum.

easel

An easel is literally a donkey, coming into English in the 1630s from Dutch *ezel*. The use is similar to that of horse in **clothes horse**, where the load-bearing object is likened to a beast of burden.

etch

This is from Dutch *etsen*, from German *ätzen*, from a base meaning 'cause to eat'. This type of engraving is done by 'eating away' the surface of metals, glass, and stone, by the application of acid.

grotesque

Nowadays something grotesque is ugly or distorted, but when grotesque first appeared in English in the 16th century it simply described the style of painting found in a grotto, specifically the murals in ancient Roman ruins. It comes from Italian *grottesca*, used in the phrases *opera* (or *pittura*) *grottesca* 'work (painting) resembling that in a grotto'. **Grotty**, meaning 'unpleasant or unwell', source of **grot** 'dirt', comes from grotesque. It was introduced to the public in 1964 in the Beatles' film *A Hard Day's Night*. **Grotto** itself ultimately comes from Greek *kruptos* 'hidden', also the source of **crypt**.

panorama

In 1787 the painter Robert Barker invented the panorama, a spectacular method for presenting a large painting of a landscape or other scene. It was either arranged inside a cylinder and viewed from the inside, or unrolled and made to pass in front of the viewer showing the various parts in succession. The first panorama was of a view of Edinburgh. By the early 1800s it had come into wider use as 'a complete and comprehensive survey or presentation' and 'an unbroken view of the whole region surrounding an observer'. Barker formed the word from Greek *pan* 'all' and *horama* 'view'. The cinematic **pan shot** following someone or showing surroundings is a shortening of panorama.

perspective

In early use this word was a name for the science of optics. It comes from medieval Latin *perspectiva (ars)* 'science of optics', from *perspicere* 'look at closely'. The notion of perspective in drawings dates from the end of the 16th century.

Bad see also CHANCE, CRIME, GOOD

bogus

Bogus was originally an American word, which first appeared meaning an apparatus for making counterfeit coins. The source could have been **tantrabogus**, a New England word for any strange-looking apparatus or object that possibly came from **tantarabobs**, which was brought over by colonists from Devon and meant 'the devil' or from another dialect name for the devil, Bogey, which gave us **bogey** and **bogeyman**. In golf a bogey is a score of one stroke over par at a hole. Also American is the modern slang sense of bogus, 'bad', which came to a wide audience in the name of the 1991 film comedy *Bill & Ted's Bogus Journey*. It seems to have originated as a term used by young computer hackers in the 1970s for anything useless or incorrect.

cheat

This started out as a shortening of **escheat**, a legal term for the reverting of property to the state when the owner dies without heirs. As an extension of this, the word came to mean 'to confiscate', and then 'to deprive someone of something unfairly'. Finally, the senses 'to practise deception' and 'to try to get an advantage by breaking the rules' came to the fore.

corrupt

Corrupt comes from Latin *corrumpere* 'mar, bribe, destroy', from *cor-* 'altogether' and *rumpere* 'to break'. Also from *rumpere* are **disrupt** 'break apart'; **eruption** a breaking out; **interrupt** 'to break between'.

desperado

It looks like a Spanish word, but desperado is almost certainly one hundred per cent English—a pseudo-Spanish alteration of **desperate**, probably created to sound more impressive and emphatic. Between the early 17th and early 18th centuries a desperate was a desperate or reckless person, just like a desperado. An earlier meaning was 'a person in despair or in a desperate situation', which developed into 'a person made reckless by despair'. In both senses desperate is earlier than desperado, but the more exotic form ousted the original. The ultimate origin of desperate is Latin *desperare* 'to deprive of hope', the source of **despair**.

diddle

In the farce *Raising the Wind* (1803) by the Irish dramatist James Kenney, the character Jeremy Diddler constantly borrows and fails to repay small sums of money. The informal term diddle, 'to swindle or cheat', appeared soon after the play's production, and is probably testimony to the impact the character made. The name

Bad

Diddler may be based on an earlier word diddle (more often **daddle**) meaning 'to walk unsteadily'.

disaster

In a disaster the stars are against you, for this is from Italian *disastro* 'ill-starred event', from *dis-* (expressing negation) and *astro* 'star' from Latin *astrum*.

sinister

In Latin sinister meant 'left' or 'left-hand', but apart from terms in heraldry such as **bend sinister**, a broad diagonal stripe from top right to bottom left of a shield which is a supposed sign of illegitimacy, sinister in English has never meant the physical left-hand side. Instead it reflects deep-rooted prejudices against left-handedness, which had associations of evil, malice, or dishonesty.

wicked

This comes from Old English *wicca* 'witch'. Wicked is one of those words, like **bad**, which has completely reversed its meaning in the slang sense 'excellent, very good', first used in the 1920s. **No peace for the wicked** is a biblical allusion, to the Book of Isaiah: 'There is no peace, saith the Lord, unto the wicked.'

Behaviour

see also CHARACTERISTICS, EMOTIONS

aloof

Aloof was originally a nautical term for an order to steer a ship as close as possible towards the wind. It literally means 'to windward', **loof** (or **luff**) being an old term meaning 'windward direction'. The idea was that keeping the bow of the ship close to the wind kept it clear of the shore.

awkward

There used to be a word *awk*, based on an Old Norse *afugr*, that meant 'turned the wrong way round'. So awkward meant 'in an awk direction', 'in the wrong direction, in reverse order, upside down'. It could be applied, for instance, to an animal that was on its back and was unable to get up. The meaning 'clumsy or ungainly' developed in the 16th century, followed by other meanings such as 'embarrassing', or 'difficult to deal with'.

bohemian

The English novelist William Makepeace Thackeray (1811–63) was apparently the first to use bohemian to mean 'a socially unconventional person'. He took it from

Behaviour

French *bohémien*, which meant 'a person from Bohemia' (now part of the Czech Republic) and also **gypsy**. Gypsies do not originate in Bohemia but people probably called them Bohemians because that was one route by which they reached western Europe.

callous

The Latin source *callosus* means 'hard-skinned', and the word was originally used in this sense. The transference to 'insensitive to others' feelings', which happened in the late 17th century, has a parallel in **thick-skinned**. **Callus**, for hardened skin, is from the same word.

candid

'The stones came candid forth, the hue of innocence', wrote the poet John Dryden around 1700. He was using candid in its original meaning 'white', from Latin *candidus*. Over time the English word developed the senses 'pure and innocent', 'unbiased', and 'free from malice', before finally settling on 'frank'. **Candour** has a similar history, developing from 'whiteness' to the current 'openness and honesty in expression'. These days someone running for office needs to be 'whiter than white'. So did the **candidates** in Roman times, since candidate is also based on *candidus*. A *candidatus* was a white-robed person, as candidates for office were traditionally required to wear a pure white toga, meant to reflect their unstained character.

desultory

Desultory 'lacking purpose or enthusiasm' also had the literal sense 'skipping about' in early use. The source is Latin *desultorius* 'superficial' (literally 'relating to a vaulter'), from *desultor* 'vaulter', from *desilire* 'to leap'.

eccentric

Eccentric started life in the astronomical sense, meaning 'a circle or orbit not having the earth precisely in its centre', before taking on its main modern meaning of 'unconventional and slightly strange' as it were 'off centre' in the mid 17th century. It comes from Greek *ekkentros*, from *ek* 'out of' and *kentron* 'centre'.

lairy

For a century or more lairy has been Australian and New Zealand slang for 'ostentatious, flashy'. British English has adopted this use, to join an earlier, originally Cockney sense 'cunning or conceited', as well as the meaning 'aggressive, rowdy'. The word is a form of **leery**, which means 'cautious or wary' and is related to **leer** 'to look at in a lecherous way', from Old English *hleor* 'cheek'.

polite

Latin *politus* 'polished, made smooth' is the source of polite, with **polish** coming from the same root via French. Polite was originally used to mean 'polished',

with the sense of something that is carefully finished
and maintained being transferred to language and
behaviour around 1500.

valiant
Early senses included 'robust' and 'well-built'. The source
is Old French *vailant*, based on Latin *valere* 'be strong'.
The sense 'courage' came in late Middle English. The
same Latin source gives **valour** which at first referred to
'worth derived from personal qualities or rank' and later
(towards the end of the 16th century) to 'courage', and
valid. Via French *valoir* 'be worth' we also get **value**
from *valere*.

 # Birds

albatross
The spelling of albatross was influenced by Latin *albus*,
'white'. The large white seabird was originally *alcatras*,
also applied to other water birds such as pelicans (who
gave their name to the prison-island of Alcatraz in San
Francisco Bay), coming via Spanish and Portuguese
alcatraz, from Arabic *al-gattās* 'the diver'. Albatross
sometimes has negative associations from Coleridge's
Ancient Mariner (1798), in which an albatross shot by the
mariner brings disaster on the rest of the crew and long-
lasting guilt to him.

canary

The canary acquired its name from the Canary Islands
where the ancestors of our cage birds originated. The
name comes from Latin *canaria insula* meaning 'island of
dogs' from *canis* 'dog', also the source of **canine** and
kennel, one of the islands having had a large population
of dogs.

cormorant

A glossy black cormorant greedily gobbling down great
quantities of fish fits the description 'sea raven', the
meaning of the Latin *corvus marinus*, the source of the
bird's name. Since the 16th century the word has also
been used to describe an insatiably greedy person or
thing.

dodo

The large, flightless dodo found on Mauritius in the
Indian Ocean was hunted to extinction, because,
apparently, it was not afraid of humans. When people
arrived in the 16th and 17th centuries they discovered it
was very easy to catch and kill and called it dodo from
Portuguese *duodo*, 'simpleton'. By the late 17th century
the dodo had died out, hence **dead as a dodo**,
'completely dead or extinct'.

flamingo

Flamingo may be connected with **flamenco**, the Spanish
Gypsy music and dance. In Spanish *flamenco* means

Birds

'flamingo', 'flamenco', and also 'like a Gypsy', 'strong and healthy-looking', and 'Flemish'. How 'Flemish' is related is unclear; perhaps from the pink cheeks of north Europeans, or the reputation the Flemish people had in the Middle Ages for flamboyant clothing. The name of the bird was probably influenced by Latin *flamma* 'flame', from its bright pink colour.

ostrich

The first part of ostrich comes from Latin *avis* 'bird'; the second goes back to the Greek for a very different bird—*strouthos* 'sparrow'. The fuller term in ancient Greek was *megas strouthos* 'large sparrow'. It was also *strouthokamelos* or 'sparrow camel', perhaps because of its long neck. A traditional belief that hunted ostriches would bury their heads in the sand, thinking this would hide them gives us 'ostrich' for someone who refuses to face facts, and to **bury your head in the sand**.

parrot

A parrot was originally a **popinjay** from French *papingay* coming, via Spanish, from Arabic *babbaga*, perhaps an imitation of the bird's cry. The French was altered to resemble the name of the jay. Popinjay for a conceited, vain person is early 16th century. The origin of parrot may lie in the tendency to give pet birds human names. It could represent French *Pierrot*, a pet form of *Pierre* 'Peter'. **Polly**, as in 'Pretty Polly' has been used since the early 19th century, although Poll is recorded as a parrot's name in 1600. **Parakeet** may similarly be based on the Spanish name *Pedro*, also 'Peter'. Alternatively it may be from a word meaning 'little wig', referring to the bird's head plumage.

pheasant

An old name for the river Rion in European Georgia was the Phasis. The Greeks believed that the pheasant originated there, and called it the 'bird of Phasis'. The region the Phasis flowed through was called Colchis by the Greeks. The modern Latin name for the common pheasant is still *Phasianus colchicus* 'pheasant of Colchis'. The autumn-flowering crocus called **colchicum**, gets its name from the same place. It was particularly common there, and its poison is said to have been used by the legendary Colchican witch Medea.

robin

People seem to like giving birds names (see **parrot**, above). The bird known as a redbreast, from its distinctive colouring was called 'Robin Redbreast'. The nickname gradually ousted the original part of the name, and today robin is the normal term.

turkey

The turkey was brought to England by merchants from the eastern Mediterranean, whom the English called

Turkey merchants because the whole area was then part of the Turkish Ottoman Empire. The new bird was called a Turkey bird or Turkey cock. Turkeys actually came from Mexico and were first brought from there about 1520.

Body

arm

Arm meaning 'part of the body' and arm meaning 'a weapon' are different words. The former is Old English, while the latter came into medieval English from French and ultimately Latin. It is also found in **armadillo**, the Spanish for 'little armed man'; **armistice** from Latin *arma* and *stitium* 'stoppage'; and **armour** and **armature**, both from Latin *armatura* and both originally meaning armour. The phrase **long arm of the law** was first recorded in *Rob Roy* by Sir Walter Scott (1817) as 'the arm of the law'. The first example of the 'long' form is in Dickens's *The Old Curiosity Shop* (1841). The traditional story explaining **costs an arm and a leg** connects the expression with portrait painting, a pose showing arms and legs making the portrait more expensive. More likely it originates in the idea that a person's arms and legs are very precious to them. There is a similar thought behind the much older expression **give your right arm** for something.

arse

Like **bum**, arse was not originally a rude word. It dates
back to before 1000 in English, and is connected to
old Germanic forms that were probably linked
to Greek *orros* 'rump, bottom'. Arse was perfectly
respectable until the 17th century. To go **arse over tip**
(the original form, rather than tit) and **not know your
arse from your elbow** are first found in the early
20th century. **My arse!** as a derisive comment is first
recorded in the 1920s, though all these expressions are
probably older.

bowel

Old French *bouel* has given bowel in English, from Latin
botellus 'little sausage', from *hotulus*, source also of
botulism, a form of food poisoning, adopted from
German **Botulismus**, originally 'sausage poisoning'.

chest

The Greek word *kistē*, 'box or basket', is the source of
chest. It was not used for the body part until the 16th
century. **Cistern** is from the same root.

coronary

In the 17th century coronary had the meanings 'like a
crown' or 'suitable for making garlands', from Latin
corona, 'a crown or wreath'. It came to refer to blood
vessels, nerves, or ligaments that encircle part of the
body like a crown, in particular the arteries surrounding

the heart. A **coronary thrombosis**, frequently
abbreviated just to coronary, is a blood clot forming a
blockage in one of these arteries.

knuckle

In medieval times a knuckle was the rounded shape
made by a joint like the elbow or knee when bent, but
over the years it became limited to the joints of the
fingers. The word may ultimately be related to **knee**. To
knuckle down to, to concentrate on a task, comes from
a game. People playing marbles in the 18th century set
their knuckles down on the ground before shooting a
marble

midriff

The second part of midriff is Old English *hrif* 'belly',
which goes back to the same root as Latin *corpus* 'body',
the source of many English words including
corporation, one of whose meanings is 'a protruding
abdomen'.

skeleton

This is modern Latin, from the Greek *skeletos* 'dried up'.
The general sense 'supporting framework' is found from
the mid 17th century.

testicle

The ancient Romans felt that a man's testicles **testified**
that he was male. They formed the word *testiculus* from

Latin *testis* 'witness', the source also of **attest**; **detest**
which originally meant to denounce; **protest**; **testify**;
and **intestate** 'without a witnessed will'. The testicles
were the 'witnesses' of the man's virility.

thumb

Thumb is Old English. It shares an ancient root with
Latin *tumere* 'to swell', probably because the thumb is a
'fat' or 'swollen' finger. **Thimble** is formed from thumb,
in the same way that **handle** is formed from **hand**. The
expressions **thumbs up** and **thumbs down**, indicating
success or failure, hark back to Roman gladiatorial
combat. Despite what many people believe, spectators
turned their thumbs down to indicate that a beaten
gladiator had performed well and should be spared, and
up to call for his death. The reversal of the phrases'
meaning first appeared in the early 20th century. In one
of the stories from Rudyard Kipling's *Puck of Pook's Hill*
(1906), a Roman centurion facing a bleak future says to
his friend, 'We're finished men—thumbs down against
both of us.' In Shakespeare's *Macbeth* the Second
Witch says as she sees Macbeth, 'By the pricking of
my thumbs, / Something wicked this way comes.'
A sensation of pricking in the thumbs was believed to
be a foreboding of evil or trouble.

Books

see also FICTION TO WORD, LITERATURE, WRITINGS

anthology

An anthology is literally a collection of flowers. The Greek word *anthologia* (from *anthos* 'flower', source also of the botanical **anther**, and *logia* 'collection') was applied to a collection of the 'flowers' of poems by various authors chosen as especially fine.

chapter

Latin *capitulum* literally 'little head' from *caput* 'head', also meant, among other things, 'a heading, a section of writing, a division of a book'. This, via Old French *chapitre*, is the origin of our word chapter. **Chapter and verse**, an exact reference or authority for a statement, originally referred to the numbering of passages in the Bible.

encyclopedia

An encyclopedia is literally a 'circle of learning'. In ancient Greece a child was expected to receive an all-round education, an *enkuklios paideia*. It came to be spelled *enkuklopaideia* and entered English in the 1530s initially as 'general course of instruction'. The meaning 'large work of reference' appeared in 1644. The Latin-style spelling **encyclopaedia** is still sometimes used, partly because some encyclopedias, notably the

Encyclopaedia Britannica (first published in 1768), use it in their title.

index

In Latin *index* meant 'forefinger, informer, sign'. Its second part is related to *dicare* 'to make known', also the source of **indicate**. The earliest uses in English refer to the index finger. Because this is used for pointing, index came to mean 'a pointer', either physical or some piece of knowledge that points to a fact or conclusion. Because a list of topics in a book points to their location in the text, publishers and scholars gave such lists the name index in the late 16th century.

lexicon

While a **dictionary** goes back to the Latin *dicere* 'to speak', lexicon comes from Greek *lexikon (biblion)* '(book) of words', from *lexis* 'word', from *legein* 'speak'.

novel

Novel first meant 'recent', entering English in the 15th century via Old French from Latin *novellus*, from *novus*, 'new'. Novel 'a book' comes from Italian *novella (storia)* 'new (story)', also from *novellus*. The first work called a novel was *The Decameron* by Boccaccio, which we would nowadays call a collection of short stories. Novel in the modern sense was first used in the 1630s. Initially it was contrasted with romance, novels being shorter and more connected to real life.

Books

page

The page of a book goes back to Latin *pagina* 'page', from *pangere* 'to fasten'. This is probably because *pagina* was originally used of a scroll, strips of papyrus glued together, and then transferred to the page of a book. The other page is first found in the sense 'youth, male of uncouth manners' and comes via Old French from Greek *paidion* 'boy, lad' also the source of the word-element *paed-* or *ped* found in **paediatrics** 'the medical care of children', **paedophile** 'child-lover', and **pedagogue**, from the Greek words for 'child' and 'leader', the word in ancient Greece for the slave who took a child to school, but 'teacher' in Latin.

pamphlet

The anonymous 12th-century Latin love poem *Pamphilus, seu de Amore* ('Pamphilius, or About Love') was popular in the Middle Ages and translated into many languages, including English. Its popular name was *Pamphilet*, which became pamphlet and lived on long after the original poem was forgotten.

stationer

In the Middle Ages stationers sold not stationery but books. Stationer comes from medieval Latin *stationarius*, a tradesman with a shop or stall at a fixed location, not one travelling around selling their wares. The ultimate source is Latin *statio* 'standing', also the root of **stationary** with an 'a', 'not moving' and **station**.

As the bookseller's trade included selling parchment, paper, pens, and ink, booksellers became known as stationers.

thesaurus

The source of thesaurus is Greek *thēsauros* 'storehouse, treasure'. In the late 16th century a thesaurus was a dictionary or encyclopedia; the current English sense comes from the title of one of the best-known reference works, *Roget's Thesaurus of English Words and Phrases*, first published in 1852.

Business see also CHANCE AND CHANGE

asset

An asset is literally something of which you have enough. It was originally a term used in connection with paying out money from a will, and comes from the old form of the French *assez* 'enough'.

bill

During the Middle Ages a bill was any written statement or list, a sense that survives in a **clean bill of health**. The master of a ship sailing from a port where infectious diseases were common was given a certificate before leaving, confirming there was no infection on the ship or in the port. The **Old Bill** is British slang for the police.

Business

The original Old Bill was a First World War cartoon character, a grumbling Cockney soldier with a walrus moustache. The 'police' meaning, found from the 1950s, may be from the use of the cartoon character, wearing police uniform, on posters in a police recruitment campaign, and then during the Second World War giving advice on wartime security. Police officers before the Second World War often wore 'Old Bill' moustaches, perhaps another connection.

business

The main early sense of Old English *bisignis*, from the Middle Ages to the 18th century, was 'the state of being busy'. The modern senses began to develop in the later Middle Ages, and the meanings existed happily in parallel for several hundred years. Then people began to feel that a distinction needed to be made between simply being busy and having business to attend to. In the early 19th century this resulted in the form busyness, the exact equivalent of *bisignis*.

consortium

A consortium is a partnership, from the Latin *consors* 'sharing, partner', from *con* 'with' and *sors, sort-* 'lot, destiny'. **Consort** is from the same word.

cost

This is from Old French *couster*, based on Latin *constare* 'stand firm, stand at a price'.

credit

People first used credit (ultimately from Latin *credere* 'to believe, trust') to mean 'belief' and 'trustworthiness'. The modern sense developed from the idea of, say, a shopkeeper's trust that a customer will pay for goods at a later time. The earlier form of the saying **give credit where credit is due** was 'honour where honour is due', a phrase from the Bible, from the Epistle to the Romans: 'Render therefore to all their dues: tribute to whom tribute is due; custom to whom custom; fear to whom fear; honour to whom honour.'

incentive

Incentive is closely related to **incantation**, 'words said as a magic spell'. The root of both is Latin *incantare* 'to chant, charm', from *cantare* 'to sing', the source also of **chant**. In the sense 'a thing that motivates someone to do something', incentive entered English in the Middle Ages, but it took until the 1940s for incentives to be offered to workers. The first **incentive payments** were proposed in early 1940 to encourage US farmers to plant new crops.

invest

The root of invest is Latin *vestis* 'clothes', also the source of **vest**, which shares an Indo-European root with **wear**. Latin *investire* meant 'put clothes on someone', the sense of invest when it entered English in the 16th century. Being formally installed in a job or office would once have

meant ceremonially dressing in special clothing, hence the
sense 'formally confer a rank or office on someone'. The
financial sense came into English under the influence of a
related Italian word, apparently through a comparison
between putting money into various enterprises and
dressing it in a variety of clothing.

manage

Managers originally managed horses. The earliest sense
in English was 'to handle or train a horse', or put it
through the exercises of the **manège**. This French word,
used in English for 'an area in which horses and riders
are trained' and 'horsemanship', is at root the same
word—both go back through Italian to Latin *manus*
'hand'.

scheme

This was originally a term in rhetoric for 'a figure of
speech'. It comes from Latin *schema*, from Greek. An
early English sense was 'diagram of the position of
celestial objects', giving rise to 'diagram, outline', which
led to the current senses.

Chance and Change

see also ADVENTURE, BAD, BUSINESS

adjust

The notion of 'bringing in close proximity' is present in adjust. The source was obsolete French *adjuster*, from Old French *ajoster* 'to approximate', based on Latin *ad-* 'to' and *juxta* 'near', source of words such as **joust** originally to 'bring near to join in battle' and **juxtapose** 'place near'.

calamity

This is from Old French *calamite*, from Latin *calamitas* 'damage', 'disaster', 'adversity'. Latin writers thought this was from *calamus* 'straw, corn stalk', linked to damage to crops by bad weather, but this is doubtful.

change

Change comes via Old French from Latin *cambire*, 'to exchange or barter', found also in **exchange**. The ultimate origin could be Celtic, which would mean that the Romans picked up the word when they invaded the lands of the ancient Gauls and Britons.

crisis

At one time a crisis was specifically the turning point of a disease, a change leading to recovery or death, coming from Greek *krisis* 'a decision', from *krinein* 'to decide, judge' also the root of **critic**, **critical**, and **criterion**. Its more general sense 'decisive point' dates from the early 17th century. **Crisis? What crisis?** is often attributed to the British Prime Minister James Callaghan, but it was in fact coined by a headline writer in the *Sun* newspaper. Returning to London from a meeting in the Caribbean in January 1979 during the 'Winter of Discontent' when the country was plagued by strikes and economic problems, Callaghan was interviewed and said 'I don't think other people in the world would share the view there is mounting chaos.' The next day the *Sun's* headline read: 'Crisis? What Crisis?'

fortune

The Roman goddess Fortuna, who personified luck or chance, gave us the English word **fortune** and **fortuitous**. The saying **fortune favours the brave** is found in English from the late 14th century, but the idea can be traced back to classical times. The Roman poet Virgil included the line *'audentes fortuna iuvat'* or 'fortune favours the brave' in his epic poem the *Aeneid*.

haphazard

This is composed of Middle English **hap** 'luck, fortune' (from Old Norse *happ*) and **hazard**, which was initially a gambling game played with two dice in which the chances are complicated by arbitrary rules. It reached English in the Middle Ages through Arabic, Spanish, and

French, but goes right back to Persian or Turkish *zar* 'dice'. In the 16th century hazard came to mean 'a chance' and 'a risk of loss or harm'.

metamorphosis

Metamorphosis came into English via Latin from Greek *metamorphoun* 'transform, change shape'. It was introduced from the *Metamorphoses*, a large collection of verse stories by Ovid (43 BC–AD 17 or 18), about transformations of gods and mortals into objects, plants, or animals. In the 1980s **morph**, derived from metamorphosis, came to be used in computer animation for the merging of one image into another, although the idea was already familiar to young television viewers in the UK from the character of Morph, a stop-motion plasticine character created by Aardman Animations from 1977, who would mutate in the same way.

nemesis

This word for someone's or something's downfall is Greek; the literal meaning is 'retribution', from *nemein* 'give what is due'.

phase

A phase first described the changing aspect of the moon, but had developed the modern sense of a distinct period by 1701. It is from French *phase*, based on Greek *phasis* 'appearance'.

Characteristics

serendipity

The delightful word serendipity, meaning 'the occurrence of events by chance in a beneficial way', was invented by the writer and politician Horace Walpole around 1754, from Serendip, an old name for Sri Lanka. Walpole was a prolific letter writer, and he explained to one of his correspondents that he had based the word on the title of a fairy tale, *The Three Princes of Serendip*, the heroes of which 'were always making discoveries, by accidents and sagacity, of things they were not in quest of'.

Characteristics

see also ANGER, APPEARANCE, EMOTIONS, FOOLS, INSULTS

character

This goes back to Greek *kharaktēr* 'a stamping tool'. The first English sense was of a distinguishing mark made on something. By the early 16th century we find 'feature, or trait' from which the modern senses have evolved.

indolent

It now means 'lazy', but indolent was originally a medical term, referring to an ulcer or tumour that caused no pain to the patient. This reflects its root, Latin *in-* 'not' and *dolere* 'to suffer or give pain'.

indomitable

'Untameable' was the early sense, from late Latin *indomitabilis* 'not able to be tamed'.

moody

In Anglo-Saxon times if you were moody you were brave, passionate, or strong-willed. The word came from *mod* source of **mood**, which had a range of meanings including 'mind', 'thought', and 'fierceness'. From this moody developed to mean 'angry', and by the 13th century had developed the modern sense.

nonchalant

This is an English use of a French word meaning literally 'not being concerned', from the verb *nonchaloir*; the *chaloir* element is from Latin *calere* 'be warm, be roused with zeal'.

pensive

Pensive is from Old French *pensif* from *penser* 'to think': this is via Latin *pensare* 'to ponder' from *pendere* 'to weigh'. The notion is of 'weighing up' the merits of various options. **Ponder** 'to consider, weigh things up' and **ponderous** 'weighty' come from the same root. The flower name **pansy** also comes from the same source, being the English spelling of the French *pensée* 'thought'. This is because of the face-like markings on the flowers, which in old varieties looked as if they were hanging down pensively.

Characteristics

phlegmatic

According to the medieval doctrine of the four humours, an excess of phlegm made people stolidly calm. The root of **phlegm**, and so of phlegmatic, is Greek *phlegma* 'inflammation', formed from *phlegein* 'to burn'. Phlegmatic had acquired the sense 'calm and self-possessed' by the late 16th century.

posh

One of the more frequently repeated explanations of the origin of a word is the story that posh comes from the initials of 'port out, starboard home'. This is supposed to refer to the location of the more desirable cabins—on the port side on the outward trip and on the starboard side on the return—on passenger ships between Britain and India in the 19th century. Such cabins would be sheltered from the heat of the sun or benefit from cooling breezes, and so were reserved by wealthy passengers. Sadly, there is no evidence to support this neat and ingenious explanation. The P&O steamship company is supposed to have stamped tickets with the letters P.O.S.H., but no tickets like this have ever been found. A more likely explanation is that the word comes from a 19th-century slang term for a dandy, from thieves' slang for 'money'. The first recorded example of posh is from a 1915 issue of *Blackwood's Magazine*.

suave

The early sense of this was 'gracious, agreeable'. It is from Latin *suavis* 'agreeable'. The current sense dates from the mid 19th century.

supercilious

A supercilious person has an air of contemptuous superiority. One way they might show this is by raising their eyebrows in disdain—a clue to the word's origin. *Supercilium*, the Latin source of the English word, means 'eyebrow'.

Chemistry

caustic

English caustic came via Latin from Greek *kaustikos*, from *kaiein* 'to burn', also the base of **cauterize**.

chemist

Alchemy was a medieval science that looked to transform matter, particularly to convert base metals into gold or find a universal 'elixir of life'. It was the medieval equivalent of chemistry, and also the origin of the word. Alchemy came via Old French and medieval Latin from Arabic *al-kīmiyā*, which was from Greek *khēmia* 'the art of transforming metals'.

Chemistry

chrome

This metal was given its name from Greek *khrōma* 'colour', because of the brilliant colours of chromium compounds.

cobalt

Cobalt is a silvery-white magnetic metal, often found alongside deposits of silver. Cobalt comes from German *Kobalt*, a variation of the word **Kobold**, 'goblin or demon', perhaps related to **goblin**. Medieval silver miners named the metal *Kobalt* because of the trouble it caused them. They believed that cobalt was harmful both to the silver ores and to their own health, though these effects were mainly due to the arsenic and sulphur with which it was frequently combined.

corrode

The second part of corrode is the same as the first part of **rodent**—a clue to the meaning of their Latin source *rodere*. It means 'to gnaw', so when something is corroded it is gradually worn away, as if by gnawing.

element

Latin *elementum* 'principle, rudiment' is the source of element. In medieval times people thought everything was made up from four elements: earth, air, fire, and water. They also believed each kind of living creature had a natural affinity with one of the elements: mostly air and water, although the salamander, for example, supposedly lived in fire. From this idea came that of a person's natural or preferred environment, of **being in your element** if you are doing something you love. **The element** was sometimes used specifically to mean 'the sky', and **the elements** became a term for bad weather. **'Elementary, my dear Watson'**, is not actually found in any of Sir Arthur Conan Doyle's Sherlock Holmes books although Holmes did say 'My dear Watson', and 'Exactly, my dear Watson'. The famous phrase does not appear until 1915, in *P. Smith, Journalist* by P. G. Wodehouse.

gas

Gas is an invented word, coined in the 17th century by the Belgian chemist and physician Joannes Baptista van Helmont (1577–1644), the first scientist to realize that there are gases other than air and discoverer of carbon dioxide. Van Helmont based the word on Greek *khaos*, chaos. Gas for lighting or heating purposes dates from the late 18th century. The first experiments using coal-gas for lighting are said to have been made by the rector of Crofton, Dr Clayton, in about 1688; gas-lighting in its practical application was due to William Murdock (1754–1839).

mercury

Mercury was the Roman god of eloquence, skill, trading, and thieving, and the messenger of the gods. His name came from Latin *merx* 'merchandise', also source of **market**, **merchant**, and **mercenary**. In later Latin *mercurius* was also the name of the metal, liquid at room temperature, probably because the fluidity of the metal was like the rapid motion associated with the god. In English it was first called mercury in the Middle Ages—its earlier name was **quicksilver**.

metal

Metal and **mettle** were once the same. Both could refer to a physical material and a quality. In the 17th century the quality came to be 'vigour, spiriteness', originally of horses but later also of people. By the 18th century mettle was restricted to this, and metal to the material. Their ultimate origin is Greek *metallon* 'mine, quarry, metal'.

uranium

A rare radioactive metal, uranium is found in the mineral pitchblende. The German chemist Martin Klaproth isolated it and called it uranium after the planet Uranus, which the astronomer Sir William Herschel had discovered less than a decade before, in 1781.

 Childhood see also FAMILY, TOYS

boy

A boy was originally 'a male servant'; the origin is obscure. It is apparently identical to East Frisian *boy* 'young gentleman' and perhaps to Dutch *boef* 'knave'. Although boy is used positively in phrases such as **that's the boy** and **one of the boys**, the lower status persisted in its use as a form of address for summoning and giving orders to slaves or servants.

child

In Anglo-Saxon times child frequently meant a newborn baby, a sense retained in **childbirth**. In the 16th century child sometimes meant a female infant: 'A very pretty bairn. A boy or a child, I wonder?' (Shakespeare, *The Winter's Tale*). Similarly, **children should be seen and not heard** was applied originally not to children but to young women. It appears early as 1400 in the form 'A maid should be seen, but not heard'. It was not until the 19th century that children became the subject.

cot

We have the British Empire to thank for the child's cot, which started life as an Anglo-Indian word for a light bedstead from the Hindi *khāt* 'bedstead or hammock'. A less familiar cot is an old word for a small, simple cottage, nowadays used for a shelter for livestock. Closely related are **cottage**, and **cote** as in **dovecote**, though that too once meant 'cottage'.

diaper

In the USA babies wear diapers not **nappies** (from **napkin**) as in England. This is because they were originally made of diaper, a fabric woven in a repeating pattern of small diamonds. Napkins, towels, and cloths could also be diapers in Britain from the late 16th century, but napkin came to predominate in babywear. The original elements of the word are Greek *dia-* 'through, across' and *aspros* 'white', the sense being either 'white at intervals' or 'pure white'.

liquorice

Liquorice has no connection with **liquor** which comes directly from Latin, but goes back to a Greek compound formed from *glukus* 'sweet' (source of **glucose**), and *rhiza* 'root' (as in **rhizome**). Liquorice is made by evaporating the juice of the root of certain members of the pea family.

lollipop

Late 18th-century children enjoyed a particular kind of sweet that dissolved easily in the mouth. Its dialect name was a lollipop, which may come from another dialect word, *lolly* meaning 'tongue', though this is not recorded until a century later. The shortened form, **lolly**, appeared in the 19th century, and is still a general word for a sweet in Australia and New Zealand.

naughty

Today naughty generally refers to children or animals misbehaving in a fairly harmless way, but until quite recently it was stronger, meaning 'wicked' or 'morally

bad'. Naughty comes from the Old English word
naught, 'nothing', and originally meant 'possessing
nothing, poor, needy'. The sense 'mildly rude or
indecent', found in expressions such as **naughty bits**,
dates from the 16th century.

scamp

Nowadays most scamps are children but in the 18th
century a scamp was a highwayman. In the 19th century
the original sense moderated into 'a swindler, cheat', a
derogatory use still found in Caribbean English. The
word probably derives from early Dutch *schampen* 'to
slip away'. This may also be the source of **scamper**
although Italian *scampare* 'decamp' is an alternative
source. The first recorded sense was 'run away'. It was
very common between 1687 and 1700, and may have
been military slang.

urchin

An urchin was originally a hedgehog, a name, based on
Latin *hericius* 'hedgehog', still used in some English dialects.
People started calling poor, raggedly dressed children
urchins in the 16th century, though this did not become
common until over 200 years later. **Sea urchin** comes from
the original sense, referring to the spines on its shell.

waif

In the 1990s a new look became popular for fashion
models—very thin, childlike girls called waifs or

superwaifs. Waif can be traced back to medieval law, where it was a term for a piece of property found without an owner, which belonged to the lord of the manor if it was unclaimed. **Waifs and strays** was an overall term for lost property and stray animals. In the 1600s waif first referred to homeless or neglected people. Waif is from Old French *gaif*, probably from Scandinavian.

Christianity
see also HEAVEN AND HELL, RELIGION

anathema
An ecclesiastical Latin word for an 'excommunicated person, excommunication', anathema comes from the Greek word meaning 'thing dedicated', later coming to mean 'thing devoted to evil, accursed thing'.

Bible
Bible has come via Old French from ecclesiastical Latin *biblia*, from Greek *(ta) biblia* '(the) books'. The singular *biblion* was originally a diminutive of *biblos* 'papyrus, scroll', of Semitic origin. There is a link with the Eastern Mediterranean port of Byblos, which was a major exporter of papyrus to Greece. Words like **bibliography** come from the same source.

cardinal

The connection between a cardinal, 'a senior Roman
Catholic priest', and cardinal, 'fundamental, most
important', is a door hinge. The word derives from Latin
cardinalis, from *cardo* 'hinge', and its senses share the
idea of something being of pivotal importance, on
which everything else turns or depends.

carnival

Originally a carnival was the period before Lent, a time
of public merrymaking and festivities. It comes from
medieval Latin *carnelevamen* 'Shrovetide'. The base
elements of the Latin are *caro, carn-* 'flesh' and *levare* 'to
put away', before the meat-free fasting of Lent began.
The popular belief that carnival is from *carne vale*,
'farewell, meat' is mistaken. Other flesh-related words
that come from *caro/carn-* include **carnivorous**,
carnage, **carnation** (from the flower's 'fleshy' colour),
carrion, and **incarnation**.

cathedral

First used in the term **cathedral church**, a church
containing the bishop's throne, cathedral comes from
the Latin word for a seat or throne, *cathedra*, which is
also the source of **chair**. The term **ex cathedra**, meaning
'with the full authority of office', is a reference to the
authority of the pope; its literal meaning in Latin is
'from the chair'.

Christianity

catholic

This comes via Latin from Greek *katholikos* 'universal', with base elements *kata* 'in respect of ' and *holos* 'whole'. The general sense is 'all-embracing'.

chapel

The first place called a chapel was named after the holy relic preserved in it, the cape of St Martin. The Latin word *cappella*, meaning 'little cape', was applied to the building itself and eventually to any holy sanctuary. **Chaplain** is related, referring initially to an attendant entrusted with guarding the cape. The Latin form remains unchanged in the musical term **a cappella**, which means 'sung without instrumental accompaniment' but is literally 'in chapel style'.

epiphany

Epiphany is the festival commemorating the manifestation of Christ to the Gentiles as represented by the Magi or three wise men who brought gifts to the infant Jesus. It is from Greek *epiphainein* 'reveal'. An alternative Greek name for the festival is *Theophania* 'divine revelation', which lies behind the personal name Tiffany, originally given to girls born at the festival.

gospel

The Good News Bible is an English translation of the Bible, published in 1976, whose name refers to the root meaning of gospel. The word is not related to **God**, but formed from Old English *gōd* 'good' and *spel* 'news, a story'. This was a translation of Greek *euangelion* 'good news', the source of our words **evangelism** and **evangelist**. The rock musical *Godspell*, based on the Gospel of St Matthew and first produced in 1971, took its title from the original spelling of the word.

pontiff

Referring to the pope, this word is from French *pontife*, from Latin *pontifex* meaning literally 'bridge-maker' but used in ancient Rome as a term for a member of the principal college of priests. This also gives us **pontificate**. The use 'express opinions in a pompous way' dates from the early 19th century. The same *pont-* 'bridge' element is found in **pontoon**.

Classical Greece and Rome
see also GEOGRAPHY, PEOPLES

aegis

An aegis was originally a piece of armour or a shield, especially a god's. It came into English via Latin from Greek *aigis* 'shield of Zeus'. It is now often met as **under the aegis of** meaning 'under the protection of'.

Classical Greece and Rome

draconian

Draco was an Athenian Greek lawmaker of the 7th century BC, who introduced notoriously severe laws. Since the late 19th century draconian has described excessively severe laws and punishments, although **draconic** was used similarly from the early 18th century.

iris

In classical mythology Iris was the goddess of the rainbow and messenger of the gods. People saw the rainbow as a bridge or road let down from heaven for her. The Latin and Greek word *iris*, taken from her name and meaning 'rainbow', is also in **iridescent** and the element **iridium**, which forms colourful compounds. The iris in the eye appears to derive from the variety of its colours. As a flowering plant, iris dates from the late Middle Ages.

meander

The River Menderes in south-west Turkey rises in the Anatolian plateau and winds some 384 km (240 miles) to the Aegean Sea. It features in Homer's *Iliad* and was known in ancient times as the *Maeander*, its winding course giving its name to meander.

muse

People musing look thoughtful and reflective, and muse probably originally referred to facial expression, as it is related to **muzzle**. It has no connection with the Muses of classical mythology—the nine goddesses regarded as inspiring learning and the arts. The Greek form *mousa*, is also the source of **music** and **museum**. An institute called the Museum was established at Alexandria *c.*280 BC by Ptolemy I of Egypt, and became the most renowned museum in the ancient world. Museum means 'seat of the Muses, place dedicated to the Muses'.

narcissus

The narcissus, a kind of daffodil, takes its name from a handsome youth in Greek mythology. Narcissus fell so deeply in love with his own reflection in a pool that he pined away and died, but the narcissus flower sprang up on the spot. **Narcissism**, 'excessive admiration of your own physical appearance', comes from the infatuation of Narcissus with his own beauty, and seems to have been invented by the poet Samuel Taylor Coleridge in 1822, although it is particularly associated with the psychotherapist Sigmund Freud. The source of narcissus is unknown, and the Greeks probably borrowed it from an earlier language, but in the past it was associated with Greek *narkoun* 'to make numb', source of **narcotic**.

nectar

Nectar was the drink of the Classical gods. In America nectar is the usual term for a thick fruit drink. The word took on its modern meaning 'a sugary fluid in flowers' in the early 17th century. **Nectarine**, a smooth-skinned kind of peach, was originally an adjective meaning 'like nectar'.

ocean

The ancient Greeks believed the world was surrounded by a great river, which they called *ōkeanos*. Ocean originally described the body of water ('the Great Outer Sea' contrasted with the Mediterranean and other inland seas) regarded as enclosing the earth's single land mass, Europe and Asia, then the only land known. The **Mediterranean** is the sea 'in the middle of the earth' or 'enclosed by land', from Latin *medius* 'middle' and *terra* 'land'.

ostracize

Ancient Athenians would meet every year to vote on whether an unpopular citizen should be expelled for ten years. They wrote the name of the person they wanted to exile on an *ostrakon*, a shell or fragment of pottery, and somebody exiled in this way was said to have been ostracized.

tantalize

In Greek mythology Tantalus was a king of Lydia (modern-day Turkey) who killed his son Pelops, and served him in a stew to the gods. His punishment was to be forced to stand for eternity up to his chin in water which receded whenever he tried to drink it and under branches of fruit that drew back when he tried to reach them. Tantalize is based on his name. The same story is reflected in **tantalus**, a stand in which decanters of whisky, brandy, and other spirits are locked out of reach but remain visible. In the early 19th century a newly discovered metal was named **tantalum** because its inability to absorb acid was similar to Tantalus's inability to absorb water.

Clothes see also FABRIC, FASHION

anorak

The anorak comes from Greenland, from the Inupiaq language of the Inuit. The shabby anoraks traditionally worn by trainspotters and others with unfashionable preoccupations led to such people being known as **anoraks** from the early 1980s.

apron

What we call an apron was known in the Middle Ages as a *naperon*, from Old French *nape* or *nappe* 'tablecloth' (also the source of **napkin** and its shortening **nappy**). The initial 'n' got lost, as people heard 'a naperon' and misinterpreted this as 'an apron'. A similar process of 'wrong division' took place with words such as adder (see REPTILES).

Clothes

buckle

This is from Old French *bocle* 'buckle, boss', from Latin *buccula* 'cheek strap of a helmet'; from Latin *bucca* 'cheek'. The verb 'to buckle' as in buckle under a weight or strain is from French *boucler* 'to bulge'.

cap

Cap comes from Latin *cappa* 'hood', which may be related to Latin *caput* 'head'. **Cape**, 'a cloak', also comes from *cappa*, while the geographical **cape** goes back to *caput*, also source of **chaperone**, which was first recorded as a hood. The sense someone providing protection or cover by accompanying another dates from the 18th century. **If the cap fits**, **wear it** goes back to a dunce's cap, the kind poor performers at school had to wear as a mark of disgrace. Americans use **if the shoe fits**, **wear it.**

cloak

The source of cloak was Old French *cloke*, a variant of *cloche* meaning 'bell' and, because of its shape, 'cloak'. The ultimate origin is medieval Latin *clocca* 'bell' (see **clock** at TIME). **Cloak-and-dagger** is used of plotting, intrigue, and espionage. As cloak-and-sword, translating French *de cape et d'épée*, it dates from the early 19th century, originally used of stories and plays featuring intrigue or melodramatic adventure, in which the main characters tended to wear a cloak and dagger or sword. The idea is older: Chaucer wrote of the smiler with the knife beneath his cloak.

jeans

In the 15th century **jean fustian** was a kind of heavy
cotton cloth, literally 'fustian (a type of cloth) from
Genoa'. Jeans as we know them today date from
the 1860s, when Levi Strauss (1829–1902), founder of the
Levi's company, made durable denim work trousers
popular with cowboys in the Wild West. **Denim** was
originally **serge denim**, from French *serge de Nîmes* 'serge
of Nîmes'.

lingerie

The original lingerie had more practical associations
than the word has today, for it comes from the French
linge 'linen' from Latin *linum* 'flax, linen', also behind Old
English **linen**, which was probably borrowed by
Germanic people before the Anglo-Saxon invasion, and
is the source of **line** in the sense 'cover the inside of'
from the use of linen as a liner. Flax could also be made
into rope or string, and this is probably the source of the
other **line**, for a straight mark or row.

petticoat

This comes from the phrase *petty coat* which means
literally 'small coat', originally a masculine garment,
a tight-fitting undercoat worn underneath a doublet or
a padded jacket to go under armour. It seems to have
been used for a similar under-garment for women.
In the late 15th century it was fashionable for women
to wear full skirts open down the front in an inverted

Clothes

V-shape, the gap filled with a contrasting underskirt, and the term petticoat was transferred to this under-garment.

trousers

Scottish Highlanders and Irishmen once wore a *trouse* or *trouses*, a kind of knee-length shorts whose name came from Irish *triús* or Scottish Gaelic *triubhas*. The same words gave us **trews**, close-fitting tartan trousers worn by some Scottish regiments. In the early 17th century people started calling the *trouse* trousers, on the analogy of **drawers** (probably from their being things that you pull or draw on). Until the late 18th century European men wore tight breeches—looser trousers were adopted by the working classes during the French Revolution, and the style imported to Britain by dandies like Beau Brummell.

turban

The words turban and **tulip** are from the same source. Turkish people compared the flower to the shape of the turban and gave it the same name, *tūlbend*, taken from Persian *dulband*. The tulip made a spectacular impression when brought from Turkey into western Europe in the 16th century. At first forms such as *tulipan* and *tulban* existed alongside turban for the headdress, whereas the flower always appeared in the -l- form, and eventually monopolized that spelling.

Colours

beige

Beige was first used for a woollen fabric which was usually undyed and unbleached, and then used for things of a similar colour. The immediate source is French, but earlier details are unknown. **Greige**, halfway between beige and grey, appears in the 1920s.

crimson

Crimson was originally a deep red dye used in colouring fine cloth and velvet and obtained from an insect called the **kermes**, whose body was dried and ground up to produce the dye. The name of the insect and of the colour came ultimately from Arabic *qirmiz*.

green

The defining characteristic of green is that it is the colour of living plants and the word shares an earlier ancestor with **grass**. Green has long been associated with a sickly complexion, and phrases such as **green and wan** and **green and pale** were once as common as **green around the gills**. An inexperienced person has been green since the Middle Ages, in reference to the colour of unripe corn. Green has also been the colour of jealousy and envy. In *Othello* Shakespeare gave us a memorable term for jealousy, the **green-eyed monster**. A person with **green fingers** (US, a **green thumb**) is

good at growing plants. This originated as the title of a
1934 book of garden verse by the British comic writer
Reginald Arkell.

maroon

The colour maroon derives from French *marron*
'chestnut'. The earliest examples in English refer to this
lustrous reddish-brown nut, with the colour dating from
the late 18th century. The noise of a chestnut bursting in
a fire accounts for maroon for a loud, bright firework
used as a signal or warning. The Maroons were
descendants of runaway slaves living in the wilds of
Suriname and the West Indies. Their name came from
French *marron* 'feral', from Spanish *cimarrón* 'wild'. In
the early 18th century to maroon someone became to
leave them on a desolate island or coast, especially as a
punishment.

puce

This colour term is from a French word for 'flea'.

purple

Just as **crimson** is named after an insect, so purple is
named after a dye from a shellfish called *porphyra* in
Greek, the source also of the name of the purple stone
called **porphyry**. At one time purple and crimson
described the same colour. The rare and expensive dye
was used for colouring the robes of Roman emperors

and magistrates. From the late 16th century purple has been used to mean 'striking' or 'ornate' in phrases such as **purple prose** or a **purple patch**. The latter, describing an over-elaborate passage in a literary composition, is a translation of Latin *purpureus pannus* and comes from the Roman poet Horace's *Ars Poetica*: 'Works of serious purpose and grand promise often have a purple patch or two stitched on, to shine far and wide'.

scarlet

Scarlet originally referred to an expensive type of cloth. Since good strong colours, particularly a fast bright red, were expensive they were only used on high-quality cloth and the word was associated with the colour rather than the cloth by the 15th century. It is a shortening of Old French *escarlate*, from medieval Latin *scarlata*: this came via Arabic and medieval Greek from late Latin *sigillatus* 'decorated with small images', from *sigillum* 'small image', which must originally have referred to embroidered or damasked cloth. The sense 'red with shame or indignation' dates from the mid 19th century.

ultramarine

Ultramarine from Latin *ultramarinus* 'beyond the sea', originally came from lapis lazuli, a rock imported from Afghanistan that was more precious than gold. It was not until the early 18th century that a reliably fast, and much cheaper, deep blue was discovered by accident by a man called Diesbach in Berlin. This was then the capital of Prussia, so the colour became known as **Prussian blue**.

vermilion

The name for this brilliant red goes back to Latin *vermis* 'a worm', source also of **vermin**, and its variant **varmint**. The reason for the unlikely connection probably lies in the red colours **crimson** and **carmine**, which were originally extracted from the kermes insect. People mistakenly thought that vermilion also came from an insect or worm, although its main early source was in fact cinnabar, a bright red mineral.

yellow

As with other colour words such as **auburn** and **brown**, the root of yellow probably referred to a wider range of colours than the modern word. It shares an ancestor with **gold**, but is also related to **gall, bile**, and the final element of **melancholy**, all of which derive from the greenish colour of bile. The yellow egg **yolk**, which could be spelt *yelk* into the 17th century, was also related to yellow. **Jaundice** is from Old French *jaune* 'yellow', from the symptomatic yellowish complexion. Yellow is associated with cowardice, a link that began in the 1850s in the USA. Since the 1920s a coward has been **yellow-bellied**.

Computers see also MATHEMATICS

cursor

Nowadays we call the movable indicator on our
computer screen the cursor. In medieval English a cursor
was a running messenger, a borrowing of the Latin
word for 'a runner', from *currere* 'to run'. From the late
16th century cursor became the term for a sliding part of
a slide rule or other instrument, marked with a line for
pinpointing the position on a scale, the forerunner of the
computing sense.

delete

'Destroy' was the early recorded sense of delete, from
Latin *delere* 'blot out, efface'.

disk

The word **disc** goes back to Latin *discus*, source of
discus, dish and Late Middle English **desk** (*discus* had
come to be used for a stool or table in medieval Latin).
Its earliest sense in English was the seemingly flat, round
form of the sun, moon, and other celestial objects. The
anatomical disc, the sort that people 'slip', dates from
the late 19th century, as does the type that turns on a
record player. In the USA the usual spelling is disk, and
this is now used everywhere with reference to
computers, in **floppy disk** and **disk drive**.

Computers

glitch

Although nowadays a glitch can be any kind of hitch or snag, the word was originally used by US electronic engineers in the 1960s to mean 'a sudden surge of electrical current'. Astronauts began using the word to talk about any sudden malfunction of equipment. It may derive from Yiddish *glitsh* 'a slippery place'.

hack

The word hack meaning 'to cut with rough or heavy blows' goes back to ancient times. Modern computer enthusiasts have used it in the sense 'to gain unauthorized access to computer systems' since the 1980s, although **hacker** appeared earlier, in the 1970s. The sense 'to cope' as in **I can't hack it** dates from the 1950s. It has no relation to hack 'a writer or journalist producing dull, uninteresting work', which originally referred to a horse, especially one hired out and consequently often tired and overworked. It is a shortening of **hackney**, probably from Hackney in East London, where horses were once pastured. This gave us the **hackney carriage**, originally a horse-drawn vehicle plying for hire and still the official term for a taxi. The idea of tiredness and overwork continues in **hackneyed**, 'overused, unoriginal, and trite'.

modem

The term modem is a blend of modulator and demodulator.

monitor

Today's familiar uses of monitor, for a computer or
TV screen or for checking the progress or quality of
something, date only from the mid 20th century. A much
earlier sense was 'a reminder or warning', reflecting its
origin in Latin *monere* 'to warn'. A **monitor lizard** is a
large tropical lizard, in Australia also called a **goanna**
(a corruption of iguana), whose name derives from the
way its reactions can warn people of the presence of
venomous creatures. In schools from the 16th century a
monitor was a pupil responsible for supervising and
disciplining other pupils.

nerd

Originally an American term, nerd in the sense of
'boring, unfashionable person' was first recorded in 1951.
The word itself appeared the previous year in *If I Ran the
Zoo* by Dr Seuss, who seems to have invented it: 'I'll sail
to Ka-Tro / And Bring Back an It-Kutch, a Preep and a
Proo / A Nerkle, a Nerd, and a Seersucker, too!' Some
think that this is its origin, but Dr Seuss used nerd as the
name of an animal, and there is no connection with the
sense we are familiar with. Another theory links the
word with the name Mortimer Snerd, a dummy used by
the American ventriloquist Edgar Bergen in the 1930s.

robot

This is one of the few English words to have come from
Czech—from *robota* 'forced labour'. The term was

coined in Karel Čapek's play *R.U.R., or 'Rossum's
Universal Robots* (1920), when it described an artificial
man or woman.

wiki

Wiki, a web page that can be edited by users, comes
from Hawaiian *wikiwiki* 'very quick'. The WikiWikiWeb
was the first such site founded in 1995, named after the
Wiki Wiki shuttle bus that runs between Honolulu
Airport terminals. This has since been eclipsed by the
collaborative encyclopedia **Wikipedia** founded in 2001.
Wiki is sometimes explained as from 'What I Know Is'
but this is what has been christened a backronym—an
acronym formed to explain an extant word.

 # Crime see also BAD, DEATH, LAW, PUNISHMENT

alibi

Alibi is recorded from the late 17th century, in the sense
'elsewhere', and was originally a Latin word with the
same meaning and spelling. A typical example of its use
comes from John Arbuthnot's *History of John Bull* (1727):
'The prisoner had little to say in his defence; he
endeavoured to prove himself Alibi.' The noun use,
'evidence that a person was elsewhere when a crime was
committed', dates from the 18th century. The weakened
sense of 'excuse' is early 20th century.

blackmail

Blackmail was originally a protection racket. Scottish chiefs in the 16th century exacted tribute from farmers and small landowners in the border counties of England and Scotland, and along the Highland border. The money was in return for protection or immunity from plunder. The second part of the word means 'tribute, rent' and comes from an old Scandinavian word *mál*, meaning 'speech, agreement'. Black may have been a joke on white money, the silver coins in which legitimate rents were paid.

contraband

This is from Spanish *contrabanda* 'smuggling', adopted from Italian *contrabando* 'unlawful dealing', from *contra-* 'against' and *bando* 'proclamation, ban'.

culprit

Formerly, in England, when a prisoner pleaded not guilty the Clerk of the Crown said: 'Culprit, how will you be tried?' This expression, first recorded in 1678, may have started out as a mistake in reading the written abbreviation *cul. prist.*, standing for Old French *Culpable: prest d'averrer notre bille*, '(You are) guilty: (We are) ready to prove our indictment.' *Cul prit* (later culprit) came to mean 'a guilty person'. Use may have been influenced by **culpable** which comes from Latin *culpa* 'fault, blame'.

Crime

mafia

The first printed reference to the Mafia dates from 1866. The secret criminal society started in Sicily where *mafia* meant 'bragging'. Other communities harboured similar organizations: a **Chinese mafia** is reported in California in 1891 and a **Russian mafia** in 1903. By the 1940s any group regarded as exerting a secret and sinister influence could be a mafia.

mayhem

Between the 15th and 19th centuries mayhem was a crime which involved maiming a person so that they could no longer defend themselves. It is a form of **maim**, which came through French but whose ultimate origin is unknown. The modern sense 'violent or extreme disorder' originated in the USA in the 19th century.

murder

The ancient root of murder is shared by Latin *mors* 'death', from which **mortal** and **mortuary** also derive. In his *Canterbury Tales* Geoffrey Chaucer wrote 'Murder will out'. The idea is older, but his concise way of expressing it ensured it became proverbial. From the 18th century blue was thought of as the colour of harmful things, and someone being attacked would **cry** or **scream blue murder** to emphasize their plight.

poison

In early use poison meant a drink or medicine, specifically a potion with a harmful or dangerous ingredient. The source was Old French *poison* 'magic potion', from Latin *potio*, also the source of **potion**. **One man's meat is another man's poison** was being described as long ago as 1604 as 'that old moth-eaten proverb'. A similar idea is found in the work of the Roman poet and philosopher Lucretius (*c.*94–55 BC): 'What is food to one person may be bitter poison to others.' A **chalice** from Latin *calix*, 'cup', (also the source of the botanical **calix**) is a large cup or goblet, and **a poisoned chalice** something that seems attractive but is likely to be a source of problems. A poisoned chalice features in Shakespeare's *Macbeth*, and is the source of our expression.

ransack

This is a word still very close to its original 14th-century sense. The Old Norse word *rannsaka* from which it comes, made up of *rann* 'house' and a second element related to 'seek', was a legal term referring to the searching of property for stolen goods.

rape

This originally meant the violent seizure of property, and later the carrying off of a woman by force. It comes via Anglo-Norman French from Latin *rapere* 'seize', also

the source of the word **rapacious**, **rapid**, and also **rapt**
and **rapture**, when you are carried away by your feelings.
In Old French *rapere* was changed to *ravir*, source of
ravish. The plant name, rape, originally referred to the
turnip, from Latin *rapum, rapa* 'turnip'.

Death see also CRIME

autopsy

In an autopsy someone seeks to find out how a person died by seeing the body with their own eyes. An early sense was 'personal observation', and this is the key to the word's origin. It comes from Greek *autoptēs* 'eyewitness', based on *autos* 'self' and *optos* 'seen', which means it is related to other English words such as **optic** and **optician**.

cemetery

A cemetery is literally a place for sleeping. The word came from Greek *koimētērion*, 'dormitory', from *koiman* 'to put to sleep'. Early Christian writers first gave it the meaning of 'burial ground', applying it to the underground cemeteries or catacombs in Rome.

coffin

Coffin comes from the Old French word *cofin* meaning 'a little basket', and in medieval English could refer to a chest, casket, or even a pie. The sense 'a box in which a dead body is buried or cremated' dates from the early 16th century. **Coffer** is closely related, both words coming from Greek *kophinos* 'basket'.

Death

corpse

At one time corpses did not have to be dead. Until the early 18th century a corpse (from Latin *corpus* 'body') could be the living body of a person or animal, as in 'We often see…a fair and beautiful corpse but a foul and ugly mind' (Thomas Walkington, 1607). You would need to specify 'a dead corpse' if you were talking about a dead body. In time, you could simply say 'a corpse' and people would assume that you meant a dead person. The 'p' used to be silent and the final 'e' was rare before the 19th century. In fact, corpse and **corps**, 'a division of an army' are basically the same word. A **corporal** is in charge of a 'body' of troops.

epitaph

Old French *epitaphe* came via Latin from Greek *epitaphion* 'funeral oration', from *ephitaphios* 'over or at a tomb', from *epi* 'upon' and *taphos* 'tomb'.

exterminate

This is from Latin 'drive out, banish', from *ex-* 'out' and *terminus* 'boundary'. This was the sense used when the word entered English. The sense 'destroy' comes from the Latin of the Vulgate Bible.

extinct

The early recorded sense of this was 'no longer alight', from Latin *exstinguere* 'to **extinguish**'. Extinct for species of animals that have died out is late 17th century.

massacre

This is from French, from Old French *macecre* 'slaughterhouse, butcher's shop'.

mortuary

In the Middle Ages a mortuary was a gift claimed by a parish priest from a deceased person's estate. The word derives from Latin *mortuus* 'dead', the source also of **mortgage**, literally a 'dead pledge' because the debt dies when the pledge is redeemed; and **mortify** 'deaden', and related to **murder**. The current sense, 'a room or building in which dead bodies are kept', dates from the mid 19th century. In Paris the bodies of people found dead were formerly taken to a building at the eastern end of the Île de la Cité, where they were kept until identified. It was called the Morgue (from a French word for haughtiness or sad expression). By the 1830s **morgue** was being used in English for other mortuaries; a use the French borrowed back from English in the 1940s.

shroud

Late Old English *scrūd* meant 'garment, clothing' and is from a Germanic source from a base meaning 'cut'; **shred** is related. An early sense of to shroud in Middle English was 'cover so as to protect'. Use for the sheet in which a corpse is laid out dates from the late 16th century.

Dirt

crap

Crap is related to Dutch *krappe*, from *krappen* 'pluck or cut off ', and perhaps also to Old French *crappe* 'siftings', and Anglo-Latin *crappa* 'chaff'. The original sense was 'chaff', and later 'residue from rendering fat' and 'dregs of beer'. Current senses meaning 'something of poor quality', 'rubbish', 'nonsense', 'excrement', date from the late 19th century and share the notion of 'rejected matter'.

defecate

This originally meant 'clear of dregs, purify' from Latin *defaecare*, formed from *de-* (expressing removal) and *faex, faec-* 'dregs'. The current sense dates from the 19th century.

dirt

The origin of dirt is old Scandinavian *drit* 'excrement'. In its earliest uses the English word retained both the meaning and the form, but gradually dirt replaced *drit*. Its history parallels that of bird (earlier *brid*). By the time **dirty** appeared in the later Middle Ages, dirt appears to have been the only form in use. The sense 'obscene, pornographic, smutty' dates from the 16th century, though familiar phrases such as **dirty joke** and **dirty weekend** are first recorded in the 20th.

dust

Dust is related to Dutch *duist* 'chaff, meal dust, bran',
and the ancient meaning appears to have been
'material that rises in a cloud of smoke'. Various
biblical uses of dust have settled in the language.
Shake the dust off your feet derives from the Gospel
of Matthew: 'And whosoever shall not receive you, nor
hear your words, when ye depart out of that house or
city, shake off the dust of your feet.' **Dust and ashes**,
for a sense of disappointment or disillusion, is found
in Genesis and Job. It refers to the legend of the
Sodom apple or Dead Sea fruit, whose attractive
appearance tempted people, but which tasted only of
dust and ashes when eaten. A **dusty answer**, a curt
and unhelpful reply, comes from the 1862 poem
'Modern Love' by George Meredith: 'Ah, what a dusty
answer gets the soul / When hot for certainties in
this our life!'

foul

The Old English word foul comes from an ancient root
shared by Latin **pus** (adopted into medieval English),
and Latin *putere* 'to stink' (source of **putrid**). The
original sense was 'stinking or disgusting'. **Foul play**,
unfair conduct or treachery, is recorded from the late
16th century, and sports players have been able to
complain of **a foul** since the 1750s.

Dirt

grunge

In the 1990s grunge became the term for a style of rock music in which the guitar is played raucously and the lyrics delivered in a lazy vocal style. Before then it was used to mean 'grime or dirt'. It was formed from **grungy**, a word coined in the 1960s, probably by blending **grubby** (from the state you get in when you **grub** or dig) and **dingy** (an 18th century word of unknown origin, but perhaps related to **dung**).

gunk

This was originally a US usage and came from the proprietary name of a detergent.

puke

This is probably imitative and was first recorded in Shakespeare's *As You Like It:* 'At first the infant, mewling, and puking in the nurse's arms'.

reek

We think of a reek as an unpleasant smell, but in Old English it meant 'smoke'. This gave us the traditional name, used since at least the early 19th century, of **Auld Reekie** ('Old Smoky') for Edinburgh.

trash

Popular culture is often called **trashy**, which goes right back to the beginnings of trash's history—one of the first things that it referred to was bad literature. Trash was originally various kinds of refuse, including cuttings from a hedge. Domestic refuse became trash at the beginning of the 20th century. People have called others trash since the early 17th century—Shakespeare wrote in *Othello* 'I do suspect this trash / To be a party in this injury'; and in the USA **white trash** is a derogatory term for poor white people living in the southern states. The verb is first recorded in the 18th century in the sense 'strip (sugar canes) of their outer leaves to encourage faster ripening'; the other senses ('vandalize', 'impair the quality of something') date from the 20th century.

Drink

alcohol

Arabic *al-kuhl* gave us the modern English word alcohol, but there were several changes in meaning along the way. *Al* in Arabic means 'the', and *al-kuhl* means 'the kohl', referring to a powder used as eye make-up. By extension, the term was applied to a fine powder and then to a liquid essence or spirit obtained by distillation.

beer

The ancestor of beer came from monastic Latin term *biber* 'a drink', from Latin *bibere* 'to drink', also behind

Drink

beverage, **bibulous**, and **imbibe**. Although beer appears in Old English, it was not common before the 16th century, the usual word in earlier times being **ale**, which now refers to a drink made without hops. The late 16th-century proverb 'Turkey, heresy, hops, and beer came into England all in one year' reflects the difference. Ale continues to be applied to paler kinds of liquors for which the malt has not been roasted. Some areas still use beer and ale interchangeably.

binge

Binge drinking is generally thought of as a modern problem, but the word binge has been around since at least the 1850s. It was originally a dialect term in the English Midlands, first meaning 'to wash or soak', which was taken up by boozy students at Oxford University.

booze

People have been boozing for a long time. The spelling booze dates from the 18th century, but as *bouse* the word entered English in the 13th century, probably from Dutch. We have been going to the **boozer**, or pub, since the 1890s.

carafe

Adopted via French from Italian *caraffa*, carafe is probably based on Arabic *garafa* 'draw water'.

cider

Cider goes back to Greek *sikera*, a word used by Christian writers to translate Hebrew *sēkār*, which meant 'strong drink'.

grog

This word for alcoholic drink is said to be from **Old Grog**, the reputed nickname (given to him because of his grogram cloak) of Admiral Vernon (1684–1757): in 1740 he first ordered diluted rum to be served out to sailors instead of the traditional neat rum. **Grogram** was a heavy fabric which got its name from French *gros grain* 'course grain', also found in the name of the lighter silk fabric **grosgrain**.

plonk

There are two different plonks. One, as in 'to plonk something down', was originally a northern English word meaning 'to hit or strike with a heavy thud', and probably comes from the sound. The other plonk, describing cheap wine, started out in Australia. It is probably humorous form of *blanc* in the French phrase *vin blanc* 'white wine', though some suggest that it might be meant to imitate the sound of a cork being taken out of a bottle. **Plonker**, meaning 'idiot', dates from the 1960s but was popularized by the 1980s BBC television sitcom *Only Fools and Horses*. It is based on the first plonk and was first used to mean 'something large or substantial' and also 'penis'.

Drink

toddy

Some palm trees have a sugary sap that is drunk in parts of Africa, South India, and the Philippines, especially when fermented into an alcoholic drink. This was the original toddy. The word comes from the Indian languages Hindi and Marathi, and goes back to a Sanskrit name for an Asian palm, the palmyra. Travellers brought it back to the colder climate of Britain, and the hot toddy of whisky or some other spirit with hot water, sugar, and spices has soothed many a cold since the late 18th century.

vodka

The name of the clear, strong alcoholic spirit claims that it is just 'water'—it is a diminutive form of Russian *voda* 'water'. Travellers to Russia brought the word back to Britain in the early 19th century.

Emotions

see also ANGER, CHARACTERISTICS, FEAR, HAPPY,
HORROR, MIND AND MENTAL HEALTH, SAD, SENSATIONS

disgruntled

Disgruntled people go round muttering and
complaining. Originally the word involved comparison
with a pig making small or subdued **grunts** (an Old
English word probably imitating the sound). The main
element is **gruntle**, a dialect word used of pigs from the
Middle Ages and of grumbling people from a little later.
In the 17th century someone added *dis-* as an intensifier.
In the 20th century the comic novelist P. G. Wodehouse
(1881–1975) removed the dis- again and introduced the
humorous **gruntled**, 'pleased'. In *The Code of the
Woosters* (1938) he wrote: 'I could see that, if not actually
disgruntled, he was far from being gruntled.'

embarrass

Although it came into English from French, embarrass
was probably based on Portuguese *baraço* 'halter'. The
first English sense was 'encumber or impede'. Notions
of difficulty or problems led to the use of embarrassed
to mean 'in difficulties through lack of money', as in
financially embarrassed. The familiar modern meaning
was not recorded until the early 19th century.

Emotions

emotion

The modern meaning of emotion is surprisingly recent
and very different from its original sense. In the
16th century it first meant 'a public disturbance or
commotion'. The root is Latin *movere*, 'to move', and the
second sense was 'a movement or migration'. The main
current meaning of 'a strong feeling' was not used in
writing until the early 1800s. The **emoticon**, a blend of
emotion and **icon** dates from the 1990s.

exasperate

Exasperate is from Latin *exasperare* 'irritate to anger',
based on *asper* 'rough'.

jealous

This comes via Old French *gelos* and medieval Latin
zelosus from Greek *zelos*, also the source of **zeal**.

livid

First recorded meaning 'a bluish leaden colour', livid
comes from Latin *lividus*, from *livere* 'be bluish'. It was
often used to describe the skin of someone cold or very
ill. The sense 'furiously angry' dates from the early
20th century.

malice

Malice goes back to Latin *malus* 'bad', source also of
malign, **malaise**, and the first part of **malevolent**, the

second half being from Latin *velle* 'to wish'. Since the 15th century malice has been a legal term, found especially in **malice aforethought**, the intention to kill or harm which distinguishes murder from manslaughter.

peace

Peace is from Old French *pais*, from Latin *pax* 'peace'. **No peace for the wicked** comes from Isaiah 48:22 ('There is no peace, saith the Lord, unto the wicked.'). In legal texts, **pacific**, from the same root, retains its early meaning 'free from strife, peaceful'. In 1520 the Portuguese explorer Ferdinand Magellan passed through the stormy waters of the strait between what is now Tierra Del Fuego and mainland Chile. He emerged to calm seas, so called the ocean *Mar Pacifico* 'tranquil sea'. The treacherous sound he passed through is still the Strait of Magellan. **Pacify** and **pacifism** go back to the same root, as does **appease**, literally 'bring to a peaceful state'.

pride

In Old English *pryde* was 'excessive self-esteem', and from medieval times pride was the first of the Seven Deadly Sins. **Pride goes** (or **comes**) **before a fall** is a version of a sentence from the biblical Book of Proverbs: 'Pride goeth before destruction, and an haughty spirit before a fall.' **Pride of place** is from falconry, referring to the height from which a falcon swoops down on its prey. It is

first recorded in Shakespeare's play *Macbeth*, suggesting
the natural order of things has been reversed following
the killing of Duncan: 'A falcon, tow'ring in her pride of
place, / Was by a mousing owl hawk'd at and kill'd.' Your
pride and joy is recorded only from the beginning of
the 20th century, but since the Middle Ages something
a person is very proud of has been their 'pride'. **Pride
and joy** may have been suggested by Sir Walter Scott's
poem *Rokeby* (1813): 'See yon pale stripling! when a
boy, / A mother's pride, a father's joy!'

resent

Resent comes from obsolete French *resentir*, from *re-*
serving as an intensifier and *sentir* 'to feel', from Latin
sentire. The early sense was 'experience (an emotion or
sensation)' which later developed into 'feel deeply',
giving rise to 'feel aggrieved by'.

 # Entertainment
see also GAMES, MUSIC, SONG, SPORT, THEATRE

acrobat

The earliest acrobats were tightrope walkers, which
explains why the word derives from Greek *akrobatos*,
'walking on tiptoe'. The *akro-* part of *akrobatos* meant
'tip, end, summit' found in several other English words.
The fortified **acropolis** of a Greek city, most famously

Athens, was usually built on a hill. **Acrophobia** is fear of heights. An **acronym** is a word formed from the initial letters of other words, and an **acrostic** is a poem or puzzle where the first letters in each line form words.

arena

Roman amphitheatres, used for staging gladiatorial combats and other violent spectacles, were strewn with sand to soak up the blood spilled by the combatants. The word for 'sand' in Latin was *harena* or *arena*, and this came to be applied to the whole amphitheatre.

audience

We generally talk about going to 'see' a play, but in former times the usual verb was 'hear'. The oldest meaning of audience is 'hearing, attention to what is spoken', based on the Latin word *audire* 'to hear' also found in **audible**, 'able to be heard'. An **auditorium**, originally a Latin word, was a place for hearing something and an **audition** was the act of hearing or listening. And an **audit** was originally a hearing, in particular a judicial hearing of some kind—it was later used as the term for the reading out of a set of accounts, hence the modern meaning.

cabaret

Samuel Pepys wrote in his diary, 'In most cabaretts in France they have writ upon the walls *"Dieu te regarde"* ['God is watching you'], as a good lesson to be in every man's mind'. He was referring to French inns, the meaning of cabaret in the 17th century. The modern sense of entertainment in a nightclub dates from before the First World War. Cabaret is from the Old French for 'shed'.

couch potato

This phrase for someone who spends all day sitting in front of the television was coined in the US around 1976. It is actually a more ingenious expression than it might seem: a potato is a type of tuber, and the slang term **boob tuber** was used at the time to refer to someone who was addicted to the **boob tube** or television. Couch is Middle English and comes via Old French from Latin *collocare* 'lay in place'.

entertain

This is based on Latin *inter* 'among' and *tenere* 'to hold'. It originally meant 'maintain, continue'. In the late 15th century it developed into 'maintain in a certain condition, treat in a certain way'. The meaning 'show hospitality' developed from this in the same period. The noun **entertainment** dates from the early 16th century; its use for a public performance is early 18th century.

jukebox

In the USA a juke was a nightclub or bar that provided food, drinks, and music for dancing. The word was based on a term from the Creole language of the Gullah, an African-American people living on the coast of South Carolina and nearby islands. In their language juke meant 'disorderly'.

television

Television was first demonstrated in 1926 by the Scottish inventor John Logie Baird, but the word was thought up before the design was perfected, in 1907. The first part of television means 'at a distance', and comes ultimately from Greek *tēle* 'far off'. The second part goes back to Latin *videre* 'to see'. C. P. Scott, editor of the *Manchester Guardian* from 1872 to 1929, was unhappy about the formation: 'Television? The word is half Greek, half Latin. No good can come of it.' It was first shortened to **TV** just after the Second World War.

ticket

This is a shortening of an Old French word *estiquette*, also the origin of **etiquette**. A ticket was originally a 'short written note' and 'a licence or permit'—the use for a piece of paper or card giving admission or permission to travel is late 17th century.

tutu

The female ballerina's costume gets its name from the French nursery. In French *tutu* is a child's alteration of *cucu*, an informal term for the bottom, from *cul*

Entertainment

'buttocks'. The outfit originally referred to was the short classical tutu, with a skirt projecting horizontally from the waist. The **leotard** sometimes worn by dancers gets its name from that of the French trapeze artist Jules Léotard (1830–1870).

Fabric see also CLOTHES, FASHION

chenille

This term for a tufty velvety yarn is from a French word meaning 'hairy caterpillar', from Latin *canicula* 'small dog', the connection being the fur of all three.

chiffon

Chiffon was originally used in the plural, for trimmings or ornaments on a woman's dress. It is from French, from *chiffe* 'rag'.

chintz

Chintz was originally a painted or stained calico imported from India. The source was the Hindi *chīnt*, literally 'spattering, stain', which in English became *chint*. The plural of this unfamiliar word, being more frequently used, came to be mistaken for a singular and written *chints* and eventually chintz. **Chintzy** means 'resembling or decorated with chintz' in British English, but in America means both 'cheap, of poor quality' and 'miserly, mean'.

ermine

This is from Old French *hermine*, probably from medieval Latin *(mus) Armenius* 'Armenian (mouse)'. White ermine fur is the winter coat of the common weasel, and it needs dependable snowfall, such as is found in Armenia, for the coat to turn white.

Fabric

fabric

Fabric comes from Latin *fabrica* 'something skilfully produced'. A fabric was originally 'a building', and then 'a machine or appliance' and 'something made', which led to the main current meaning 'cloth, textile'. The related **fabricate** originally meant 'to manufacture, construct', but towards the end of the 18th century began to be used in the sense 'make up facts that are not true'.

flannel

Ever since the Middle Ages we have worn flannel, which probably comes from Welsh, from the word *gwlân* 'wool'. In 1920s the sense of 'bland, vague talk used to avoid a difficult subject' developed from the idea of soft, warm fabric—it seems to have started as military slang.

lace

This comes from Latin *laqueus* 'noose' also found as an early sense in English and still the basic sense of the Spanish-American equivalent, **lasso**. The fine openwork fabric of looping threads was called lace from the middle of the 16th century. The verb lace, 'fortify, flavour' as in to **lace a drink**, is from the late 17th century. **Lacerate** is unrelated, coming from Latin *lacerare* 'to mangle, tear'.

satin

Satin came via Old French from Arabic *zaytūnī* 'of Tsinkiang', a town in China. In the past satin was a silk fabric and China the main and at one time only source of silk. Late 19th-century **sateen** is an alteration of satin, on the pattern of velveteen.

tweed

Tweed was originally produced in Scotland, where it was called *tweel*, a Scots form of **twill**, a word based on **two** and like **twine** indicating two-ply yarn. Around 1830 a cloth merchant misread this as tweed, a mistake perpetuated by association with the River Tweed, on the border between England and Scotland. Tweed is traditionally worn by the English country gentry, and **tweedy** has been used since the early 20th century to suggest a robust, traditional kind of Englishness.

velvet

Velvet is noted for its smoothness and softness. Latin *villus*, 'tuft, down', is the source of it and of **velour**. An **iron fist in a velvet glove**, 'firmness or ruthlessness cloaked in outward gentleness', has been current in English since the 1830s when it appeared as a saying of Napoleon's. People gave the name **velvet revolution** to the relatively smooth change from Communism to a Western-style democracy in Czechoslovakia at the end of 1989. The similarly trouble-free division of Czechoslovakia into Slovakia and the Czech Republic in 1992 was the **velvet divorce**.

Family see also CHILDHOOD, MARRIAGE

bastard

Bastard probably derives from medieval Latin *bastum* 'packsaddle' (a saddle adapted for loads); the French equivalent was *fils de bast* or 'packsaddle son'. The reference was to a loose-living mule driver who used a packsaddle for a pillow and the next morning was off to the next town.

clan

Clan is from Scottish Gaelic *clann* 'offspring, family', from Old Irish *cland*, derived from Latin *planta* 'sprout'.

cousin

Cousin comes via Old French *cosin*, from Latin *consobrinus* 'mother's sister's child'. By the time the word entered English it could be used for the child of an aunt or uncle. It came to be used of any relative more distant than your brother or sister, particularly in the past to a nephew or niece: 'How now brother, where is my cosen, your son?' (Shakespeare, *Much Ado About Nothing*).

family

Someone's family was originally the servants of their household. It then came to be 'all the people who live in one house, including parents, children, and servants', before it settled on its modern meaning. The word is from Latin *famulus* 'household servant', as is **familiar**. Family is also used, chiefly in the US, as a slang term for the members of a local unit of the Mafia; a use popularized in the 1972 film *The Godfather*. The phrase **in the family way** meaning 'pregnant' dates from the late 18th century, but was in use earlier meaning 'in a domestic way, in a domestic setting'.

infant

This is from Latin *in-* 'not' and *fari* 'to speak'. According to law, an infant is someone who has not reached the age of legal majority, so is unable to speak for themselves in law. The Italian equivalent *infante* meant 'youth' and also 'foot soldier', from which arose *infanteria*, a body of foot soldiers. English adopted this as **infantry** in the late 16th century.

kid

Kid for a young person developed in the 19th century, but probably looks back to late 17th-century slang use to mean a baby or young child. The verb **kidnap**—its second syllable a slang word, **nap**, meaning 'to take or seize'—originally referred to the 17th-century practice of stealing children to provide servants or labourers for the new American plantations. Young goats are traditionally a source of soft pliable leather for fine gloves, which gave **handle with kid gloves** 'to deal very tactfully and gently with'.

Family

lass

The word lass is based on the Old Norse feminine adjective *laskura* 'unmarried'.

maiden

The ancient root of maiden is also that of Scottish and Irish Gaelic **mac** 'son', the element in surnames beginning Mac- or Mc-, and seems to have referred to a young person of either sex. In the Middle Ages maiden was also shortened to **maid**, both meaning 'a young female' and 'a virgin of any age', and also 'a female servant', for which maid is now the usual term. This ambiguity led to words and phrases such as **girl** or **young lady** replacing maiden and maid in the 'young female' sense.

nephew

A nephew could originally also be a grandson—the word coming via Old French *neveu* from Latin *nepos* 'nephew, grandson'. **Nepotism**, favouritism towards friends or relations, also comes from *nepos*, referring to the privileged treatment formerly given to the 'nephews' of popes, who were often their illegitimate sons. **Niece** comes from Latin *neptis* the feminine of *nepos*.

tribe

In the early days of ancient Rome the people fell into three political divisions. This division into 'three' (*tri-* in

Latin) may be the origin of *tribus*, from which tribe
descended, along with **tribunal**, **tribune**, **tribute**, and
retribution 'paying back'. In English tribe initially
referred to the twelve ancient tribes of Israel claiming
descent from the sons of Jacob. From tribute comes
tributary, found from the 15th century for someone
paying tribute. The sense of a smaller river adding its
contribution to a bigger developed from this in the early
19th century.

Fashion see also CLOTHES, FABRIC, SHOPPING

bigwig

Important people in the 17th and 18th centuries wore
large wigs that came down to their shoulders. These
were the original 'big wigs'. In Britain this headdress can
still be worn by judges, the Lord Chancellor, and the
Speaker of the House of Commons. In the 18th century
bigwig began to refer to the person wearing the wig, and
the word outlived the fashion.

bikini

In 1946 the USA exploded an atom bomb at Bikini,
an atoll in the Marshall Islands in the western Pacific.
Not long after, a scanty two-piece swimming costume
caused a sensation on French beaches. Its effect was
so great that the French called it the bikini. The word

Fashion

seems to have appeared first in English in a US newspaper, the *Waterloo Daily Courier*, on 26 June 1947. In an article it reports: 'The French, it seems, have a new suit planned that is about twice as wide as a piece of string. It's so explosive that they call it the Bikini.'

bloomers

Bloomers were first trousers gathered at the ankle and worn with a short skirt. They were named after Mrs Amelia J. Bloomer (1818–94), an American social reformer who advocated this type of clothing. In the late 19th century, bloomers were considered appropriate for activities such as cycling. In the early 20th century the name started to be applied to loose knee-length knickers and then colloquially to any knickers.

boutique

Small shops started being called boutiques in French in the 18th century. The French word goes back through Latin to Greek *apothēkē* 'a storehouse'. This is ultimately the source of **apothecary**, and of **bodega**, a shop in Spain selling wine. In the 1950s boutique came to be used particularly of a shop selling fashionable clothes. Other small businesses claiming exclusive clienteles began to call themselves boutiques: the **boutique winery** appeared in the USA in the 1970s, and a **boutique hotel** in New York in 1989.

dandy

Dandies emerged in the late 18th century. The word is perhaps a shortened form of **Jack-a-dandy**, a 17th-century term for a conceited fellow, where dandy is a pet form of Andrew. The original dandies, such as Beau Brummel, were not flamboyant, but understated and elegant, reacting against the wigs and knee breeches of an older generation. They pioneered the forerunner of the business suit. Dandy quickly became a term of approval for anything high quality, a use found in US expressions such as **fine and dandy**.

fashion

If you were out of fashion in the early 1500s you were not outmoded, you were 'out of shape'. Fashion originally meant 'make, shape, or appearance' as well as 'a particular style'. It was not until the 16th century it developed the sense of 'a popular style of clothes or way of behaving'. **In fashion** and **out of fashion** were both used by Shakespeare to mean 'in vogue' and 'out of vogue'.

gown

Old French *goune* is the source of gown, from late Latin *gunna* 'fur garment'.

sideburns

The 19th-century American general Ambrose E. Burnside sported muttonchop whiskers and a moustache, with a clean-shaven chin. By the 1870s people were calling this style a Burnside. Changing fashion did away with the moustache and burnsides became strips of hair in front of a man's ears. Fame fades fast, and the general's name must have puzzled many, though they understood the 'side' part. In the 1880s the elements reversed order to form sideburns. This still left 'burns' as a puzzle, and the more familiar **sideboards** was sometimes substituted as an alternative.

tattoo

Tattoos on the skin came into English in the 18th century from the Polynesian languages of the Pacific Islands—Captain Cook's journals are the first to record the word. The military tattoo sounded by drum or bugle to recall soldiers to their quarters in the evening was originally written **tap-too**. It comes from Dutch *doe den tap toe*, literally 'close the tap'. The tap was on a cask, closing it signalled time for drinking was over and soldiers should go home.

vogue

Fashion and rowing may not appear to have much in common, but Italian *voga*, from which vogue came derives from *vogare* 'to row, go well'. During the 17th century vogue was definitely **in vogue**, developing most of its current meanings. In the 1980s dancers in clubs began to vogue, imitating the poses struck by a model on a catwalk or in the glossy fashion magazine

Vogue, which started life as a weekly New York society paper before the US publisher Condé Nast bought it and transformed it from 1909.

Fear
see also HORROR, MIND AND MENTAL HEALTH

abhor
Abhor literally means something that makes you shudder. It comes from Latin *ab-* 'away from' and *horrere* 'to shudder with fright', also the basis of **horror**. In Shakespeare's day abhor could also mean 'to cause horror': 'It does abhor me now I speak the word' (*Othello*).

abominable
People once thought abominable came from Latin *ab-* 'away from' and *homo* 'human being', and so meant 'inhuman, beastly'. Consequently, it was frequently spelt *abhominable*, a spelling found in Shakespeare. In fact, it comes from Latin *abominari*, 'to regard as a bad omen', so is related to **omen** and **ominous**. The name **Abominable Snowman** (or Yeti) was brought back by the 1921 Royal Geographical Society expedition to Mount Everest, which found mysterious footprints in the snow. It translates Tibetan *Meetoh Gangmi*. **Yeti** is from Tibetan *yeh-the* 'little man-like animal'.

Fear

aghast

Gast (originally *gaestan*) was an Old English word meaning 'frighten, terrify', still used in Shakespeare's day: 'Or whether gasted by the noise I made, Full suddenly he fled' (*King Lear*). This gave rise to *agast*, which had the same meaning. The spelling (probably influenced by **ghost**) was originally Scottish but became general after 1700. **Ghastly** comes from the same word.

agoraphobia

Agoraphobia is literally 'fear of the market place', from Greek *agora* 'a market place' and the English suffix *-phobia* (from Greek *phobos* 'fear'). In ancient Greece an agora was a public open space for markets and assemblies.

alarm

Alarm started out as the exclamation 'to arms!'; coming via Old French *alarme*, from Italian *all' arme!*. The spelling **alarum** existed in English in early times because the 'r' was rolled when pronouncing the word; this form became restricted to the peal of a warning bell or clock. The original exclamation is seen in **alarums and excursions**, a stage direction found in Shakespeare's *Henry VI* and *Richard III*.

dread

The original word for 'to fear greatly, regard with awe' was *adread*, shortened to dread in the Middle Ages.

Among Rastafarians dread is dread of the Lord, and more generally a deep-rooted sense of alienation from contemporary society. Rastafarians wear **dreadlocks**, sometimes simply **dreads**, where hair is washed but not combed, and twisted while wet into tight braids. These terms were originally Jamaican, but came to wider attention in 1974 in 'Natty Dread', sung by Bob Marley and the Wailers. **Dreadnought** is a large, fast battleship equipped with large-calibre guns, the first of which, HMS Dreadnought, was launched in 1906. In the early 19th century, a dreadnought was a very warm coat or a fearless person.

fraught

Something fraught is now usually filled with danger or anxiety, but at first the word simply meant 'laden' or 'equipped'. It comes from medieval Dutch *vracht* 'ship's cargo', source also of **freight**.

panic

Pan, the Greek god of flocks and herds, had horns, ears, and legs like a goat's on a man's body. His sudden appearance was supposed to cause terror like that of a frightened, stampeding herd. In Greek his name probably originally meant 'the feeder' from his role as god of flocks, but was early on interpreted as *pan* meaning 'all' and he was identified as a god of nature or the universe. **Panic button** originated in the US Air

Fear

Force. Second World War bombers had an emergency bell system used if the aircraft was so badly damaged by enemy action it had to be abandoned—the pilot gave a 'prepare-to-abandon' ring and then a ring meaning 'jump'.

phobia

An independent usage of the suffix *-phobia* (via Latin from Greek) meaning 'fear'. Modern psychologists have ransacked Greek and Latin as new fears are uncovered, including **brontophobia**, 'fear of thunder' from Greek *bronte* 'thunder' also in **brontosaurus**, 'thunder lizard'; **heliophobia** from *helios* Greek for 'sun', also in **heliotrope**, plants that turn their flowers to follow the sun; and **nomophobia**, a joking coinage of 2008 for feeling anxious without a mobile phone.

terror

Like **terrible**, terror comes from Latin *terrere* 'to frighten'. The **Terror** was the period of the French Revolution marked by extreme bloodshed. **Reign of terror** was originally coined to describe this and **terrorist** used to describe the Jacobins, the revolutionary group responsible for the Terror. **Terrible** once meant 'causing terror or awe', a meaning reflected in the feared 16th-century Russian tsar **Ivan the Terrible**. The weakened sense 'very bad, appalling' gradually evolved from the early 17th century.

Fiction to Word see also LITERATURE

blatant

A word first used by the Elizabethan poet Edmund Spenser (c.1552–99) in *The Faerie Queene*, for a thousand-tongued monster, offspring of the three-headed dog Cerberus and the fire-breathing Chimera. Spenser used this 'blatant beast' to symbolize slander. He may have invented the word, or taken it from Scots *blatand* 'bleating'. Blatant was subsequently used to mean 'clamorous, offensive to the ear', and did not take on its modern meaning 'unashamedly conspicuous' until the late 19th century.

gargantuan

Gargantua is a giant with a huge, insatiable appetite from the book of the same name, published in 1534, by the French satirical writer Rabelais. In one episode Gargantua accidentally swallows six pilgrims while eating a salad. Gargantuan, meaning 'enormous, gigantic', comes from Rabelais's colossal guzzler.

Jeep

The name of the Second World War Jeep originally came, in American English, from the initials 'GP', standing for 'general purpose'. It was probably also influenced by the name of 'Eugene the Jeep', a resourceful creature with superhuman powers that first appeared in the Popeye comic strip in 1936.

Lolita

In Vladimir Nabokov's novel *Lolita* (1958), Humbert Humbert, a man in his late 30s, becomes sexually obsessed with Dolores Haze, a 12-year-old girl whom he dubs Lolita, a pet form of Dolores. The book's disturbing subject matter created a scandal when it was published in the USA, but it gave the world two words for 'a sexually precocious young girl', Lolita itself and **nymphet**.

mascot

The French operetta *La Mascotte* by Edmond Audran had its première on 29 December 1880. The next year the word made its first appearance in English. French *mascotte* derives from *masco* 'witch' in southern French dialect. Initially mascot meant simply 'someone or thing supposed to bring good luck' and did not have to be carried or displayed.

paparazzi

Paparazzo was the name of a society photographer in Frederico Fellini's 1960 film *La Dolce Vita*. By the following year paparazzo was appearing as a general name in English for a press photographer, and it had acquired a plural paparazzi.

quixotic

A quixotic person is idealistic, unrealistic, and impractical, like the hero of the Spanish novel *Don Quixote* (1605–15) by Miguel de Cervantes. Don Quixote, a middle-aged country gentleman obsessed with tales of chivalry, decides to become a knight and rides out with his squire Sancho Panza in search of adventure.

Scrooge

Charles Dickens's *A Christmas Carol*, published in 1843, shows the transformation of the bad-tempered, miserly Ebenezer Scrooge into a kind and philanthropic old gentleman. On Christmas Eve the ghost of Marley, his former business partner, shows him visions of the past, present, and future, including what his own death will be like if he does not mend his ways. On Christmas Day Scrooge sends a turkey to his abused clerk Bob Cratchit, subscribes to charities, and is genial to all. Since the mid 20th century any miserly killjoy has been a Scrooge.

Tweedledum and Tweedledee

The English poet John Byrom coined Tweedledee and Tweedledum in a satire of 1725 about the composers George Frederick Handel and Giovanni Battista Bononcini, musical rivals who were both enjoying success in London at the time. To **tweedle** is to play a succession of shrill notes or to play carelessly. Lewis

Food

Carroll picked up the names and used them for two identical characters in *Through the Looking-Glass*, and now they apply generally to any virtually indistinguishable pair. **Twiddle** is a variant of tweedle, and **twiddle your thumbs** dates from the late 19th century.

yahoo

The fourth part of Jonathan Swift's satire *Gulliver's Travels*, published in 1726, describes the country of the intelligent horses, the Houyhnhnms. Their simplicity and virtue contrasts with the disgusting brutality of the Yahoos, beasts in the shape of men. Soon yahoo was being used for a coarse person or lout. In Australia the Yahoo is a large, hairy, man-like monster supposedly inhabiting the east of the country. It is recorded from the mid 19th century, and may be an Aboriginal word, though Swift's Yahoos influenced the English form. In the internet site Yahoo!, Yahoo stands for Yet Another Hierarchical Officious Oracle, but was chosen partly because of the associations of yahoo.

 Food see also FRUIT, PLANTS, SENSATIONS

aspic

This jelly gets its name from a French word for the snake which appears in English as 'asp'. There has been much debate why. The best suggestion is that it is from a

French expression *froid comme un aspic* 'as cold as an asp', from the coldness of aspic. Other suggestions are that it is from the colour or patterns in 18th-century jellies or the shape of the moulds used.

chipolata

Chipolata sausages have nothing to do with chips—their name comes from Italian *cipollata*, 'flavoured with onion' (the Italian for 'onion' is *cipolla*, related to English **chives**).

garnish

Garnishing a food with a sprig of parsley is a far cry from the word's medieval meaning, 'to equip or arm yourself'. Over time the sequence of meanings evolved like this: 'to equip or arm yourself', 'to fit out with something', 'to decorate or embellish', and finally 'to decorate a dish of food for the table'. The source, Old French *garnir* (also the root of **garment**), meant both 'to fortify or defend', and 'to provide, equip, or prepare'.

junket

Originally, junket was a rush basket, going back to Latin *juncus* 'a rush'. In early translations of the Bible it was used for the little boat of bulrushes the infant Moses was placed in by his mother. It came to mean 'cream cheese' or 'sweetened curds', because they were at one time drained in a rush basket. Junkets might be served at a feast, and by the 16th century the sense 'a feast, a party' arose, from which came, in the early 19th century, 'a pleasure trip'. The meaning 'a trip or excursion made by government officials and paid for by public funds' developed more recently.

marmalade

Early marmalade was a solid quince jelly; in 1524 King Henry VIII was given 'a box of marmalade'. The word is recorded in English in the late 15th century, and comes from Portuguese *marmelada* 'quince jam'. The story that marmalade was originally made for Mary Queen of Scots when she was ill and comes from *marie malade* 'ill Mary' has no foundation. The Scots are, however, generally credited with inventing the kind of orange marmalade we are familiar with, and the first marmalade factory was built in Dundee in 1797, by the Keiller family.

mayonnaise

Most books say that mayonnaise comes via French *mahonnais* from Port Mahon, the capital of Minorca, captured by the French in 1756. The first reference to mayonnaise anywhere is only in 1804, when the success was hardly recent, and the spelling has always been with 'y' rather than 'h'. The chef M. A. Carême (1784–1833) explained the word as from French *manier* 'to handle' from the method of preparation. It could also be a corruption of French *bayonnaise*, meaning 'from the town of Bayonne'.

praline

This chocolate filling is named after the French Marshal de Plessis-Praslin (1598–1675), soldier, diplomat, and politician, whose cook, Lassagne, is credited with having invented it. It is said that the delicious results were influential in his diplomatic successes.

stew

When stew entered the language it referred to a cauldron or large cooking pot, not to what cooked in it. The source was Old French *estuve*, probably based on Greek *tuphos* 'smoke or steam', which is also where the fevers **typhus** and **typhoid** come from, because they create the kind of stupor that is associated with smoke inhalation. The verb 'to stew' originally referred to bathing in a hot bath or steam bath. It was not long before the idea of heating people in a bath had changed to heating food in an oven. **Stifle** probably comes from the same root, and **stove**, originally a 'sweating room' in a steam bath, may be related.

treacle

Now a kind of syrup, treacle was originally an antidote against poison. The word entered medieval English from Old French *triacle*, from Greek *thērion* 'wild beast', as a term for an ointment made with many ingredients that counteracted venom. The sense antidote was extended to medicine, then, by way of sugar syrup used to make medicine more palatable, into the current sense by the late 17th century. Lewis Carroll played on the healing sense when he wrote about treacle wells in *Alice in Wonderland*, for he was referring to a real, ancient healing well at Binsey just outside Oxford.

vindaloo

Vindaloo is one of the hottest curries in the British Indian restaurant's repertoire, but the word was not originally Indian and did not imply spiciness. It probably derives from Portuguese *vin d'alho* 'wine and garlic sauce'. An English recipe of 1888 describes it as a Portuguese curry, but it did not become familiar until Indian restaurants spread widely in the 1960s.

 # Fools see also INSULTS

clown

The earliest uses of clown mean 'an unsophisticated country person'. Before long it was applied to any rude or ill-mannered person, and by 1600 was also being used to refer to the character of a fool in a stage play, from which the comic entertainer in a circus developed. Quite a few people are afraid of clowns, and a word for the

condition has been coined **coulrophobia**, the first
element borrowed from the Greek for a stilt-walker,
clowns being unknown in the classical world.

dunce

The 13th-century Scottish theologian and scholar John
Duns Scotus was a profoundly influential figure. His
works were university textbooks, his followers so
numerous they had a name, Scotists. But from the
16th century the Scotists' views became old-fashioned
and they were attacked and ridiculed, especially for
making unnecessarily fine distinctions. The Scotists
acquired a new name: Dunsmen or Dunses. A Duns
was a 'hair-splitter', 'a dull pedant', and 'a person who
is slow at learning'. The last is the sense which
survives to this day.

idiot

This comes via Latin *idiota* 'ignorant person', from
Greek *idiōtēs* 'private person, layman, ignorant person'
based on *idios* 'own, private', reflecting the attitude in
the ancient world to those who did not take an active
part in public life.

imbecile

Originally an imbecile was physically weak. The root
meaning may be 'without a supporting staff', from Latin
baculum 'stick, staff'. The current sense dates from the
early 19th century.

Fools

inane

This is from Latin *inanis* 'empty, vain'. The sense 'silly, senseless' dates from the beginning of the 19th century.

moron

Early use was as a medical term for an adult with a mental age of about 8–12. It comes from Greek *mōron*, the neuter of *mōros* 'foolish'.

nincompoop

The word nincompoop perhaps came from Nicodemus, the name of a Jewish Pharisee in the New Testament who became something of a byword for slow-wittedness. Nicodemus secretly visited Jesus one night to hear his teachings. Jesus explained, 'Except a man be born again, he cannot see the Kingdom of God', which puzzled Nicodemus, who took Jesus literally and said 'How can a man be born when he is old?'. The *-poop* part may come from the old verb **poop**, 'to deceive or cheat'. In a similar vein **ninny** may be a pet form of the name Innocent.

nit

Nit, the tiny egg of a human head louse, was in use for something small or insignificant by Shakespeare's day. However, **nitwit** is not recorded until the 1920s and **nit-picking** or pedantic fault-finding did not enter English until the 1950s. The idea here is of painstakingly searching through someone's hair for nits. In Australia children shout 'nit!' to warn when a teacher is approaching. Nit here is probably an alteration of **nix**, from German *nichts*, 'not'.

oaf

Oaf goes back to Old Norse *alfr* 'elf'. It originally meant 'elf's child, changeling', and from this 'an idiot child', then 'fool' or 'halfwit'. Finally, in the early 20th century, it acquired the general sense of 'large clumsy man', a sense used by Rudyard Kipling in *The Islanders* (1903) when he called cricketers and footballers 'flannelled fools at the wicket' and 'muddied oafs at the goals'.

stupid

Our word stupid comes from French *stupide* or Latin *stupidus*, from *stupere* 'to be amazed or stunned', also the source of **stupor** and **stupendous**. The 'slow-witted, foolish' sense eventually became the main meaning.

Fruit see also FOOD, GARDENING, PLANTS

apple

Originally apple was used for any fruit. The **forbidden fruit** eaten by Adam and Eve in Eden is generally thought of as an apple but the 1611 King James Version of the Bible simply calls it fruit. A **rotten apple** (or a **bad**

Fruit

apple), a bad influence on others, goes back at least to
the early printer William Caxton in the 15th century. The
apple of your eye, once a term for the pupil, was later
applied to anything similarly delicate and precious. The
Australian expression **it's** (or **she's**) **apples** means
'everything is fine, nothing to worry about' is from
apples and rice (or spice), rhyming slang for 'nice'. Also
rhyming slang is **apples and pears** for 'stairs'. New York
has been the **Big Apple** since the 1920s, possibly from
the idea that there are many apples on the tree but New
York is the biggest.

apricot

The Romans called the apricot *malum praecocum*, 'the
early ripening apple'. The second element, meaning
'early ripening', also gives us **precocious**. Over the
centuries *praecocum* gradually mutated: into Byzantine
Greek *perikokkon*, to Arabic *al-birquq*, to Spanish
albaricoque, and Portuguese *albricoque*. In the 16th century
albricoque was adopted into English as *albrecock*. The
modern spelling was probably influenced by French
abricot, and perhaps Latin *apricus* 'ripe'.

avocado

Avocado in the Aztec language Nahuatl was *ahuacatl*,
'testicle', applied to the fruit because of its shape. The
16th century Spanish conquerors of Central America
converted *ahuacatl* to *aguacate*, then to avocado, Spanish

for 'lawyer' (related to English **advocate**). Avocado entered English in the 17th century.

banana

Banana travelled to English through Portuguese and Spanish from Mande, a language group of West Africa, arriving in the 16th century. Americans began to **go bananas** in the 1950s. The **top banana**, 'the most important person in an organization', derives from US theatrical slang for the comedian with top billing in a show, first recorded in 1953. People have been slipping on a **banana skin** since the beginning of the 20th century. The **banana republic**, a small state, especially in central America, whose economy is dependent on fruit exporting, was referred to as early as 1904.

grape

Grape originally referred to the whole bunch of berries. It goes back to Old French *grap* 'hook', specifically a vine hook for harvesting grapes. **Grapple**, first found as **grappling hook**, has a similar origin, while **grapefruit** are so called because they grow in clusters like grapes. To hear something **on the grapevine** comes from the American Civil War, when news was said to pass 'by grapevine telegraph'. **Bush telegraph**, originally an Australian term, is a similar idea. **Sour grapes** comes from Aesop's fable of the fox and the grapes: a fox tries to reach a bunch of grapes hanging from a vine above his head. After several attempts he gives up muttering that they were probably sour anyway.

orange

Orange, first recorded in English in medieval times, goes back through Arabic to Persian. The Arabs brought what we now call the Seville or bitter orange to Sicily in the Middle Ages. From Sicily it was introduced to the rest of Europe. In the 16th century the Portuguese brought the sweet orange from China, at first distinguished as a **China orange**. The **Orangemen** of Northern Ireland are supporters of the Orange Order, a Protestant political society supporting continued union with Britain. They wear orange badges to symbolize adherence to King William III, also called William of Orange from the southern French town which was home to his ancestors. He defeated the Catholic James II at the Battle of the Boyne in 1690.

peach

Peach is from Old French *pesche*, from medieval Latin *persica*, a shortening of *persicum (malum)*, literally 'Persian apple'. Peaches are natives of China, but were introduced to Europe via the Middle East.

pear

A word adopted before the Anglo-Saxons arrived in England from the Latin *pirum*. **Go pear-shaped**, 'go wrong', is RAF slang. Although the first written examples are from the early 1980s, around the time of the Falklands War, it was probably used several decades earlier. It may be a darkly humorous reference to the shape of a fighter plane which has nose-dived into the ground. More cheerfully it may describe a novice pilot's attempts to produce a perfect circle when performing a loop in the air.

pineapple

The Latin *pinus* gave us 'pine tree', and originally a pine apple was the fruit of the pine tree, a pine-cone. When the pineapple was introduced in the early 17th century the shape and segmented skin was felt to resemble a pine cone and the name transferred to it.

pomegranate

Old French *pome grenate*, was from *pome* 'apple' and *grenate* based on Latin *granatum*, 'having many seeds'. Similarly, **pomander**, a perforated container of sweet-smelling substances, is from Old French *pome d'embre*, from medieval Latin *pomum de ambra* 'apple of ambergris'. Apples are again found in **pommel**. This once described a decorative ball or finial at the top of something and is from Old French *pomel* 'little apple'.

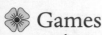

Games

see also CHILDHOOD, ENTERTAINMENT, SPORT, TOYS

billiards

French *billard*, 'little tree trunk' was originally the name of the cue for the game, but was soon transferred to the game itself. The word is also the source of **billet**, a thick piece of wood. The French comes from medieval Latin *billa, billus* 'branch, trunk', probably from a Celtic root.

card

A medieval word that comes via French *carte* from Latin *charta* 'papyrus leaf or paper', the source of **chart**, and **charter**. Its first recorded sense was 'playing card'. If you **play your cards right** you make the best use of your assets and opportunities to get what you want, whereas to **lay your cards on the table** is to be completely open and honest in saying what your intentions are. **On the cards** (in the US, **in the cards**), 'possible or likely' refers to cards used for fortune-telling. In Britain someone **given their cards** is sacked from their job, from the National Insurance and other documents formerly held by the employer. **Play the race card** originates in a letter written by Lord Randolph Churchill (1849–95) in 1886 on the question of Irish Home Rule. Charles Dickens (1812–70) provides the first written use of card in the sense 'an odd or eccentric person', in his *Sketches by Boz* (1836). It comes from **sure card**, a person who was sure to succeed. **Discard** was originally used in relation to rejecting a playing card.

casino

A casino was originally a public room used for dancing and music, rather than gambling. It is borrowed from the Italian for 'little house', ultimately from Latin *casa* 'cottage', the source of **chalet**.

croquet

Croquet and **crochet** are probably the same word. Croquet is thought to be a form of French *crochet* 'hook, shepherd's crook', which means 'hockey stick' in parts of France, and in English a handicraft where yarn is made into fabric with a hooked needle. The lawn game seems to have been invented in France but introduced to Ireland, from where it spread to England in the 1850s. The French is also the source of the musical note the **crotchet**, from its shape, and also the old-fashioned term meaning a perverse or twisted belief, in use since Middle English, and giving the term **crotchety** in the 19th century.

dice

Originally—and still in the USA—a gambler would throw two dice but one **die**. This singular form is now rare in British English, surviving mainly in **the die is cast**, 'something has happened that cannot be undone' said by Caesar when he crossed the Rubicon. Dice came from Latin *datum* 'something given, starting point', a form of *dare* 'to give', interpreted as 'something given by chance or fortune'. Journalists began to use the expression **dicing with death** in the early 20th century of the risks taken by racing drivers. It is probably the source of the adjective **dicey** meaning 'dangerous', first used by RAF pilots in the 1950s.

pawn

There are two separate words here. The pawn in chess came via Anglo-Norman French *poun*, from medieval Latin *pedo* 'foot soldier', from Latin *pes, ped-* 'foot' (source of **pedal**, **pedestal**, and **pedestrian**). Figurative use 'someone used by others for their own purposes' is recorded from the late 16th century. The sense 'to deposit an object as security for money lent' is from French *pan* 'pledge, security'.

polo

The name for this game (originally played in the East) is from a Balti Tibetan word meaning 'ball'.

scrabble

Scrabble the game was registered as a trademark in January 1950, but the word is 16th century, from early Dutch *schrabben* 'to scrape'. The original meaning was 'to scrawl or scribble', followed by 'to scratch or grope about'.

snooker

Both the game and the word snooker originated among British army officers serving in India in the 1870s. Colonel Sir Neville Chamberlain (not the future British prime minister) is said to have coined it for a fast-moving version of billiards that he and his officers' mess had devised. Snooker was already army slang for 'a newly joined cadet', and the name may have referred to the inept play of a fellow officer.

trump

The word trump, 'a playing card of the suit ranking above others', is an alteration of **triumph**. The Latin source, *triumphus* probably came from Greek *thriambos* 'hymn to the god Bacchus'. In some games the trump suit it is the suit of the last card dealt, which is turned over to show its face, giving us **come** or **turn up trumps**, 'to produce a better outcome than expected'. In the **last trump**, trump is a form of **trumpet** which comes ultimately from the same source as trump.

Gardening see also FRUIT, PLANTS

bloom

The word for 'flower' in English was **blossom**. Old Norse *blóm* 'flower, blossom', was the source of bloom

Gardening

in English, which shares a base with **blow** 'to burst into flower', most often met in **overblown**. A **bloomer** is from the use of blooming for 'bloody' in **blooming error** and is probably Australian prison slang. In the 1930s another bloomer appeared, for a type of loaf, but it is not clear where from.

compost

Garden compost and fruit **compôte** both derive from French *compôte* 'stewed fruit', from Old French *composte*, from Latin *compositum* 'something put together'—source of **compose**, **decompose**, and **component**. The Latin was formed from *com-* 'with' and the irregular verb *ponere* 'put, place'. From this we get **impose** 'place (up) on'; **oppose** 'place against'; and **posture**.

garden

Garden comes from Old French *jardin* and has an ancient root that is also the ancestor of **yard. Everything in the garden is lovely** (or **rosy**) is an early 20th-century catchphrase from a song popularized by the English music hall star Marie Lloyd (1870–1922).

orchard

In Old English orchard was simply a name for a garden. The first part of the word probably comes from Latin *hortus* 'garden'. The second part is **yard**.

pergola

This is an English use of an Italian word which came from Latin *pergula* 'projecting roof, vine arbour', from *pergere* 'to come or go forward'.

pink

Pink for the colour beloved by little girls actually comes from the Dianthus flower, rather than the other way round. Similarly, several languages use the **rose** as their source for the colour. Shakespeare uses the pink flower to signify the supreme example of something in *Romeo and Juliet*: 'I am the very pink of courtesy', probably making a pun on 'the flower of', meaning 'the finest example'. This Shakespearean phrase led to the expression **in the pink of condition**, which by the early 18th century was shortened to **in the pink** 'in very good health and spirits'. The plant name's origin is not known for certain. It may be short for **pink eye** 'small or half-shut eye', like its French equivalent *oeillet*, 'little eye'. Pink in the sense of the sound a cooling engine makes is early 20th century and imitates the sound.

rake

The rake used by gardeners is an Old English word, from a root meaning 'heap up'. **Thin as a rake** is a comparison used since Geoffrey Chaucer's day. The phrases **rake over old coals** and **rake over the ashes** come from searching a dead or dying fire to see if a spark remains. Rake for a rich, immoral man is an abbreviation of the old word **rakehell**: the kind of sinful person likely to be found if you searched through Hell with a rake.

spade

A spade for digging is related to Greek *spathē* 'blade or paddle' and has been in the language since Anglo-Saxon times. The spade on a playing card dates from the 16th century and is based on Italian *spada* 'a broad-bladed sword'. **Call a spade a spade**, 'to speak plainly' dates from the mid 16th century. A tongue-in-cheek variation, from the early 20th century, is **call a spade a shovel**. **In spades** meaning 'to a very high degree', comes from the card game bridge, where spades are the highest-ranking suit.

topiary

Topiary is from French *topiaire*, from Latin *topia opera* 'fancy gardening'.

trellis

This once referred to any latticed screen, from Old French *trelis*, from Latin *trilix* 'three-ply', from *tri-* 'three', and *licium* 'warp thread'. This was used in France for a strong fabric and then something woven from wire. The word is found in gardening contexts from the early 16th century.

Geography
see also HARD AND EASY, WEATHER

antipodes

Think of someone standing on the other side of the world, exactly opposite the point where you are standing, the soles of their feet facing the soles of yours. This is the idea behind the Antipodes, which came via French or Latin from the Greek word *antipous*, meaning 'having the feet opposite'. Writing in 1398, John de Trevisa described the Antipodes who lived in Ethiopia as 'men that have their feet against our feet'.

arctic

Arctic ultimately comes from Greek *arktos* 'bear', but not because of the polar bears living in the Arctic. The bear in question is the Great Bear, the constellation *Ursa Major*, which can always be seen in the north.

atlas

Atlas was a Titan, or giant, in Greek mythology punished for taking part in a rebellion against the gods by being made to bear the weight of the world on his shoulders. He gave his name to the Atlas Mountains in Morocco, which seemed so high they were imagined to hold up the sky. A collection of maps is called an atlas because early atlases were published with an illustration of Atlas, the world on his back, on the title page. The first person to use the word this way was probably the map-maker Gerardus Mercator in the late 16th century. The Atlantic Ocean also gets its name from Atlas. Atlantic originally referred to the mountains, then to the sea near the west African coast, and later to the whole ocean.

climate

This is from late Latin *clima, climat-*, from Greek *klima* 'slope, zone'. Climate originally meant a zone of the earth between two lines of latitude, then any region of the earth, and later its atmospheric conditions.

epicentre

This is from Greek *epikentros* 'situated on a centre', from *epi-* 'upon' and *kentron* 'centre'. It originally meant the point immediately above an earthquake, but has been used as an emphatic form of 'centre' since at least 1970.

estuary

This was originally a tidal inlet of any size. The source is Latin *aestuarium* 'tidal part of a shore' from *aestus* 'tide'. **Estuary English** was coined by David Rosewarne in 1984 for an accent which developed along the Thames Estuary from London English and which has rapidly become the dominant urban accent in southern England.

gulf

The Greek word *kolpos* had a number of meanings relating to a curved shape, including 'bosom', 'the trough between waves', 'the fold of a piece of clothing', and 'gulf or bay'. This is where gulf came from, via Italian and Old French. We can talk about a **gulf between** two groups, meaning a great difference between them. This was probably influenced by a passage in the Gospel of Luke: 'Between you and us there is a great gulf set'.

swamp

Swamp is first found in the compound 'swampwater' and probably goes back to a Germanic root with the senses 'sponge, fungus'. **Sump** is probably related, as it is first found with the meaning 'swamp'.

volcano

In Roman mythology Vulcan was the god of fire and metalworking. A conical mountain with erupting lava, rock fragments, hot vapour, or gas must have suggested his forge, and Italians named such a feature *volcano* or *vulcano* after him.

zone

Zone is from Greek *zōnē*, 'girdle'. It was first used to refer to each of the five belts or encircling regions (differentiated by climate) into which the surface of the earth is divided by the tropics and polar circles. From this, zone came to be applied to areas defined by certain boundaries or subject to certain restrictions.

Good see also BAD, HAPPY

benefit

The source of benefit is Latin *benefactum*, 'a good deed', which was the original English meaning. The modern sense is recorded from the early 16th century. To give someone **the benefit of the doubt** originally meant a verdict of not guilty when the evidence was not conclusive.

benevolent

This comes, via Old French, from Latin *bene volent-* 'well wishing'.

good

The ancient root of good probably meant 'to bring together, unite' also the source of **gather**. In 1957 British Prime Minister Harold Macmillan said, 'Let us be frank about it: most of our people have **never had it so good**'. 'You Never Had It So Good' was the US Democratic Party slogan during the 1952 election campaign. **Good Friday**, the Friday before Easter Day, on which Christ was crucified, uses good in the old sense 'observed as holy'. **Goodbye** is a shortened form of the phrase 'God be with you'. In time good replaced God, in line with phrases such as **good morning** and **goodnight**. Sweets and cakes have been **goodies** since the mid 18th century, and the childish exclamation **goody** is first recorded not much later.

halcyon

The halcyon was a bird that in the past was thought to breed in a nest floating on the sea, and to charm the wind and waves so that the sea was calm. It was identified as a kingfisher, the word coming from the Greek for a kingfisher, *alkuōn*. The **halcyon days** were originally 14 days of calm weather which were supposed to occur when the halcyon was breeding. Today the phrase refers to a period of time in the past that was idyllically happy and peaceful.

kind

In Old English the original senses of kind were 'nature, the natural order', and 'innate character', which led to our use 'a class or type of similar people or things'. Kind is also related to **kin** and through it to **king**. In medieval times it was used to mean 'well born'. The association of good breeding with good manners gives the meaning 'considerate and generous'.

nice

In medieval English nice meant 'foolish, silly, ignorant', from its Latin source *nescius* 'ignorant'. It developed a range of negative senses, from 'dissolute', 'ostentatious, showy', 'unmanly, cowardly', and 'delicate, fragile' to 'strange, rare', and 'coy, reserved'. In *Love's Labour's Lost* Shakespeare talks of 'nice wenches', meaning 'disreputable women'. Nice was first used in the more positive sense 'fine or subtle' (a **nice distinction**) in the 16th century, and the current meanings, 'pleasant' and 'kind', seem to have been in common use from the 18th century. **Nice guys finish last** is credited to Leo Durocher, manager of the Brooklyn Dodgers baseball team from 1951 to 1954. In his 1975 autobiography *Nice Guys Finish Last* he is quoted as saying of a rival team: 'Take a look at them. All nice guys. They'll finish last. Nice guys. Finish last.'

paragon

A paragon, a 'perfect example', is from an obsolete French word, from Italian *paragone* a 'touchstone to try good gold from bad', which came from Medieval Greek *parakonē* 'whetstone'.

silly

A medieval Englishman would be pleased to be described as silly—you would mean he was happy or lucky. Silly is an alteration of earlier *seely*, from an ancient root meaning 'luck, happiness'. The Old English *seely* meant 'happy, fortunate, blessed by God'. This developed into 'holy', then 'innocent, defenceless, deserving pity'. Cynical people regard goodness and simplicity as showing lack of intelligence, and since the late 16th century the primary sense has been 'foolish'. The first **silly billy** was either William Frederick, the Duke of Gloucester (1776–1834), or King William IV (1765–1837) who became unpopular when he intervened in politics, imposing the Conservative Robert Peel as prime minister despite a Whig majority.

splendid

Early 17th-century examples of splendid, ultimately from Latin *splendere* 'to shine brightly', describe a grand place or occasion. **Splendid isolation** was first used at the end of the 19th century for the diplomatic and commercial non-involvement of Great Britain in Europe.

superb

The first things described as superb were buildings and monuments. Later the word described a haughty person. From the early 18th century people started using superb in the sense 'very fine, excellent'. It comes from Latin *superbus* 'proud, magnificent'.

Happy see also GOOD, SAD

bliss

This word from a Germanic root is related to **blithe** 'happy'. **Bless** and bliss have influenced each other from an early period, resulting in a gradual distinction between blitheness as an earthly lightness of heart and the heavenly bliss of the 'blessed'.

content

Two words are spelt content in English; one stressed on the second syllable meaning 'happy' from Latin *contentus* 'satisfied', the other stressed on the first syllable meaning 'things included' from Latin *contenta* 'things contained'. Both Latin words go back to *continere* 'hold, contain' which also gives us **contain**.

ecstasy

The base of the word ecstasy is Greek *ekstasis*, meaning 'standing outside yourself'. Ecstasy first referred to frenzy or distraction, of literally being 'beside yourself' with strong emotion. This meaning is now rare, but was famously used by Wilfred Owen in his war poem 'Dulce et Decorum Est' (written in 1917): 'Gas! Gas! Quick, boys!—An ecstasy of fumbling, Fitting the clumsy helmets just in time.' Ecstasy came during the 16th and 17th centuries to mean emotional or religious frenzy or heightened emotion. The drug Ecstasy is first referred to in 1985. It gained its street name because of its euphoric effects.

exuberant

'Overflowing, abounding' were the early senses recorded for exuberant from French *exubérant*, from the Latin verb *exuberare* 'be abundantly fruitful'. The base is Latin *uber* 'fertile'. The current sense 'overflowing with delight', is first recorded in the 16th century.

grin

When grin entered English in the 11th century it meant 'to bare the teeth in pain or anger', preserved in **grin and bear it**, 'to suffer stoically'. In the 15th century grin began to be used for various sorts of smile. **Groan** is related.

happy

Before the 14th century you could be **glad** but not happy. Happy comes from *hap* 'fortune, chance', which entered English a century or more earlier and is now obsolete, except in **hapless** 'unfortunate', **happen** and **perhaps**. **Happy as a sandboy** is because sandboys (who were grown men as well as boys) were 'happy' or 'jolly' because they were habitually drunk. A dictionary of slang published in 1823 explains this. Sandboys sold sand for building, cleaning pots and pans, and spreading on pub floors to soak up spillages.

Hard and Easy

jest

In the Middle Ages a jest was not a joke but a notable exploit. Spelled *gest*, it came from the Latin word *gesta* 'actions, exploits'. Jest came to be used for a narrative of someone's deeds, then for 'an idle story' then 'a joke'.

jovial

When we describe someone as jovial, we are looking back to the Latin word *jovialis* 'of Jupiter'. This refers to the supposed influence of the planet Jupiter on those born under it. Jove is a poetical equivalent of Jupiter, the name of the most important god of the ancient Romans.

joy

Joy is from Old French *joie*, from Latin *gaudium*, from *gaudere* 'rejoice'. In **rejoice** the *re-* makes the sense more intense; **enjoy** comes from the Old French *enjoier* 'give joy to'.

 # Hard and Easy

adamant

The Greek word *adamas*, originally 'invincible or untameable', came to be applied to the hardest metal or stone, and to diamond, the hardest naturally occurring substance. Via Latin it was the source **diamond** (see below). In Old English adamant was a legendary rock so hard that it was believed to be impenetrable. Early medieval Latin writers mistakenly explained the word as coming from *adamare* 'take a liking to', associating adamant with the lodestone or magnet which 'takes a liking' to iron, and adamant passed into modern languages with this confusion of meaning. The notion of unyielding conviction is much more recent, probably dating from the 1930s.

cinch

The first recorded use of cinch, 'something that is easy to achieve', was as a term for a girth of a saddle that was made from separate twisted strands of horsehair. It was used in Mexico and the western USA, and is a Spanish word. The link between the original meaning and the modern one is the idea of having a firm or secure hold on something.

diamond

The name of the gem derives from a medieval Latin alteration of Latin *adamans* **adamant** (see above). Adamant was a legendary rock or mineral with many supposed properties. One of these was hardness, which was a reason why people sometimes identified it with diamond. A **diamond is forever** was used as an advertising slogan for De Beers Consolidated Mines from the late 1940s onwards, and in 1956 Ian Fleming used *Diamonds are Forever* as the title of his latest James Bond thriller, but the idea was first expressed by the American writer Anita Loos, in *Gentlemen Prefer Blondes* (1925). 'Diamonds are a Girl's Best Friend' was a song written by Leo Robin and Jule Styne for the 1949 stage musical of *Gentlemen Prefer Blondes*.

durable

This came via Old French from Latin *durabilis*, from *durare* 'to last, harden'. **Obdurate** comes from the same root.

easy

Both easy and **ease** go back via Old French *aisier* to Latin *adjacens* 'lying close by', source also of **adjacent**. **Easy-peasy** 'childishly easy' is only recorded from the 1970s. The 'peasy' is simply a rhyme and the childish word intensifies the sense.

glib

Glib is of Germanic origin and related to Dutch *glibberig* 'slippery', and German *glibberig* 'slimy'. In the late 16th century, one of its first meanings was 'smooth or unimpeded'. To **give a glib answer** is to speak fluently but insincerely and shallowly. A number of other words, such as **greasy**, **oily**, and **slimy**, link smoothness and slipperiness with insincere speech or behaviour.

petrify

The original sense of petrify was 'to convert into stone', from the Latin and Greek root *petra* 'rock'. The sense 'to terrify, astonish' dates from the mid 17th century.

problem

A problem was initially a riddle, puzzle, or question put forward for academic discussion. 'Put forward' are the key words here, as its ancestor is the Greek verb *proballein*, 'to throw out or put forth', based on *pro* 'forward' and *ballein* 'to throw', also the source of **ballistic**.

quartz

Quartz, a hard mineral consisting of silica, comes via German from Polish dialect *kwardy*, corresponding to Czech *tvrdý* 'hard'.

rock

The rock that makes the earth came into medieval English from Old French *rocque*, which can be traced back to medieval Latin *rocca* but no further. The classical Latin word was *petra*, the source of **petrify** (see above). People have been **caught between a rock and a hard place** since the 1920s, first of all in Arizona and California. Also American is **on the rocks** 'on ice', first recorded in 1946, while the slang term for a precious stone is 1920s. In France the modern form of *rocque, roc*

developed the form *rocaille* for decoration using shells
and pebbles, fashionable in the 18th century. 19th-century
French workmen changed this to **rococo**, originally
meaning old-fashioned, but now used to describe
18th-century art. Rock meaning 'to move to and fro' is
an Old English word.

 # Heaven and Hell
see also CHRISTIANITY, RELIGION

angel

Angels are messengers from God, the word coming
ultimately from Greek *angelos* 'messenger'. **On the side
of the angels**, on the side of what is right, comes from a
speech given in 1864 by the British statesman Benjamin
Disraeli during the controversy about Charles Darwin's
On the Origin of Species: 'Is man an ape or an angel?...I
am on the side of the angels.' The plant **angelica** is the
'angelic herb' because it was believed to work against
poison and disease.

demon

The Greek word *daimōn* is the root of demon. In ancient
Greece a demon or **daemon** was a divine or
supernatural being somewhere between a god and a
human; an attendant spirit or inspiring force, as in
Philip Pullman's *His Dark Materials* books. Demons were

not evil until the writing of the Septuagint, a Greek
version of the Hebrew Bible, in the 3rd and 2nd
centuries BC.

devil

The English word devil goes back to Greek *diabolos*
'accuser, slanderer', the source also of **diabolic**, and
similar words. In the Septuagint, a Greek version of the
Hebrew Bible written in the 3rd and 2nd centuries BC,
diabolos translated the Hebrew for 'Satan'. **The devil
finds work for idle hands** appears first in English in
the *Divine Songs* of the 18th-century hymn writer
Isaac Watts, but goes back to the letters of St Jerome
(c.342–420). **Why should the devil have all the best
tunes?** is a question that has been attributed to the
Victorian evangelist Rowland Hill, who encouraged the
singing of hymns to popular melodies. **Speak** or **talk of
the devil**, when a person appears just after being
mentioned, comes from the superstition that if you
speak the devil's name he will suddenly appear. **The
devil to pay**, 'serious trouble to be expected', is often
said to have a nautical origin. The seam near a ship's keel
was sometimes known as 'the devil', and because of its
position was very difficult to 'pay', or seal with pitch or
tar. There is not much evidence for this theory, and more
probably it was a reference to a pact made with Satan,
like Faust's, and to the inevitable payment to be made to
him in the end. The **devil's advocate** was an official of
the Roman Catholic Church who challenged proposals

to make a dead person a saint. His job was to present everything, good and bad, known about the person, to make sure the case was examined from all sides. The official is now called the Promoter of the Faith.

heaven

The ultimate origin of heaven is unknown, although parallel forms exist in related languages. Heaven has always referred both to the sky and to the abode of God. Some Jewish and Muslim people believe there are seven levels of heaven, of which the seventh is the highest. There souls enjoyed a state of eternal bliss, and so **in seventh heaven** came to mean 'very happy, ecstatic'.

hell

Hell descends from an ancient Indo-European root with the sense 'to cover, hide' which also gave rise to Latin *celare* (root of **conceal** and **occult**) and to English **hole** and **helmet**. The infernal regions are regarded as a place of torment or punishment, giving us many curses and exclamations, such as a **hell of a . . . .** These expressions were considered shocking until the early 20th century, so alterations such as **heck** were used to soften the effect. **Hell hath no fury like a woman scorned** is a near quotation from a 1697 play by William Congreve. Grumpy and misanthropic people everywhere will agree with the French philosopher Jean-Paul Sartre who wrote in 1944: '**Hell is other people.**'

limbo

In some Christian theologies limbo is the abode, on the border of hell, of the souls of unbaptized infants and of just people who died before Christ's coming. It comes from Latin *limbus* 'edge, hem, border'. There is no linguistic connection with the West Indian dance the limbo, which is an alteration of **limber** 'lithe, supple'.

Lucifer

This is a Latin word originally, meaning 'light-bringing, morning star', from *luc-* 'light' and *-fer* 'bearing'. It was sometimes used in poetry for the planet Venus appearing in the sky before sunrise. Its use for the rebel archangel (Satan) is from the biblical quotation 'How art thou fallen from heaven, O Lucifer, son of the morning' (Isaiah 14:12).

paradise

Paradise goes back to the ancient Iranian language Avestan, in which the sacred texts of the Zoroastrian religion were written. *Pairidaēza* meant 'an enclosure, park'. It was used in the sense paradise in the Greek translation of the Bible, and through Latin entered Old English, where it meant 'the Garden of Eden' and later 'heaven'.

Satan

This has goes back to Hebrew *sātān*, which literally meant 'adversary'. William Blake's great poem 'Jerusalem', which became a popular hymn, is the source of the phrase **dark satanic mills**. 'Jerusalem' also gave us '**England's green and pleasant land**'.

tempt

Tempt goes back to Latin *temptare* 'to test, try', which is the sense in **tempt Providence**. In the Middle Ages temptation was particularly used of the biblical story of Jesus being tempted to sin by the Devil during 40 days in the wilderness. Modern temptations are generally more trivial. In 1892 Oscar Wilde wrote: 'I can resist everything except temptation' (*Lady Windermere's Fan*). **Attempt** is from the same root.

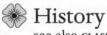

History

see also CLASSICAL GREECE AND ROME

antiquity

This comes from Latin *antiquitas*, from *antiquus* 'old, former' from *ante* 'before'. **Antics** is from the same source by way of Italian *antico* 'antique', used to mean 'grotesque', and as a term for the grinning faces carved on architecture fashionable at the time, before coming to describe grotesque behaviour.

chivalry

This springs from the fact that knights rode horses. Chivalry came into English from medieval Latin *caballerius*, based on Latin *caballus* 'horse'. **Cavalry**, **cavalier**, and **cavalcade** come from the same word. Originally chivalry described knights, noblemen, and horsemen collectively. Later it referred to the qualities associated with ideal knights: courage, honour, loyalty, and courtesy.

damsel

In early romances any knight in shining armour worth his salt searched for a **damsel in distress** to rescue. Damsel is based on Latin *domina* 'mistress', which is also the source of **dame** and of French **mademoiselle**.

dinosaur

Dinosaur was coined in 1841, from Greek words meaning 'terrible lizard'. The *-saurus* is also found in **saurian** 'lizard-like'. People or things that have not adapted to changing times have been condemned as dinosaurs since the 1950s.

fossil

Fossils are the petrified remains of ancient creatures that are dug up, and fossil comes from Latin *fodere* 'to dig'. It was originally used for fossilized fish which were found in the earth. In those days before the theory of evolution, people believed that they had lived underground too. The use of the word for a person or organization seen as outdated or resistant to change is found from the mid 19th century.

History

knight

To Anglo-Saxons knight meant 'boy, youth, servant', but in medieval times this developed into a term for a man of honourable military rank. Knights in traditional stories are rescuers of people in danger or distress, giving us a **knight in shining armour**. A **white knight** is, in Stock Exchange language, a person or company that makes an acceptable counter-offer to a hostile takeover bid from a **black knight**. Highwaymen were called ironically **knights of the road** which survives as a jokey term for someone who habitually travels the roads for work.

mammoth

In Siberia people dig up fossil remains and frozen carcasses of a large elephant-like hairy mammal with long curved tusks. They call these in Russian *mamont*, which probably came from a Siberian word meaning 'earth horn'. English acquired this as mammoth. The word began to refer to anything of a huge size in the early 19th century.

nostalgia

As the saying goes, 'Nostalgia isn't what it used to be'. Nostalgia first meant 'acute homesickness', from the Greek words *nostos*, 'return home', and *algos*, 'pain', a translation of the German *Heimweh* or 'homesickness'. The modern meaning, 'longing for the past', was established by the early 20th century. A number of medical terms also derive from *algos*, such as **neuralgia** 'pain in a nerve', and **analgesia** 'relief of pain'.

posse

This evokes the image, familiar from Westerns, of men being recruited by a sheriff to pursue outlaws or other wrongdoers. The key element in its meaning is the fact that the sheriff has empowered this group to enforce the law. Medieval Latin *posse* meant 'power', from earlier Latin *posse* 'to be able'. Posse was first used in Britain, to mean 'an assembled force or band' specifically 'local able-bodied men summoned by a sheriff to stop a riot or pursue criminals'. **Possible** comes from the same root.

pyramid

Pyramid was first used in English in the geometrical sense. It came via Latin from Greek *puramis*, which also meant a type of cake. This may be the earlier sense, the geometrical sense coming from a resemblance in shape. An Egyptian origin is now generally rejected. **Pediment**, the triangular upper part of a building, was once *periment* and may be an alteration of pyramid.

Home see also ARCHITECTURE

boudoir

Etymologically, a boudoir is a place where someone sulks. The word was adopted from French in the late

18th century, and literally means 'sulking place', from *bouder* 'to sulk, pout'.

counterpane

This is an alteration of *counterpoint*, from Old French *contrepointe*, based on medieval Latin *culcitra puncta* 'quilted mattress' (*puncta*, literally meaning 'pricked'). The change in the ending was due to association with the word *pane* in an obsolete sense 'cloth'.

cushion

You can tell that the Romans knew a thing or two about reclining in comfort when you discover that they had separate words for a hip cushion (*coxinum*) and an elbow cushion (*cubital*). The former word, from Latin *coxa* 'hip or thigh', gave rise to Old French *cuissin*, from which we get cushion.

divan

The divan travelled across Europe from the court of the Ottoman Empire in the East. The Ottoman divan was its privy council, presided over by the sultan or his highest official, the grand vizier. Turkish *dīvān* came from a Persian word with a range of meanings: 'brochure', 'anthology', 'register', 'court', and 'bench'. The last gave rise to the usual sense of divan in English, a piece of furniture. Originally, a divan was a low bench or raised part of a floor forming a seat against the wall of a room, common in Middle Eastern countries. European imitations of this led to the sense 'a low flat sofa or bed' in the late 19th century. **Ottoman** was used for a similar object.

economy

Like **ecology**, economy comes from Greek *oikos* 'house', and in the past they were spelled *oikonomy* and *oecology*. Economy was then 'the art or science of managing a household'. The sense expanded to cover the management of a country's finances. Being **economical with the truth** is a euphemism for lying or deliberately withholding information. Mark Twain commented in *Following the Equator* (1897), 'Truth is the most valuable thing we have. Let us economize it.' The phrase itself did not gain widespread popularity until its use in 1986 during a government attempt to prevent the publication of *Spycatcher*, a book by a former MI5 officer, Peter Wright. Giving evidence at the trial, the head of the British Civil Service reportedly said of a letter: 'It contains a misleading impression, not a lie. It was economical with the truth.'

emulsion

Nowadays we tend to think of emulsion as a household paint for walls and ceilings, whose name comes from the scientific sense of 'a fine dispersion of minute droplets of one liquid in another'. However, emulsion was originally a milky liquid made by crushing almonds in water. Its root is the Latin word *mulgere* 'to milk'.

Home

mansion

The rich person's mansion and the minister's **manse** have the same origin, both deriving from Latin *mansio* 'place where someone stays', from *manere* 'to stay' (the source of **remain** and **manor**). A mansion was originally the home of a medieval lord of the manor, but the word was later extended to any impressive house. 'The principal house of an estate' was the original sense of manse; after becoming increasingly restricted to an ecclesiastical residence, it is now a house occupied by a Church of Scotland or other Nonconformist minister.

mattress

The word mattress came via Old French and Italian from Arabic *matrah* 'carpet or cushion', from *taraha* 'to throw'.

nimby

Nimby, short for Not In My Back Yard, refers to a person who objects to the siting of something unpleasant in their own neighbourhood while not objecting to similar developments elsewhere. It was first recorded in 1980, in the USA.

veranda

This is from Hindi *varaṇḍā*, which was borrowed from Portuguese *varanda* 'railing, balustrade'.

Horror

see also FEAR, MIND AND MENTAL HEALTH

appal

Appal has its origin in the physical effect of being
horrified. Old French *apalir* meant both 'to grow pale'
and 'to make pale', and these senses were carried over
into the English word. As shock or disgust can make the
colour drain from your face, appal soon acquired its
current meaning.

atrocious

Whereas nowadays atrocious tends to describe
something such as bad weather or poor English, it was
once a stronger word describing great savagery, cruelty,
or wickedness, as in Charles Darwin's reference to
'Atrocious acts which can only take place in a slave
country' (1845). It is from Latin *atrox* 'fierce or cruel',
from *ater* 'black', and literally means 'black-looking'.
Atrocity has not had its sense weakened in the
same way.

cannibal

The explorer Christopher Columbus brought the word
cannibal to Europe. In the West Indies he encountered
the warlike Caribs, and believed they were cannibals.
He called them *Canibales*, which entered English
in a translated account of his voyage written in 1553.

Horror

The Caribs also gave their name to the **Caribbean** sea and region.

eerie
The word eerie 'strange and frightening' was originally northern English and Scots in the sense 'fearful'. The focus then moved from feelings of fear to the cause of the fear. It probably comes from Old English *earg* 'cowardly'.

gruesome
Although gruesome first appeared in English in the late 16th century, based on Scots *grue* 'to feel horror, shudder', it was rare before the late 18th century. It was popularized in the novels of Sir Walter Scott: 'He's as grave and grewsome an auld Dutchman as e'er I saw' (*Old Mortality*, 1816). *Grewsome* was the more common spelling until around 1850.

horror
The Latin word *horror* was formed from *horrere*, meaning 'to stand on end' (of hair), and 'to tremble, shudder'. This is the source of our word horror and of related words such as **horrible** and **horrify**.

macabre
One of the medieval miracle plays presented the slaughter of the Maccabees, family members and

supporters of Judus Maccabaeus, who led a religious revolt in Judaea in 165 BC. This gruesome event probably gave rise to macabre, 'disturbing, horrifying', originally in the phrase **dance macabre**, a term for the dance of death. The name Maccabaeus may come from a Hebrew word meaning 'hammer'.

uncanny

The Scots originally used uncanny, just as they did its positive equivalent **canny**, 'shrewd, cautious', 'clever' or 'nice, pleasant'. Uncanny has always had overtones of the occult, and originally implied 'malignant, malicious', but during the 19th century the word left Scotland to develop its usual modern meaning 'mysterious, weird, strange'.

vampire

The best-known vampire is Count Dracula in *Dracula* by Bram Stoker, but these blood-sucking corpses of folklore had caught the public imagination long before the book was published in 1897. They have appeared in English since the mid 18th century. In 1819 *The Vampyre* by John William Polidori was a huge popular success. The word is from Hungarian *vampir*, perhaps from Turkish *uber* 'witch'. The 20th-century film industry gave vampires and vampirism a great publicity boost, as well as introducing the **vamp** or **vampish** heroine.

Horses see also ON THE FARM

canter

This began as a shortened form of **Canterbury pace**
or **Canterbury gallop**, the term for the gentle rate
at which medieval mounted pilgrims made their way
to the shrine of St Thomas à Becket at Canterbury.
To win **at a canter** is to do so with the greatest ease.
In horse-racing a horse easily wins a race if it is
able to run the final stretch cantering rather than
galloping.

jade

Since the Middle Ages a worn-out horse has been a jade,
although the origin is unknown. When a tired person
describes themselves as **jaded** it is in this sense, rather
than the sense of 'a headstrong or disreputable woman',
which developed from it. Jade the green precious stone is
a different word, from Spanish *piedra de ijada*, literally
'stone of the side or flank', from the belief that it was a
cure for colic.

mare

Old English *mearh* 'horse', *mere* 'mare' are from a
Germanic base with related words in Celtic languages
meaning 'stallion'. The sense 'male horse' died out at the
end of the Middle Ages. The same root lies behind
marshal, originally someone in charge of horses.

palfrey

A palfrey is literally an 'extra horse' but came to be used for an ordinary riding horse rather than a warhorse. It goes back via Old French *palefrei*, to late Latin *paraveredus*, from Greek *para* 'extra' and Latin *veredus* 'light horse'. This word was of Gaulish origin, and was used for the fast horses used by couriers, who might need an extra horse to ride when the first tired.

palomino

This term for a light-coloured horse comes via Latin American Spanish from Spanish *palomino* 'young pigeon' used to describe the colour.

pillion

The first people to ride pillion were not necessarily sharing their horses. In the 15th century a pillion was a light saddle, especially one used by women. Pillion is one of the earliest words to have entered English from Gaelic, coming from Scottish Gaelic *pillean* and Irish *pillín* 'small cushion', the root of which is Latin *pellis* 'skin', the source also of **pelt**.

pony

Different as they seem, pony and **poultry** have the same origin. Latin *pullus* meant 'young animal', but it tended to be applied specifically to young horses and young chickens. The 'young horse' strand became Old French *poulain* 'a foal', and the diminutive form of this, *poulenet*, was adopted into Scots in the early 18th century as *powny*, coming into general English as pony. The 'young chicken' strand is the source of Old French *pouletrie*, from which we get poultry.

ride

A word related to **road**, from a time when horses were the usual means of transport. A person who behaves in a way that invites failure is sometimes said to **ride for a fall**. This comes from hunters riding in a way likely to lead to an accident. To **ride herd** on someone, to watch over them, comes from the idea of cowboys guarding or controlling a herd of cattle by riding round its edge. A happy conclusion, **riding off into the sunset**, is a reference to the traditional closing scene of a Western, when the main characters ride off towards the setting sun. Yorkshire's East, North, and West **Riding** are unconnected to horses. The word for these three former administrative divisions goes back to Old Norse *thrithjungr* 'third part', from *thrithi* 'third'. Over time the 'th' was lost, so that the 'third part' became a riding.

stable

The French *estable*, from which we get stable, could refer to a shelter for pigs or for horses, and in English a stable originally housed any domestic animal. The saying **shut** (or **lock**) **the stable door after the horse has bolted**—take preventive measures too late, once the damage has already been done—dates back to medieval times, though until the late 19th century it referred to horse-stealing and was **shut the stable door after the steed is stolen**. **Stable** 'firmly fixed' is a quite different word, which goes back to Latin *stare* 'to stand'.

steeplechase

A steeplechase was originally a horse race across country over hedges, walls, and ditches. The term dates from the late 18th century and comes from the idea of using a distant church steeple to mark the finishing point of the race, which you have to reach by clearing any intervening obstacles. **Steeple** comes from the same Old English root as the adjective **steep**.

Hygiene see also MEDICINE

bath

The city of Bath in the west of England gets its name from its hot springs, where people immersed themselves for health reasons. The city gave its name to the **bath chair** in which its invalids were transported. The British order of knighthood, the **Order of the Bath**, has this name because recipients took a ritual bath before being installed. If sports players **take an early bath** they have been sent off by the referee.

bidet

Originally in both French and English bidet meant 'pony, small horse'—the link was the way people sat astride both.

detergent

This was formed from the Latin verb *detergere*, from de- 'away from' and *tergere* 'to wipe'.

fastidious

This comes from Latin *fastidiosus*, from *fastidium* 'loathing'. The word originally meant 'disagreeable, distasteful', later 'disgusted'. Current senses ('attentive to accuracy', 'concerned about personal cleanliness') date from the 17th century.

fumigate

We would fumigate a room today if we wanted to disinfect it, but the earliest use was 'to **perfume**', of which it is also the root, from the pleasant smell of incense. It comes ultimately from Latin *fumus* 'smoke', which also gives us **fume**.

hygiene

The word hygiene goes back to Greek *hugieinē (tekhnē)* meaning '(art) of health', from *hugiēs* 'healthy'.

lather

Old English *læthor* was 'washing soda' or its froth. Of
Germanic origin, lather is related to the Old Norse noun
lauthr, from an Indo-European root shared by Greek
loutron 'bath'. The sense 'agitation' as in **get into a
lather** dates from the early 19th century.

launder

In the sense 'to wash clothes or linen', launder was
originally a contracted form of *lavender*, a medieval
word meaning 'a person who washes clothes'. It goes
back to Latin *lavare* to wash. This is also the source of
lava, originally an Italian word for 'stream' narrowed
down to mean a stream of lava, **lavatory**, and **lavish**,
where the sense of 'profusion' comes from the French
for a deluge of rain; and **lotion** which in the past could
also be used for the action of washing as well as for a
liquid rubbed on. **Lavender**, the plant, probably does not
come directly from *lavare*, but its form was altered to
look as if it did, because lavender was used to scent
washing. The Watergate scandal in the USA in the early
1970s, in which an attempt to bug the national
headquarters of the Democratic Party led to the
resignation of President Richard Nixon, gave the world
money laundering. Before bathrooms and running
water, people washed from a basin or bowl. This is what
a **lavatory** originally was—a vessel for washing. In the
mid 17th century the word came to refer to a room with

washing facilities, from which developed the modern
sense of a toilet.

scald

To scald comes from Anglo-Norman French *escalder*,
from late Latin *excaldare* 'wash in hot water' formed
from Latin *ex-* 'thoroughly' and *calidus* 'hot'.

swab

A swab was initially a 'mop for cleaning the decks'. It
was formed from **swabber** 'a sailor detailed to swab
decks': this derives from early modern Dutch *zwabber*,
from a Germanic base meaning 'splash' or 'sway'. The
medical sense dates from the mid 19th century.

Insects

antenna

On old Mediterranean sailing ships certain types of
triangular sail, called lateen sails, were supported by long
yards or poles at an angle of 45 degrees to the mast,
which reminded the ancients of an insect's antennae.
The Latin word *antenna* was an alteration of *antemna*
'sailyard', and was used by writers to translate the Greek
keraioi 'horns of insects'. When Marconi and others
developed radio in the 1890s the word was quickly taken
up to refer to a rod or wire by which signals were
received.

butterfly

The word **butter**, known in Britain since Anglo-Saxon
times, goes back to Greek *bouturon*, and before that
possibly to the Scythians, an ancient people from the
area of the Black Sea. The butterfly may get its name
from the brimstone butterfly and other yellow or cream-
coloured butterflies. The boxing strategy of Muhammad
Ali was famously described as 'Float like a butterfly, sting
like a bee'. The quote first appeared in *The Cassius Clay
Story* (1964—Cassius Clay was Ali's original name), and is
thought to have been coined by Ali's trainer Drew
'Bundini' Brown.

Insects

caterpillar

The caterpillar first appeared in English in the form *catyrpel*, probably an alteration of the Old French word *chatepelose*, literally 'hairy cat'. English used to have a word *piller*, meaning 'a plunderer or ravager' (related to **pillage**) and, given the damage that caterpillars do to plants, it is likely that this influenced how the word is spelt.

cockroach

The early written form of cockroach was *cacaroch*, from the Spanish *cucaracha* 'cockroach'. People adapted the spelling to make it fit in better with the more familiar English words **cock**, which probably comes ultimately from the sound it makes, and **roach**, the freshwater fish, whose origin is unknown.

earwig

Earwigs have nothing to do with wigs. The -wig bit is related to **wiggle**, which makes a lot more sense. It was once thought that earwigs crawled into people's ears, an idea found in other languages: in French an earwig is a *perce-oreilles*, 'ear-piercer'; in German it is *Ohrwurm*, 'ear worm'. The Germans also used *Ohrwurm* for those irritating snatches of music that stick in your head, and **ear worm** is now used in this sense. These tunes are also called sticky tunes or a cognitive itch, while the Brazilians call them *chiclete de ouvido* or ear chewing gum.

fly

In Old English a fly was any winged insect. In the 17th century Edward Topsell wrote of 'the black flies called beetles'. **A fly in the ointment**, a minor irritation that spoils the success or enjoyment of something, goes back to the biblical book of Ecclesiastes, 'Dead flies cause the ointment of the apothecary to send forth a stinking savour.' To **fly a kite** now means 'to try something out to test public opinion', but in the 19th century it was to raise money on credit. In the USA **go fly a kite** means go away. The **flies** on trousers or in a theatre come from the idea that they are only partly attached to their base, as if they could fly off.

insect

Insects have bodies that are divided into segments, the basic idea behind the word. Insect was formed from Latin *animal insectum* 'segmented animal', and originally referred to any small cold-blooded creature with a segmented body. The root word is *secare* 'to cut', which also gave us **dissect**, **section**, and **segment**.

larva

'A disembodied spirit or ghost' was the first use of this Latin word which means literally 'ghost, mask'. The modern use as a term for the active immature form of an insect is due to the Swedish botanist Linnaeus (1707–78).

mite

Old English *mīte*, a tiny arachnid related to the ticks, is of Germanic origin. Mite used in phrases such **as poor little mite** is probably from the same word but was also the name, during the Middle Ages, a small Flemish copper coin. The 'small size' is reflected in the phrase the **widow's mite**, from Mark 12:42 'And there came a certain poor widow, and she threw in two mites, which make a farthing'.

wasp

Wasp can be traced back to an ancient root that also produced the Latin word for 'wasp', *vespa*. The ultimate origin may be a word that meant 'to weave', from the way wasps chew up wood into a papery substance to construct their nests. The Latin *vespa* was carried forward into Italian and used for the Vespa, the little motor scooter beloved by Italians, named for its hyperactive buzzing.

Insults

see also FOOLS, REPTILES AND AMPHIBIANS, SLANG, TROUBLE

gormless

The original spelling was *gaumless*, formed from dialect *gaum* 'understanding' from Old Norse *gaumr* 'care, heed'.

lackadaisical

'Feebly sentimental' was among the early meanings of lackadaisical, which comes from the archaic interjection **lackaday** (earlier *alack-a-day*), and its extended form **lackadaisy**.

loon

This word for a 'silly person' comes from the North American loon, a large water bird also known as a diver which gets its name from its distinctive cry. The sense silly is from the bird's actions when escaping from danger, perhaps influenced by **loony**, the abbreviation of **lunatic** from Latin *luna* 'moon'. In the past people thought that the phases of the moon could affect people.

ludicrous

The early sense of ludicrous was 'sportive, intended as a jest': it is based on Latin *ludicrus*, probably from *ludicrum* 'stage play'.

po-faced

The po in po-faced, 'humourless and disapproving', probably comes from the use of po to mean 'chamber pot', though it might also have been influenced by the exclamation '**poh**!', used to reject something contemptuously. It is first recorded in the 1930s and was probably modelled on the expression **poker-faced**. This comes from the need to keep a deadpan face when

171

playing poker. The game, first recorded in the 1830s in the USA probably gets its name from the German word *pochen* 'to brag'.

prude

The old French word *prudefemme*, which was applied to a modest and respectable woman, was the source of prude. This was the female equivalent of French *prud'homme* 'a good man and true'. The English word was used in a more negative sense than the French one, describing an excessively prim and demure woman, and is now applied to either sex.

scruff

As an insult for a person with a dirty or untidy appearance, scruff is an alteration of **scurf** meaning dandruff or a similar skin condition, which comes from the same root as Old English words meaning 'to gnaw' and 'to shred'. The reversal of letters from scurf to scruff is also seen in **bird** and **dirt**, originally *brid* and *drit*. The **scruff of the neck** was originally the *scuff*—the word is recorded from the late 18th century, but its origin is obscure.

toady

In the 17th century one way unscrupulous charlatans and quacks tried to sell their supposed cures was to have an assistant take the medicine and then eat, or pretend to eat, a toad—people thought that toads were poisonous and so were likely to attribute the assistant's survival to the charlatan's wares. The assistant was a **toad-eater**. In the 18th century this term also came to mean 'a fawning flatterer', and in the early 19th it was shortened to toady. **Toad** is an Old English word, and **toadstool** is apparently from the fungus being the right size and shape to be a toad's stool.

twit

The kind of twit that is a silly or foolish person dates only from the 1930s and comes from an English dialect use that meant 'a tale-bearer'. This may go back to twit in the sense 'to tease or taunt someone, especially in a good-humoured way', which is a shortening of Old English ætwītan 'reproach with'.

wimp

Wimp seems to have originated in the USA in the 1920s, although it was not really used much until the 1960s. There was an earlier slang term **wimp** which meant 'woman', used at Oxford University in the early years of the 20th century. This could be the origin, or wimp could simply be an alteration of **whimper**. Like **bonk**, **drum**, and **hoot**, whimper is another of those words suggested by the sound it represents. 'This is the way the world ends / Not with a bang but a whimper' is from 'The Hollow Men' (1925) by T. S. Eliot.

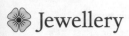 Jewellery

amber

Amber comes from Arabic *'anbar*, which also meant 'ambergris' a wax-like substance used in the manufacture of perfume that originates as a secretion of the sperm whale. Much more appealing is **amber nectar**, which was popularized as an advertising slogan for Fosters lager from 1986. It goes back much further than that, though, and has been a slang term for beer since the 1890s, especially in Australia.

amethyst

It was traditionally believed that putting an amethyst in your drink could prevent you getting drunk, through an association of the colour of the stone and the colour of red wine. The word comes from the Greek *amethustos*, meaning 'not drunken'.

aquamarine

In Latin *aqua* means 'water' and *marina* means 'of the sea, marine'. Put them together and you get aquamarine, a precious stone the blue-green colour of sea water. Other words from *aqua* include **aquarium**, **aquatic**, and **aqueduct**, which is combined with Latin *ducere* 'to lead'

brilliant

This is from French *brillant* 'shining' which is probably from Latin *beryllus* 'beryl'. The abbreviation **brill** meaning 'great, wonderful' came into use in the 1980s.

carat

This measure of the purity of gold and a unit of weight for precious stones comes via French from Italian *carato*, from Arabi *kīrāṭ*, a unit of weight. The base is Greek *keration* used for both a carob seed and a unit of weight but literally 'little horn' describing the carob's elongated seedpod.

emerald

The word emerald can be traced back to Greek *smaragdos*, and ultimately to an ancient Hebrew verb meaning 'flash or sparkle'. In early English examples the word's meaning is vague, and does not necessarily refer to a green stone. Ireland has been called the **Emerald Isle**, on account of its lush greenery, since as long ago as 1795.

ivory

The Latin word *ebur*, from which ivory derives, is related to ancient Egyptian *āb* or *ābu* 'elephant'. Before poachers reduced elephant numbers, ivory was an important item of commerce, used for many functional items as well as for ornaments. The 'white' piano keys were made of ivory, and to **tickle** or **tinkle the ivories** is a familiar expression for 'to play the piano'. An **ivory tower** is a state of privileged seclusion or separation from the facts and practicalities of the real world. The phrase is an early 20th-century translation of French *tour d'ivoire*, used in 1837 by the critic and writer Charles Augustin Sainte-Beuve.

jet

The name jet for a hard black semi-precious mineral comes ultimately from the Greek word *gagatēs* 'from Gagai', a town in Asia Minor. When we refer to a jet of water or gas, or a jet aircraft, we are using a quite different word. It comes from a late 16th-century verb meaning 'to jut out', from French *jeter* 'to throw', which goes back to the Latin *jacere* 'to throw'. **Jut** is a variant of jet in this sense. *Jacere* is found in a large number of English words including **abject** literally 'thrown away'; **conjecture** 'throw together'; **deject** 'thrown down'; **ejaculate** from *jaculum* 'dart, something thrown'; **eject** 'throw out'; **inject** 'throw in'; **project** 'throw forth'; **subject** 'thrown under'; **trajectory** 'something thrown across'; and **jetty** which is something thrown out into the water. In the 1950s the idea of flying abroad by jet aircraft was new and sophisticated. At the start of that decade people who flew for pleasure came to be known as the **jet set**.

pearl

Pearl is from Old French *perle* and may be based on Latin *perna* 'leg', extended to mean a leg-of-mutton-shaped water mussel (mentioned by Pliny). The Romans greatly prized freshwater pearls, Britain's reputation as a good source of pearls being one of the motives behind their invasion. Matthew 7:6 has provided a common idiomatic expression: 'Neither cast ye your **pearls before swine**'. In Romance languages the usual word for pearl comes via Latin, from Greek *margeron*, possibly from some Eastern language. The word became *marguerite* in French, which was also used for a variety of daisy-like flowers, because they are pearly white. This is also the source of the name **Margaret**.

ruby

This is the English form of *rubinus*, the Latin name of the precious stone. This comes from *rubeus* 'red'. This is also the source of **rubric** which goes back to Latin *rubrica (terra)* 'red (earth or ochre as writing material)', from the fact that rubrics were originally written in red ink.

Jobs

abbot

This comes from Aramaic *'abbā* 'father' introduced through its use in the Bible.

Jobs

charwoman

The first element of this word is from obsolete *char* or *chare* meaning 'a turn of work, an odd job, chore'. **Chore** is a variant.

chauffeur

Early cars could be steam-driven rather than have petrol engines, which explains why this French word literally means 'stoker' from *chauffer* 'to heat'.

detective

The development of an organized police force demanded a word such as detective, and it was duly formed in the 1840s from **detect**. The first occurrences are in **detective police** and **detective policeman**; simple detective is a shortening of the latter. Charles Dickens was one of the earliest to draw attention to this innovation, reporting in his magazine *Household Words* in 1850 that 'To each division of the Force is attached two officers, who are denominated "detectives".'

guard

An Old Germanic element meaning 'to watch, guard' lies behind both guard and **ward**. Ward came into English from Old English *weard* 'watchman, guard'. The sense 'child protected by a guardian' is medieval, and the sense of a hospital ward, where you are watched over by nurses or wardens, is mid 18th century. Meanwhile,

Germanic-speaking Franks had taken over areas of Europe that were mainly Romance speaking, and introduced the word into Romance. The *w* became a *g(u)* and the word became *g(u)arde* in Old French from which the g- forms were introduced into English. The g- and w- forms (found as alternatives in other words in modern French and English, as in the name William or Guillaume) are also found in **warden** and **guardian**. **Wardrobe**, a place where you look after clothes, has an alternative **garderobe**. These were once interchangeable. However, garderobe is now mainly restricted to a term for a medieval lavatory. Wardrobe could have this sense in the past, for both words developed the sense of a small room where you could be private, and from there somewhere you could do something in private.

henchman

The original sense of this was probably 'a groom'. It is from Old English *hengest* 'stallion', and man. The first part also features in the names of the semi-mythological leaders Hengist and Horsa (meaning 'horse'), who supposedly came to Britain at the invitation of the British King Vortigern in 449 to assist in defeating the Picts. From the Middle Ages a henchman was a squire or page of honour to a person of great rank; in Scotland he was the principal attendant of a Highland chief. The word was taken up by Sir Walter Scott, whose novels were hugely popular throughout the 19th century, and

Jobs

Scott gave henchman to the wider world. The current sense, 'a criminal's follower', began in the mid 19th century in the USA.

navvy

A navvy is a labourer employed in building a road or railway. The word is a 19th-century shortening of **navigator**, which in the 18th century was a labourer employed in the rapidly expanding enterprise of canal construction (in parts of England a canal is known as a **navigation**). Navigate comes from the Latin word for ship, *navis*, which gave rise to **navy**, and also, because of its shape, to the **nave** or long central part of a church. The ultimate root of *navis* is the Greek word for ship, *naus* (also source of **nausea**, which originally meant seasickness).

pundit

A modern pundit is an expert in a particular subject called on to give their opinions about it to the public. The source of the word is Sanskrit *pandita* 'learned', used to describe a learned man versed in Sanskrit law, philosophy, and religion. The 'learned expert or authority' sense dates from the early 19th century.

tailor

A tailor's work is indicated in the source of the word, which goes back to Latin *taliare* 'to cut'.

valet

Rich men who could afford to employ a valet to look
after their clothes had to be careful that he was also not
a **varlet**, 'an unprincipled man', as the words are
essentially the same. French *valet* 'attendant' and its early
variant varlet are related to **vassal**, from medieval Latin
vassallus 'retainer', which derived from a Celtic word.
The first valets were 15th-century footmen who acted as
attendants on a horseman.

Language see also LITERATURE, SLANG

Babel

Genesis 11 tells the story of the Tower of Babel, where God, angered by the arrogance of its builders who thought they could reach heaven by erecting a tower, confused their language so that they could no longer understand each other. Babel was originally the Hebrew form of 'Babylon', a name meaning 'gate of God' in the Babylonian Akkadian language. The Bible story led to its use in English in the general sense of 'a confusion of sounds'.

bombastic

Although it now means 'high-sounding language with little meaning', **bombast** originally referred to raw cotton or cotton wool used as padding. The source is Old French *bombace*, from medieval Latin *bombax*, an alteration of *bombyx* 'silk'.

cockney

A cockney was originally a pampered or spoilt child. It may come from a similar word, *cokeney* 'a cock's egg', which, since cocks do not lay eggs, actually meant a small and misshapen hen's egg. The 'pampered child' meaning developed into an insulting term for someone who lives in the town, regarded as effeminate and weak, in contrast to hardier country dwellers. By the early

17th century cockney was being applied to someone from
the East End of London, traditionally someone born
within the sound of Bow Bells (the bells of St Mary-le-Bow
church in the City of London).

gossip

In Old English *godsibb* or gossip meant a godparent,
literally 'a person related to one in God'. It came from
god 'God' and *sibb* 'a relative', the latter found in **sibling**.
Gossip came to be applied to a close friend, especially a
female friend invited to be present at a birth. From this
developed the idea of someone who enjoys idle talk, and
by the 19th century idle talk or tittle-tattle itself.

idiom

This goes back to Greek *idioma* 'private or peculiar
phraseology', from *idiousthai* 'make one's own' from
idios 'own, private'. **Idiosyncrasy** is from *idios* combined
with *sun* 'with' and *krasis* 'mixture', and originally meant
'physical constitution peculiar to an individual'.

jargon

Modern life is full of jargon, language used by a particular
group that is difficult for other people to understand. It
comes from Old French *jargoun* 'the warbling of birds',
and in medieval English meant 'twittering, chattering' and
also 'gibberish'. Our current sense had developed by the
17th century.

Language

laconic

The Spartans or Laconians of ancient Greece were known for their austere lifestyle and pithy speech. When Philip of Macedon threatened to invade Laconia in the 4th century BC, he wrote to its governing magistrates trying to frighten them into submission, saying that if he entered Laconia he would raze it to the ground. They are reported to have sent a one-word reply—'If'. Since the 16th century laconic has meant 'using very few words'.

palaver

When early Portuguese traders in West Africa had disputes or misunderstandings with the locals they used the Portuguese word *palavra*, literally 'word, speech', to mean 'a talk between local people and traders'. Africans picked up the term from them, and later passed it on to English sailors. In English palaver first meant a prolonged and tedious discussion, then in the late 19th century a fuss, commotion, or rigmarole. The Portuguese *palavra* developed from Latin *parabola* 'parable'.

syllable

Syllable comes via Old French and Latin from Greek *sullabē*, from *sun-* 'together' and *lambanein* 'take'. A syllable is basically a group of sounds 'taken together' and uttered with a single effort.

waffle

Someone who waffles rambles on in a vague or trivial
way, but in the 17th century to waffle was 'to yap or
yelp', and then 'to dither'. It came from English dialect
waff 'to yelp' (the same word as **woof**, both imitating
the sound), and was used mainly in northern England
until the modern meaning developed in the early
20th century. Waffle 'a small crisp batter cake'
is quite different: it comes from Dutch *wafel* from
Old French *gaufre*, the root of **wafer**. *Gaufre* also
meant 'honeycomb', and this is probably the basic
idea—the indentations on a waffle or wafer look like
a honeycomb.

 Law see also CRIME, PUNISHMENT

affidavit

A legal term from medieval Latin, affidavit means
literally 'he has stated on oath'.

affray

Although an affray is now a disturbance of the peace
caused by fighting in a public place, its first meaning
was 'alarm, fright or terror' or 'frighten'. Its root is the
old Norman French word *afrayer*, which also gives us
afraid.

Law

arson

This was an Anglo-Norman legal term which came from Latin *ardere* 'to burn'.

bequeath

The Old English form *becwethan* is composed of *be-* 'about' and *cwethan* 'say'. This and the related **bequest** are both Middle English and reflect a time when wills were often spoken rather than written. **Quoth**, an old term for 'he/she said' also comes from *cwethan*.

copper

The verb **cop** meaning 'to catch', comes from a northern English dialect word cap meaning 'to capture or arrest'. This probably goes back to Latin *capere*, 'to take or seize'. So a copper was a catcher, which is why it became an informal word for a police officer in the 1840s. Apprehended villains have been saying '**it's a fair cop!**' since the 1880s. Copper, the reddish-brown metal, comes from Latin *cyprium aes* 'Cyprus metal'. The island of Cyprus was the Romans' main source of copper.

curfew

Today a curfew is sometimes imposed during periods of emergency or conflict, as a way of keeping people off the streets, usually at night. In the Middle Ages, though, the curfew was the time by which people had to put out or cover the fire in their hearth—the objective was not to keep order but to stop houses burning down. Curfew is an Old French word, from *cuvrir* 'to cover' and *feu* 'fire'.

jeopardy

The early spelling of jeopardy was *iuparti*. The word comes from Old French *ieu* (modern *jeu*) *parti* 'an evenly divided game', and was originally used in chess and similar games to mean a problem or position in which the chances of winning or losing were evenly balanced. This led to the modern sense 'a dangerous situation' and the legal use 'danger arising from being on trial for a criminal offence'.

libel

When first used a libel was 'a document, a written statement': it came via Old French from Latin *libellus*, a diminutive of *liber* 'book', source of **library**. Used as a legal term referring to a published false statement damaging to someone's reputation, libel dates from the early 17th century. Libel contrasts with **slander** which is spoken.

ombudsman

There are not many words in English that come directly from Swedish, but this is one of them. In the 1950s we adopted the Swedish word for 'legal representative' as a term for an official appointed to investigate individual complaints against companies or the government, though the British Parliamentary Commissioner for Administration, as the office is formally known, dates from 1967.

reprieve

Some words have not just changed their meaning, but reversed it. When reprieve came into English from Old French, based on Latin *reprehendere* 'to seize, take back', it meant 'to take back to prison'. In the mid 16th century it referred to postponing or delaying a legal process, before developing into the current sense of cancelling an impending punishment.

 # Light

blaze

The blaze meaning 'a bright flame' and the one referring to a white streak on a horse's face are probably related, through the idea of shining or brightness.
In America the second came to apply to a white mark chipped in a tree to indicate a path or boundary in the mid 17th century. This is where we get to **blaze a trail**, 'to set an example by being the first to do something'. Cricketers and other sportsmen wore a type of brightly

coloured, often striped jacket called a **blazer** in the late
19th century. The name came from the brightness of
the cloth.

halo

This was originally a circle of light such as that around
the sun; it came via medieval Latin from Greek *halōs*
which referred to the 'disc of the sun or moon'. From
around the middle of the 17th century, the word came to
be applied to the circle of light depicted around Christ's
head or those of the saints. Its use for an effect in
photography is found from the 1940s.

incandescent

This comes via French, from Latin *incandescere* 'glow',
based on *candidus* 'white'. The prefix *in-* here intensifies
the meaning. The **incense** that you burn comes from
the related *candere* 'to glow', while the sense meaning 'to
inflame with anger' comes from the related *incendere* 'set
fire to' also found in **incendiary**.

inferno

In the early 14th century the Italian poet Dante Alighieri
wrote *The Divine Comedy*, describing his journey through
hell and purgatory and finally to paradise. The description
of hell in particular, the 'Inferno', had a lasting impact
on the European imagination. The word came to mean
'hell' and then any 'fire raging out of control'. Italian

Light

inferno comes from Latin *infernus* 'below, subterranean', which is also the source of **infernal**, and is related to **inferior**.

limelight

Before electricity or gas lighting, theatres lit up important actors and scenes using limelight. This was an intense white light produced by heating up a piece of lime in a flame of combined oxygen and hydrogen, a process invented around 1825 by Captain T. Drummond of the Royal Engineers. From the end of the 19th century, as modern lighting ended the need for real limelight, the word came to be more common in the sense 'the focus of public attention'.

luminous

Luminous is from Old French *lumineux* or Latin *luminosus*, from *lumen, lumin-* 'light'.

minaret

This word for a slender tower (for example, part of a mosque) comes via Turkish from Arabic *manār(a)* 'lighthouse, minaret', based on *nār* 'fire or light'.

neon

This gas, used in fluorescent lamps and illuminated advertising signs, was named in 1898 by its discoverers, the scientists Sir William Ramsay and M. W. Travers.

Neon is simply the Greek word for 'new thing'. The same Greek word is the source of the many English words that start with neo- and refer to a new or revived form of something, such as **neoclassical**, **neocolonialism**, and **neo-Nazi**, a word that appeared in 1944 before the Nazis had even been ousted from power.

tinsel

Sparkly tinsel comes from Latin *scintilla* 'a spark', which is also the source of **scintillate**. In medieval times tinsel was fabric woven with metallic thread or spangles—it became something like our familiar shiny strips in the late 16th century. The idea of glitter was picked up during the 1970s in **Tinseltown**, a nickname for Hollywood and its cinema.

twinkle

As well as its original sense 'to sparkle, glimmer', twinkle also meant 'to wink, blink the eyes' from the 14th to the early 19th century. The meaning 'the time taken to wink or blink'—a very short time, in other words—is just as old, but it survives only as **in the twinkling of an eye**, 'very quickly'. This is probably because the phrase appears in various passages in the Bible, including Corinthians: 'In a moment, in the twinkling of an eye, at the last trump.' A similar expression containing the same idea is **in the blink of an eye**.

Literature

see also BOOKS, FICTION TO WORD, LANGUAGE, WRITING

anecdote

This is from Greek *anekdota* 'things unpublished'. It came to be used for any short story from its use by Byzantine historian Procopius (*c.*500–*c.*562) for his *Anekdota* or 'Unpublished Memoirs' (also called *The Secret History*) of the Emperor Justinian, tales of the private life of the court.

bathos

A Greek word first recorded in English in the literal Greek sense 'depth'. The literary sense was introduced by Alexander Pope in the early 18th century. He published the *Bathos* in his *Miscellanies* (third volume) in 1728, which was a lively satire giving descriptions of bad authors, identified by initials. **Bathysphere** for a spherical chamber that can be lowered into the depths of the sea, comes from the same source.

epilogue

An epilogue, a comment or conclusion at the end of a piece, comes via Latin from Greek *epilogos*, from *epi* 'in addition' and *logos* 'speech'.

lampoon

The source of English lampoon meaning 'publicly criticize using ridicule or irony' is French *lampon*. This is said to be from the refrain of popular French drinking songs in the 1600s *lampons* 'let us drink!', from *lamper* 'gulp down'.

plagiarism

This term for passing someone's ideas off as one's own is from Latin *plagiarius* 'kidnapper'. The Latin poet Martial (AD 40–*c*.102) used the term in one of his poems for a literary thief.

poet

A poet is literally 'a maker' (a term also used for 'poet' in the Middle Ages) from Greek *poētēs*, 'maker, poet'. A fitting or deserved retribution is **poetic justice**. Alexander Pope used the phrase in his satire *The Dunciad* (1742), where he depicts 'Poetic Justice, with her lifted scale'.

rhyme

Both rhyme and **rhythm** come from the same source, Greek *rhuthmos*. Before it referred to a musical beat rhythm meant 'rhyme'. Since the 16th century a person complaining that something lacked logical explanation might say that there was **no rhyme or reason to it**.

Literature

romance

The Romance languages are the European languages descended from Latin, romance coming via Old French from Latin *Romanicus* 'Roman'. A romance became a story in the local language describing the adventures of a hero of chivalry. These were often wild and improbable so the word became associated with any narrative depicting fantastic events or, because love was often the subject, with love. The senses 'idealized or sentimental love' and 'a love affair' are Victorian. In the late 18th century the **Romantic movement** arose, exemplified by the writers Wordsworth, Coleridge, Shelley, and Keats and painters such as William Blake and J. M. W. Turner.

story

Story, **storey**, and **history** come from Latin *historia* 'history, story'. A story was initially a historical account or representation, usually involving passages of bible history and saints' legends. From the 1500s story became used of entertaining fiction. **Storey** is essentially the same word. It may have originally referred to tiers of painted windows or sculptures decorating the fronts of buildings, showing historical subjects. Each tier was a different 'story' or, once the spelling changed, 'storey'. Eventually it came to refer to a level of a building. Some time in the 1930s or before, someone told a long, rambling anecdote about a dog with shaggy hair. It must have caught the public imagination, as ever since any similar story that only amuses because it is absurdly inconsequential or pointless has been a **shaggy-dog story**.

verse

In his poem 'Digging' (1966), Seamus Heaney resolves to carry on the family tradition of digging the soil by 'digging', not with a spade like his father and grandfather, but with a pen. The link between agriculture and writing poetry goes back to the origin of verse, as Latin *versus* meant both 'a turn of the plough, furrow' and 'line of writing'. The idea here is that of a plough making another line or furrow. *Versus* also gives us **versatile** and **version**. It is based on Latin *vertere* 'to turn', source of **vertebra**, **vertical**, **vertigo**, and **adverse**, **convert**, and also **pervert** 'turn bad'. **Versed**, as in **well versed in**, is different, coming from Latin *versari* 'be engaged in'.

Machines see also COMPUTERS, TOOLS

crank

The mechanical crank is found in Old English *cranc* recorded in *crancstæf*, a weaver's implement. The primary notion is 'something bent together' and it is related to *crincan* 'to bend', probably also the source of **cringe**. **Crank** and **cranky** meaning an eccentric or bad-tempered person are from a dialect word originally meaning 'weak, in poor health'.

damper

It stops the vibration of piano strings, absorbs shock in cars, and regulates the draught in chimneys, but originally a damper was a person or thing that dampened the spirits. This is what **to put a damper on** refers to. In Australia and New Zealand an unleavened loaf or cake of flour and water has been called a damper since the early 19th century.

engine

Engine is from Old French *engin*, from Latin *ingenium* 'talent, device', the source also of **ingenious**. Like many English words that now start with *en-*, it could also be spelled *in-*. Its original senses were 'ingenuity, cunning', and 'natural talent, wit, genius', which survives in Scots as **ingine**. From there it became 'the product of ingenuity, a plot, or snare', and also 'a tool or weapon', specifically a large mechanical weapon, such as a battering ram or heavy catapult, constructed by **engineers**. By the first half of the 17th century something like our idea of an engine had arisen, a fairly complex device with moving parts that worked together.

gadget

Sailors were the first people to talk about gadgets. The word started out in nautical slang as a general term for any small device or mechanism or part of a ship. This is the earliest recorded use, dated 1886: 'Then the names of all the other things on board a ship! I don't know half of them yet; even the sailors forget at times, and if the exact name of anything they want happens to slip from their memory, they call it a chicken-fixing, or a gadjet, or a gill-guy, or a timmey-noggy, or a wim-wom.' The word is probably from French *gâchette* 'a lock mechanism' or *gagée* 'tool'.

gasket

A gasket was at first a cord securing a furled sail to the yard of a sailing ship. It may come from French *garcette* 'thin rope'. The term for a flat ring used as a seal in an internal combustion engine dates from the early 20th century.

ignition

Ignition initially meant heating something to the point of combustion or chemical change. The Latin *ignire* 'set

on fire', from *ignis* 'fire' is also found in **igneous** rock for
solidified magma.

piston

The Latin *pistullum* meant **pestle** and is the source of
the botanical **pistil** from its similar shape. From the
same source Italian formed *pestone* for a large pestle or
rammer, and this, via French, is the source of piston.

technology

This is from Greek *tekhnologia* 'systematic treatment',
from *tekhnē* 'art' and *–logia* 'speaking, discourse'.
Technique comes from the same source via French.

valve

Latin *valva* meant a leaf of a door and valve entered the
language with this sense. Towards the end of the 18th
century it was used to describe a door or flap controlling
the flow of water and modern senses developed from
this.

widget

The widget is first recorded in the 1920s in the USA, in
the general sense 'a small gadget', and is probably an
alteration of gadget. In the early 1990s a widget became
a specific sort of device used in some beer cans to
introduce nitrogen into the beer, giving it a creamy
head.

Magic see also MYTH

charm

In the Middle Ages a charm was an incantation or magic spell, and did not mean 'a quality of fascinating or being attractive to people' until the 17th century. It comes from Latin *carmen* 'song, incantation'. **Charm offensive**, a campaign of flattery and friendliness designed to gain support, dates from the late 1970s. This is a fine example of an oxymoron, a figure of speech in which apparently contradictory terms appear together.

conjure

The earliest meanings of conjure were 'to call in the name of some divine or supernatural being; to appeal solemnly, entreat'. The -*jure* bit is from Latin *jurare* 'to swear', which gave us **jury**. Another early meaning was 'to call on a supernatural being to appear by magic ritual', which became 'make something appear as if by magic'.

enchant

Enchant is from French *enchanter*, from Latin *incantare*, based on *cantare* 'to sing'. The Latin gave us **chant**, **canticle**, a 'little song', and **incantation**. The original meanings of enchant were 'put under a spell' and 'delude'. **Enchanter's nightshade** was believed by early botanists to be the herb used by the enchantress Circe of Greek mythology, who turned Odysseus's companions into pigs.

Magic

glamour

Although rarely associated, glamour and **grammar** are related. Glamour was originally a Scots word meaning 'enchantment, magic' or 'a spell, charm' and was an altered form of grammar. Greek *gramma* 'a letter of the alphabet, something written down' was the source of grammar, which in medieval times meant 'scholarship, learning'. These were associated with astrology and occult practices, so connected with magic. 'Magical beauty' became associated with glamour in the mid 19th century, and from the 1930s the word was particularly used of attractive women.

magic

The **Magi** were the 'wise men' from the East who visited Jesus soon after his birth. They were said to have been kings, called Caspar, Melchior, and Balthasar, bringing gifts of gold, frankincense, and myrrh. The singular, **magus**, was originally a member of a priestly caste of ancient Persia credited with unusual powers. This, filtered through Greek and Latin, gave us magic and **magician**.

sorcerer

A sorcerer was originally a *sorser*, coming via Old French *sorcier* from Latin *sors* 'lot, fortune', the root of **sort**. The Latin comes from the use of oracles and casting lots to foretell the future. **Sorcerer's apprentice**, someone who starts something they cannot control without help, translates French *L'apprenti sorcier*, the title of an

1897 symphonic poem by Paul Dukas based on *Der Zauberlehrling*, a ballad written in 1797 by the German author Goethe. In this the apprentice's use of magic when his master is absent starts a series of events which he cannot control.

wand

A word from Old Norse, related to **wend** and **wind** 'to move in a twisting way'—the basic idea seems to be of a supple, flexible stick. Wand had no connection with wizards and spells until about 1400, some 200 years after it was first used. **Wander**, 'to move in a leisurely or aimless way', comes from a similar root.

warlock

This is not connected with war or locks, and not originally connected with magic. For Anglo-Saxons a warlock was 'an evil person, traitor', 'monster, savage', and 'the Devil'. The sense 'sorcerer, wizard' was originally Scottish, and only became widely known when used by the novelist Sir Walter Scott in the early 19th century. It comes from Old English words meaning 'agreement, promise' and 'deny'.

whammy

A whammy is an evil influence or hex, formed from **wham**, an imitation of the sound of a forcible impact which has only been used since the 1920s. Whammy has been around since the 1940s but is particularly associated with the 1950s cartoon strip 'Li'l Abner', where the hillbilly Evil-Eye Fleegle could shoot a single whammy to put a curse on somebody by pointing a finger with one eye open, and a **double whammy** with both eyes open.

witch

For Anglo-Saxons witches were of both sexes. The masculine was *wicca*, the source of **wicked**, which was revived by modern pagans for their religion, **Wicca**. A female witch was a *wicce*. A male witch is now a **wizard**, which comes from wise—Medieval wizards were wise men, only becoming magicians in the mid 16th century. **The witching hour**, midnight, when witches are active, is from Shakespeare's *Hamlet*. Hamlet declares: Tis now the very witching time of night, / When churchyards yawn, and hell itself breathes out / Contagion to this world.' George Orwell first used **witch-hunt** to mean 'a campaign directed at people considered unorthodox or a threat to society', of Communists being persecuted in the Spanish Civil War (1936–9).

 # Mammals

see also ON SAFARI, ON THE FARM, PETS

badger

Badger is probably based on **badge** (of unknown origin), from the animal's distinctive facial markings. Use as a verb arose in the late 18th century and reflects the popularity then of badger-baiting, when badgers were drawn from their setts by dogs and killed for sport (illegal in the UK since 1830). The alternative name **brock** is the Old English for badger, one of the few words the Anglo-Saxons adopted from Celtic.

deer

In Old English a deer was not just the animal we are familiar with now, but any four-footed creature. The meaning was narrowed down to its modern sense in the Middle Ages. The word goes back to Indo-European, to a root meaning 'breathing creature'.

gopher

This animal may get its name from Canadian French *gaufre* 'honeycomb': the gopher 'honeycombs' the ground with its burrows.

mammal

This is an anglicized form of modern Latin *mammalia*, from *mamma* 'breast', the ability to produce milk being one of the distinguishing features of mammals.

porcupine

An early form of porcupine was *porke despyne*, which possibly came from Latin *porcus spinosus* 'prickly pig'. The word appeared in many forms between the

15th and 17th centuries, including *portepyn*, *porkpen*, *porkenpick*, and *porpoynt*. Shakespeare called it a *porpentine*. In his plays, it is often the name of an inn. The ghost of Hamlet's father tells Hamlet that his story could make his son's hairs 'stand on end, / Like quills upon the fretful porpentine'.

rodent

The teeth of rodents such as rats and mice grow continuously and must be worn down by gnawing, which gives a clue about the origin of rodent. The word comes from Latin *rodere* 'to gnaw', which is related to **erode**, **corrode**, **root**, and **rostrum**. The original sense is preserved in that unpleasant affliction the **rodent ulcer**.

shrew

Old English *scrēawa* is from a Germanic source related to words with senses such as 'dwarf', 'devil', or 'fox'. No one knows for certain whether a bad-tempered woman is a shrew because people compared her to the animal or whether the animal is a shrew because it was considered venomous and dangerous, like an aggressively assertive woman. When **shrewd** first appeared it shared these negative associations, but as connection with the shrew and belief in its evil weakened, it developed the sense 'cunning' and then the modern positive meaning 'having sharp powers of judgement, astute'.

squirrel

A squirrel is literally a 'shadow-tail', an appropriate description if you picture one holding its long bushy tail over its back like a sunshade. The English name evolved from the Greek *skiouros*, based on *skia* 'shadow' and *oura* 'tail'.

weasel

The sneaky characteristics of weasels were not transferred to people until the late 16th century. Its bad reputation comes from the belief that weasels creep into birds' nests and suck their eggs, leaving the empty shell behind. This lies behind the originally US phrase **weasel words** for words used to reduce the force of a concept being expressed; verb sense 'extricate' (weaseled his way out of doing the chores) arose in the 1950s.

wolf

The Indo-European root of wolf also became Greek *lukos* and Latin *lupus*, source of **lupine**, 'like a wolf'. The Greek word gave us **lycanthropy**, the mythical transformation of a person into a wolf or **werewolf**. The *were-* part of werewolf is probably from *wer*, Old English for 'man, person', just as the second half of the Greek comes from *anthropos* 'man'. The story of the shepherd boy who falsely **cried 'wolf'!** is one of the fables of Aesop, the Greek storyteller of the 6th century BC. To **keep the wolf from the door**, to have enough to avoid starvation, has been used since the 15th century. To **throw** someone **to the wolves** is surprisingly recent, though, found only from the 1920s. The image is of travellers on a sledge set upon by a pack of wolves, deciding to throw out one of their number to lighten the load to escape. **Wolf in sheep's clothing**, someone who appears harmless but is really hostile, comes from the Sermon on the Mount, in the Gospel of Matthew, when Jesus says: 'Beware of false prophets, which come to you in sheep's cloth, but inwardly they are ravening wolves.'

 # Marriage see also FAMILY

alimony

Today alimony means 'provision for a husband or wife after divorce' (what is usually called maintenance in Britain). Originally, though, in the early 17th century, it simply meant 'nourishment or means of subsistence'. It comes from Latin *alere* 'nourish', which is the root of words such as **adolescent**, **alimentary**, and also **coalesce** 'grow up, nourish together'.

annul

Introduced into English via Old French from late Latin *annullare*, annul is based on the Latin elements *ad-* 'to' and *nullum* 'nothing', the source also of **null**.

bachelor

The word bachelor was adopted from French in the early Middle Ages. The earliest meaning was 'a young knight serving under another's banner', one who was not old or rich enough to have his own band of followers. The sense 'unmarried man' is known from the late Middle Ages— Geoffrey Chaucer (c.1343–1400) wrote in *The Canterbury Tales* that 'bachelors have often pain and woe'.

conjugal

Conjugal is based on the Latin word *jugum* 'yoke'. The word comes from Latin *conjugalis*, from *conjux* 'spouse'.

divorce

In early times divorce covered many ways of ending a marriage: one spouse could simply leave or send the other away; the marriage could be annulled, declared invalid from the beginning (as in the divorce of Henry VIII from Catherine of Aragon); or the couple could formally enter into a legal separation. The word came from Latin *divortium*, based on *divertere* 'to turn in separate ways'. A divorced person has been a **divorcee** since the early 19th century. This term came from French, and at first usually appeared in its French forms, *divorcée* for a woman and *divorcé* for a man.

engage

Gage is an old word that means 'a valued object deposited as a guarantee of good faith' and, as a verb,

Marriage

'to give as a pledge'. An Old French word related to **wage** and **wedding**, it is the root of engage. Engage originally meant 'give as a pledge' and 'pawn or mortgage', later coming to express the ideas 'to pledge or guarantee' and 'to enter into a contract'. People have been getting **engaged** to be married since the beginning of the 18th century: the first recorded example is by Henry Fielding (1707–54), author of *Joseph Andrews* and *Tom Jones*.

husband

In Old English a **wife** was simply 'a woman', and a **husband** was 'a male head of a household' or 'a manager or steward', a sense preserved in expressions such as to **husband your resources**. The word is from Old Norse *húsbondi* 'master of a house'. Not until the 13th century or so did a husband become the married partner of a woman. Around then the word also took on the meaning 'a farmer or cultivator' and also the verbal use 'to cultivate', both of which are no longer used but are preserved in **husbandry** 'the cultivation and care of crops and farm animals'.

trousseau

The romantic trousseau conjures up an image of a blushing bride in flowing white or smart honeymoon outfit, but the original meaning was simply a bundle or package, and it did not acquire its modern meaning until the 1830s. The word derives from French *trousse*, an earlier

form of which gave us **truss** 'a supporting framework',
and 'a surgical support for a hernia'.

widow

Widow is descended from an ancient root meaning 'to be
empty', which may also the source of **divide**. A **grass
widow** is now a woman whose husband is away often or
for a prolonged period, but originally it was an unmarried
woman who had been the mistress of more than one
man: the term may have come from the idea of a couple
having lain on the grass instead of in bed. **Widow's
weeds** dating from the early 18th century was expressed
earlier as mourning weeds: here weeds is in the obsolete
general sense 'garments' from Old English wǣd(e).

wife

The original meaning of wife was simply 'woman', a
sense still used in Scotland, and in terms such as **fishwife**
and **midwife**. **All the world and his wife**, meaning
'everyone' or 'a great many people', is first recorded in
Jonathan Swift's *Polite Conversation* (1738).

Mathematics see also COMPUTERS

algebra

Bone-setting does not seem to have much to do with
mathematics, but there is a connection in the word

algebra. It comes from the Arabic *al-jabr* 'the reunion of broken parts', used specifically to refer to the surgical treatment of fractures and to bone-setting. Algebra was used in this meaning in English in the 16th century. The mathematical sense comes from the title of a 9th-century Arabic book *ilm al-jabr wa'l-mukābala*, 'the science of restoring what is missing and equating like with like', written by the mathematician al-Ḵwārizmī (*c.*790–*c.*840).

average

Originally a shipping term, meaning either the duty payable by the owner of goods about to be shipped or the financial liability for any goods lost or damaged at sea, average came into English in the 15th century from French *avarie* 'damage to a ship or cargo, customs duty'. The ultimate source was Arabic *'awār* 'damage to goods'. All this may seem a long way from the modern meaning of average, but the word came to be applied to the fair splitting of the financial liability between the owners of the vessel and the owners of the cargo, which in time led to the modern senses.

calculate

The Latin word *calculus* meant 'a small pebble', specifically one used on an abacus. This is the base of Latin *calculare* 'to count', from which calculate comes. **Calculator** first meant a person who calculates. **Calculus** has become an English word in its own right, as the name of a branch of mathematics, since the late 17th century.

computer

The first computers were not machines, but people. In the 17th century a computer was a person who made calculations, particularly someone employed to do this in an observatory or in surveying. The word was used in the late 19th century as a name for a mechanical calculating machine, and the modern sense dates from the 1940s. Its base is Latin *computare*, 'to calculate'.

count

The verb to count is from Latin *computare* 'to calculate', the root also of **account**, and **recount** 'tell' (which can also be used for both 'narrate' and 'count'). **Counters** were originally used to help in counting; in the late 17th century the word came to be used for a surface across which goods were exchanged for money. The noble title **count** is a completely different word, which was introduced by the Normans and comes from Latin *comes* 'companion, overseer, attendant'. **County** is from the same root, and seems originally to have referred to the lands or territory of a count.

cylinder

The shape and movement of a cylinder are captured in the word's origin. Cylinder comes via Latin from Greek *kulindros* 'roller'.

Mathematics

data

Originally recorded as a term in philosophy referring to 'things assumed to be facts', it is the Latin plural of *datum* 'a piece of information', literally 'something given'. Although plural, data is often treated in British English as a singular meaning 'information', although Americans and Australians use 'the data are...'. In the Middle Ages letters could be headed with the Latin formula *data (epistola)*...'(letter) given or delivered...' at a certain day or place. From this comes **date** in the time sense. The date you eat comes from Greek *daktulos* 'finger', because of the finger-like shape of the plant's leaves.

digit

We all count on our fingers. This is how Latin *digitus*, 'finger, toe', came down to us as digit, 'numeral', in the late Middle Ages. **Digital** dates from the late 15th century, and the technical use of the word in communications arose in the mid 20th century.

fraction

Medieval mathematicians called numbers that were not whole numbers fractions. The name came from Latin *frangere* 'to break', also the root of **fracture**, **fragile**, and **fragment** and ultimately of **frail**. People who struggled to learn about fractions may not be surprised to learn that the word is also linked to **fractious**, or 'bad-tempered'.

Medicine

see also HYGIENE, MIND AND MENTAL HEALTH

cataract

Latin *cataracta* (from Greek *kataraktēs*, 'rushing down')
meant both 'waterfall or floodgate' and 'portcullis'.
The first meaning led to the 'large waterfall' sense of
the English word cataract, and the second is probably
behind the medical sense describing the clouding of
the lens of the eye. A person's vision is blocked by this
condition as if a portcullis had been lowered over the
eye. Other words in English containing *kata* 'down'
include **cataclysm** from *kluzein* 'to wash'; **catapult**
from *pallein* 'hurl'; and **catastrophe** from *strophē*
'turning'.

disease

At first disease was 'lack of ease, inconvenience, trouble',
the meaning of the word in French, from which English
adopted it in the early Middle Ages. The 'lack of ease'
soon became associated with illness, and the original
sense became obsolete.

germ

This came via Old French from Latin *germen* 'seed,
sprout'. At first it meant a portion of an organism
capable of developing into a new one or part of one.
The sense 'microorganism' dates from the late 19th

213

century when it was first used vaguely to mean the 'seed' of a disease. **Germinate** is from the same root.

influenza

Italy saw an outbreak of a severe respiratory ailment in 1743. The English minister to Tuscany, Sir Horace Mann, wrote of Rome that 'Everybody is ill of the Influenza, and many die'. The epidemic spread throughout Europe, and in English influenza became the general term for this type of contagious viral infection. The English shortened influenza to the more familiar **flu** in the mid 19th century. Italian influenza means 'influence' and derives from Latin *fluere* 'to flow'. The Italian word also had the sense 'an outbreak of an epidemic', and so 'an epidemic'.

inoculate

Originally inoculation was a task of gardeners rather than of doctors and nurses. To inoculate something was to graft a bud or shoot into a plant of a different type. This corresponds to its Latin source *inoculare* 'to graft', from *in-* 'into' and *oculus* 'eye, bud' (as in **binocular** and **ocular**). As a medical procedure people could inoculate a person from the early 18th century—its first uses referred to the treatment of smallpox.

malaria

Before people understood that malaria was transmitted by mosquitoes, they attributed the disease to an unwholesome condition of the atmosphere in marshy districts. It was particularly prevalent in Italy, and especially near Rome. In a letter of 1740 the writer and statesman Horace Walpole wrote of 'A horrid thing called the mal'aria, that comes to Rome every summer and kills one'. Italian *mal'aria* is a contraction of *mala aria* 'bad air'. **Malady** comes from a similar source, being from Lain *male* 'ill' and *habitus* 'having (as a condition)'.

measles

The medieval spelling was *maseles*, probably from Middle Dutch *masel* 'pustule'. The spelling change was from association with Middle English *mesel* 'leprous, leprosy'. **Measly** dates from the late 16th century when it described a pig or pork infected with measles; the current sense 'contemptibly small, mean' dates from the mid 19th century.

rheumatism

People have been **rheumatic** in the sense of suffering from too much rheum, or watery discharge since the Middle Ages but doctors have only been diagnosing rheumatism in their patients since the 17th century. The disease was originally supposed to be caused by watery fluids in the body, and the word comes from Greek *rheumatizein* 'to snuffle', from *rheuma* 'stream'.

surgeon

The key thing about surgeons in terms of word history is that they work with their hands, using manual skill to cure or treat people rather than giving them drugs. Surgeon is a shortening of Old French *serurgian*, which came via Latin *chirurgia* from Greek *kheirourgia* 'handiwork', from *kheir* 'hand' and *ergon* 'work'.

virus

A virus was originally the venom of a snake, and was an English borrowing of a Latin word meaning 'slimy liquid' or 'poison', that is also the source of **virulent**. Early medical practitioners used the word for a substance produced in the body as the result of disease. The modern meaning dates from the late 19th century. The computer virus dates from the early 1970s.

 Military see also ARMY

admiral

The first recorded meaning of admiral is an emir or Muslim commander. The word ultimately comes from Arabic *'amīr* 'commander'. The Arabic word was used in various titles of rank, such as *amir-al-bahr* ('commander of the sea') and *amir-al-ma* ('commander of the water'). Christian scholars, not realizing that -al- simply meant 'of the', thought that *amir-al* was a single word meaning 'commander', and anglicized it as admiral. The modern maritime use comes from the

office of 'Amir of the Sea', created by the Arabs in
Spain and Sicily and later adopted by the Genoese, the
French, and, in the form 'Amyrel of the Se' or 'Admyrall
of the Navy', by the English under Edward III. From
around 1500 the word admiral on its own has been used
as the naval term.

amok

If someone **runs amok** they rush about behaving
uncontrollably and disruptively. The word amok comes
via Portuguese from a Malay word *amuk* meaning
'fighting furiously' or 'rushing in a frenzy'. It was first
used in English in the 17th century, referring to a Malay
person in a murderous frenzy after taking opium.

berserk

A **berserker** was an ancient Norse warrior who fought
with wild, uncontrolled ferocity. It came from an old
Scandinavian word, *berserkr*, which probably meant 'bear
coat' or 'bearskin', a suitably rugged garment for a
terrifyingly unhinged Viking. An alternative possibility is
that the first element is the equivalent of 'bare', referring
to fighting without armour. The phrase to **go berserk** is
first recorded in 1896.

camouflage

This was adopted during the First World War from
French, from *camoufler* 'to disguise', which was

originally thieves' slang. It comes from Italian *camuffare* 'to disguise'.

detonation

Detonation comes via French from Latin *detonare* 'thunder down'.

manoeuvre

Soldiers, sailors, and farmers come together in the words manoeuvre and **manure**, which share the Latin origin *manu operari* 'to work with the hand', from *manus* 'hand' (found also in **manage** and **manner**). The earliest sense of manoeuvre, which came into English via Old French was 'a planned movement of military or naval forces'. Old French also gave us manure. Originally it had the senses 'to cultivate land' and 'to administer or manage land or property'—the use for dung used on the land dates from the mid 16th century.

rifle

The Old French *rifler* meant both 'to plunder' and 'to scratch'. The plunder sense of rifle developed via 'to search thoroughly' into 'to search for valuables'. The word was then re-borrowed from French in the 'scratch' sense for the making of grooves in the barrel of a gun. These guns then became known as rifles. **Riff-raff**,

'disreputable people', formerly written as *riff and raff*,
is probably also from *rifler* combined with *raffler* 'to
carry off'.

sabotage

French peasants and workers traditionally wore *sabots*,
wooden clogs. When they took action against new
technologies by destroying machines and tools in the
19th century, people called the action sabotage.
The word first appeared in English in the first decade
of the 20th century, referring to a court case in Paris.
By 1916 the *Sydney Morning Herald* could report a
labourer on an Australian sheep farm threatening
sabotage against politicians and employers.

strafe

This term for 'to attack from low-flying aircraft' was
a humorous adaptation of the German First World
War catchphrase *Gott strafe England* 'may God punish
England'.

torpedo

Although we think of a torpedo as speeding through the
water towards its target, at the heart of the word's origin
is slowness and paralysis. The electric ray, a sluggish flat
fish living in shallow water, produces an electric shock to
capture prey and for defence. Its Latin name was *torpedo*,

from *torpere* 'to be numb or sluggish', source also of
torpid. When first used in English in the early 16th
century torpedo referred to this ray. In the late 18th
century the inventor of a timed explosive for detonation
underwater, the ancestor of the modern device, gave it
the name torpedo from the fish.

 # Mind and Mental Health
see also EMOTIONS, FEAR, HORROR

delirium

This is a Latin word adopted into English, from the verb
delirare 'deviate, be deranged'. The literal meaning is
'deviate from the furrow', from *de-* 'away' and *lira* 'a
ridge between furrows'.

gaga

Gaga 'slightly mad', introduced in the early 20th century,
is from the French for 'senile, a senile person'. and is a
based on *gâteux*, a variant of the hospital slang word
gâteur 'bed-wetter'.

hallucination

The word hallucination is from Latin *hallucinari* 'go
astray in thought', from Greek *alussein* 'be uneasy or
distraught'.

hysteria

In ancient times doctors (all male) regarded hysteria as a
disease of women cause by a disturbance of the womb.
In the early 19th century English pathologists (also male)
formed the English name from Greek *hustera* 'uterus,
womb'. Earlier terms for the condition had been **hysteric**
or **hysterical passion**, reflecting the same view, and the
vapours.

melancholy

According to the medieval theory of the four humours,
melancholy or black bile caused depression. The word
goes back to Greek *melankholia*, from *melas* 'black'
(source of **melanin** and **melanoma**) and *kholē* 'bile'
(source of **cholera**, **choleric**, and **cholesterol**). Today it
tends to refer to a pensive or moody sadness rather than
deep depression.

migraine

People unfortunate enough to suffer from migraine
know that this sort of throbbing headache usually affects
one side of the head—reflected in the origin of the
word. It is a highly shortened form of Greek *hemi-* 'half'
and *kranion* 'skull', the source of English **cranium**.
Until the 20th century the form **megrim**, also used for
a fit of being difficult, was more common than
migraine.

Mind and Mental Health

obsess

The word obsess had the early sense 'haunt, possess', referring to an evil spirit. It comes from Latin *obsidere* 'besiege'.

paranoia

This word is modern Latin, from Greek *paranoos* 'distracted', from *para* 'irregular' and *noos* 'mind'.

psyche

We associate psyche with things of the mind, but to the Greeks *psukhē* meant 'breath, life, soul', which then developed into the idea of 'self'. This base is involved in the first element of the science terms **psychology** and **psychiatry** (from Greek *psukhē* and *iatreia* 'healing'). **Psychedelic** was coined in the 1950s from *psyche* and Greek *delos* 'clear, manifest'. The tale of Cupid and Psyche, a folk tale turned into an allegory of love and the soul, dates from the 2nd century AD, but probably has an earlier source.

sanity

Latin *sanus* meant 'healthy' which is the first recorded sense of sanity in English. Current meanings date from the early 17th century when **sane** was first recorded, although **insane** dates from the mid 16th century. **Sanitary**, **sanitation**, and **sanatorium** where you go to recover your health, all 19th century, come from the same root.

Music see also ENTERTAINMENT, SONG

bugle

The earliest English sense of bugle was 'wild ox', giving
the compound bugle-horn for the horn of an ox used
to give signals, originally during hunting. The word comes
via Old French from Latin *būculus*, 'little ox' from *bōs* 'ox'.

clarinet

This comes from French *clarinette*, a diminutive of
clarinet, a kind of bell. It is related to **clarion**, originally 'a
shrill narrow-tubed war trumpet', from medieval Latin
clario(n-), from Latin *clarus* 'clear'. From the same source
come **claret**, **clarity**, **clarify**, **clear**, and **declare**.

cymbal

This comes via Latin *cymbalum* from Greek *kumbalon*,
from *kumbē* 'cup', from the instrument's shape. **Chime**
was first recorded as meaning 'cymbal' and 'ring'. It is
probably from the Old English form of cymbal, *cimbal*
(which would have been pronounced with a 'ch' sound,
the modern 's' sound coming from French), later
interpreted as 'chime-bell'.

fiddle

In Old English fiddle was the usual word for a stringed
instrument like a violin, from Latin *vitulari* 'to celebrate,
be joyful', which may come from *Vitula*, the name of a

Music

Roman goddess of joy and victory. The sense 'to swindle' probably came from the idea that the 'fiddler' or player could make people 'dance to his tune'. Expressions like **fiddle-de-dee** and **fiddle-faddle**, meaning 'nonsense', come from the idea of violin-playing being trivial. Fiddle-faddle is the origin of **fad**. When someone concerns themselves with trivial affairs while ignoring serious matters, they are **fiddling while Rome burns**. This looks back to a story about the Roman emperor Nero, that when Rome suffered from a disastrous fire Nero reacted by singing a song about the fall of Troy and accompanying himself on some instrument—not a fiddle, which had not been invented then.

jazz

We have been enjoying jazz since the early years of the 20th century, but no one is sure about the word's origin, although an enormous number of suggestions have been made, including an African origin. The original meaning may have been something like 'liveliness, energy, spirit'—in 1912 a baseball player said of his new way of pitching: 'I call it the Jazz ball because it wobbles and you simply can't do anything with it.' The first known musical use came in 1915 in Chicago. Jazz was also used with sexual connotations, and its source could be the slang word *jism* (of unknown origin) 'semen'. **All that jazz**, meaning

'and all that stuff, et cetera', has been around since
the 1950s.

melody

This goes back to Greek *melos* 'music, song'. **Melodrama**
was adopted from French and is a blend of *melos* and
French *drame* 'drama'.

reggae

This word for a popular style of music may be related to
Jamaican English **rege-rege** 'quarrel, row'. At one time
reggae was strongly associated with **Rastafarians**. They
got their name from their belief that Ras Tafari, another
name for the Emperor Haile Selassie of Ethopia (1892–
1975), was God Incarnate. This word has been a model for
new coinages, of which the best known is **trustafarians**—
young people who can spend their time having fun
because they have an income from a trust fund.

syncopate

This comes from late Latin *syncopare* 'to swoon'. The
notion of temporary loss of consciousness led to
associations of weakening and strengthening of musical
beats or omission of sounds.

ukulele

The ukulele is a development of a Portuguese
instrument called the *machete* that appeared in Hawaii

in the late 1870s. Around that time a British army officer, Edward Purvis, acted as vice-chamberlain of the court of King Kalakaua. According to the story, local Hawaiians gave Purvis, a small, energetic, and agile man, the nickname *ukulele* 'jumping flea'. When he took up the instrument he played with typical liveliness and with such success that his nickname became the name of the instrument.

waltz

This word is from German *Walzer*, from *walzen* 'revolve'. The transferred verb use 'move nimbly' (**waltzed off down the road**) arose in the mid 19th century.

 # Myth see also HORROR, MAGIC

banshee

A banshee in Irish legend is a female spirit who wails a warning of an imminent death in a house; the word is ultimately from Old Irish *ben síde* 'woman of the fairies'.

dragon

Dragon goes back to Greek *drakōn* 'serpent', which was one of the first senses in English in the Middle Ages. In early texts it can be difficult to distinguish the genuine large snake or python (at that time known only from

report) from the mythical fire-breathing monster.
The Chinese dragon is behind the expression **chase the dragon**, 'to smoke heroin'. A 1961 Narcotic Officer's Handbook explains: 'In "chasing the dragon" the heroin and any diluting drug are placed on a folded piece of tinfoil. This is heated with a taper and the resulting fumes inhaled through a small tube of bamboo or rolled paper. The fumes move up and down the tinfoil with the movements of the molten powder, resembling the undulating tail of the mythical Chinese dragon.'

elf

A word related to German *Alp* 'nightmare'. Elves were formerly thought of as more frightening than they are now, producing diseases, causing nightmares, and stealing children, substituting changelings in their place. Later they became more like fairies, dainty and unpredictable, and in the works of J. R. R. Tolkien (1892–1973) they are noble and beautiful. Originally an elf was specifically male, the female being **elven**: Tolkien revived **elven** and used it to mean 'relating to elves'. **Elfin**, also meaning 'relating to elves' and used to describe a small, delicate person, was first used by Edmund Spenser in *The Faerie Queene* (1590–96).

fairy

Although we now think of fairies as small, delicate creatures, they come from a powerful source—Latin *fata* 'the Fates'. The old spelling **faerie** is first recorded

Myth

in *The Faerie Queene*, a poem by Edmund Spenser celebrating Queen Elizabeth I (the figure of the 'Faerie Queene' herself stood for Elizabeth). Faerie was originally the collective form, with **fae** or nowadays **fay** as the singular.

ghoul

Ghoul is from Arabic *ḡūl*, a desert demon believed to rob graves and devour corpses.

gnome

The terms gnome and pygmy are closely related. It was probably the Swiss physician Paracelsus (*c.*1493–1541) who coined gnome as a synonym of *Pygmaeus*, the name given to a mythical race of very small people believed to live in parts of Ethiopia and India. The **gnomes of Zurich** are Swiss bankers, thought of as having a sinister influence over international monetary funds. Former British Prime Minister Harold Wilson popularized the phrase in 1956: 'All these financiers, all the little gnomes in Zurich and other financial centres about whom we keep on hearing'. **Gnomic** meaning 'clever but hard to understand', as in 'gnomic utterances', is a different word, from Greek *gnōmē* 'thought, judgement', related to *gignōskein* 'to know'.

goblin

This is from Old French *gobelin*, from *Gobelinus*, a mischievous spirit said to haunt the region of Évreux in northern France in the 12th century. The term may be related to German **Kobold** (see also **cobalt** under METALS), the name of a German spirit that haunted houses or lived underground in caves and mines, although another possible source is Greek *kobalos* 'goblin'.

gremlin

Pilots first talked about gremlins, mischievous sprites responsible for any unexplained mechanical problems suffered by planes. The earliest mention of them comes from the USA in the 1920s, but they are particularly associated with the Second World War. The word may be a combination of goblin and Fremlins, a type of beer—so these were the sort of creatures you see when you have had one too many.

hag

This word, often used disparagingly (**old hag**), is literally 'an evil spirit in female form, witch'. It derives perhaps from Old English *hægtesse, hegtes*, related to Dutch *heks* and German *Hexe* 'witch', source of **hex**. (See also **whammy** under MAGIC.)

orc

In J. R. R. Tolkien's *The Lord of the Rings* the orcs are malevolent, goblin-like creatures that attack in hordes and ride wolves. The word was not invented by Tolkien; for the Anglo-Saxons, an *orc* was 'a demon'. It had died out by AD 1000, but came back into English in the

Myth

17th century from Italian *orco* 'man-eating giant', also
the root of **ogre**. The source was *Orcus*, the name of a
Roman god of the underworld. When Tolkien was
writing in the 1930s he revived the rare word—as a noted
scholar he knew the earlier Old English use.

On Safari
see also MAMMALS, ON THE FARM, PETS

antelope
Before 17th-century zoologists gave this name to the
fast-running horned animal, an antelope was a fierce
mythical creature with long serrated horns that
was believed to live by the River Euphrates and often
appeared in heraldic designs. It was said to use its
saw-like horns to cut down trees. Although the word
came into English via Old French and medieval Latin
from Greek *antholops*, the origin and meaning of the
Greek word is a mystery.

baboon
Baboon was originally used for a carving such as a
gargoyle, and probably comes from Old French *baboue*
'muzzle' or 'grimace'. By about 1400 it was being used
for the long-snouted monkey.

camel
Our term for the camel comes from Greek *kamēlos*,
which probably came from an Arabic or Hebrew word.
When it was adopted into Old English it replaced the
existing word for the animal, *olfend*, which sounds
suspiciously like elephant. It seems that people often
got the two animals confused, not being familiar with
either. Alec Issigonis, the designer of the Morris Minor

and Mini cars, coined 'A camel is a horse designed by a committee'.

elephant

Surprisingly, elephant did not come to us from an African or Indian language, but via Latin from Greek. The Greek word *elephas* meant both 'ivory' and 'elephant'. It is found in the work of the poet Homer, who probably lived in the 8th century BC, and may have been taken up by the Greeks from an ancient language of the Middle East. Elephant appeared in English in the 14th century; before that people called them *oliphants* or *elps*.

giraffe

The giraffe was known in Europe in the medieval period, but people then called it the **camelopard** from Greek *kamēlopardalis*, from *kamēlos* 'camel' and *pardalis* 'female panther or leopard'(see **camel**, above). People thought a giraffe's spotted skin looked like a leopard's. Giraffe is from Arabic *zarāfa*.

gorilla

In the 5th or 6th centuries BC the Carthaginian explorer Hanno wrote about his voyage along the north-west coast of Africa. In the Greek translation, there appears a supposedly African name *gorillai* for a wild or hairy people. This was adopted in 1847 by the US missionary Thomas Savage as the name of the large ape.

monkey

The origin of monkey seems to go back to a name given
to the monkey character in medieval beast epics, which
may ultimately be Arabic. Historically, **ape** was used as
the general term for all apes and monkeys. Monkeys are
associated with mischief and mimicry. British **monkey
tricks** 'mischievous behaviour' are **monkeyshines** in the
USA, while **monkey business** seems to have come from
India. If you **don't give a monkey's** you do not care at all.
This phrase, recorded from the late 19th century, is a
politer shortening of don't give a monkey's ass or f—.
Monkey, slang for £500 (or, in Australia, $500) goes right
back to the 1830s, while **pony**, for £25, is late 18th century.

orang-utan

The orang utan provides one of the few contributions of
the Malay language to English. It comes from Malay
orang hutan meaning 'forest person'.

rhinoceros

The look of the rhinoceros provides its name, which
comes from Greek *rhino-* 'nose' and *keras* 'horn'. It has
been known in English since the late 14th century,
but the first reference to it calls it a kind of unicorn.
Rhino- is familiar to gardeners from the **antirrhinum** (or
snapdragon), which means 'counterfeiting a nose' from
its appearance. *Keras* appears in **keratin**, the substance
from which horn is made.

zebra

Zebra is not from an African language, as once thought, but via Italian, Spanish, or Portuguese from Latin *equiferus* 'wild horse', from *equus*, as in **equestrian**. The **zebra crossing**, named because of its black and white stripes, was introduced in Britain in 1949.

On the Farm
see also HORSES, MAMMALS, PETS

aftermath

The aftermath was originally the crop of new grass that springs up after a field has been mown in early summer. John Buchan (1874–1940), the Scottish writer of adventure stories such as *The Thirty-Nine Steps*, wrote about 'Meadowland from which an aftermath of hay had lately been taken'. *Math* was an old word meaning 'a mowing'. The modern meaning of aftermath developed in the 19th century.

barn

A barn was originally somewhere for storing **barley**, from Old English *bere* 'barley' and *ern* 'house'. In the 1940s barn started to be used in particle physics as a unit of areas, apparently from the phrase as **big as a barn door**, a long established measure of size.

donkey

Before the late 18th century a donkey was an **ass**. At first donkey was used only in slang and dialect, and its origin is lost. Early references indicate it rhymed with monkey, and some have suggested that it comes from the colour **dun** or the man's name **Duncan**. The expression **for donkey's years**, 'for a very long time', is a pun referring to the length of donkeys' ears playing on an old pronunciation of ears which was the same as years. The British expression **yonks**, with the same meaning, may derive from it.

ferret

Latin *fur* 'thief' is the root of ferret, which entered English from Old French *fuiret*. Ferrets are known for stealing birds' eggs, and this was probably why they got their name.

hen

Ultimately the word hen is related to Latin *canere* 'to sing'. Singing hens are **as rare as hen's teeth**. As hens do not have teeth this is tantamount to saying non-existent. The phrase was used in the USA from the mid 19th century. The **henpecked** husband goes back to *The Genuine Remains* (1680) by Samuel Butler and comes from the way that hens will sometimes peck at the feathers of other birds.

On the Farm

hive

This Germanic word is probably related to Old Norse *húfr* 'hull of a ship' and Latin *cupa* 'tub, cask'. Early hives were conical and made of straw.

mule

A mule results from crossing a male donkey and a female horse (the technical name for the offspring of a female donkey and a stallion is **hinny** from Latin *hinnus*). Mules have traditionally been regarded as stubborn. Someone stubborn, stupid, or physically tough has been called a mule since the 15th century. As a name for couriers of illicit drugs, mule dates from the 1920s in US slang. The name of the animal goes back to Latin *mulus*. It has no connection with mule in the sense 'a slipper or light shoe without a back'. This comes from a term for the reddish shoes worn by magistrates in ancient Rome, Latin *mulleus calceus*.

pasture

Pasture comes via Old French from late Latin *pastura* 'grazing', from the verb *pascere* 'to graze'. A clergyman is the shepherd of his flock, and **pastor** is the Latin for 'shepherd, feeder'. **Pastoral** is from Latin *pastoralis* 'relating to a shepherd'. Its use in literary, artistic, and musical contexts dates from the late 16th century.

pigeon

Pigeon comes from French *pijon*, meaning a young bird, especially a young dove. It is an alteration of Latin *pipio*, imitating the piping or cheeping of a nestling. **To be someone's pigeon**, their concern or responsibility, has nothing to do with birds but is a respelling of **pidgin** and thus means 'business'. The pigeon's distinctive walk gave us **pigeon-toed**, meaning 'having the toes or feet turned inwards', and **pigeon-chested** or **pigeon-breasted**, 'having a protruding chest'.

plough

The spelling plough was not common until the 18th century. Previously the noun was spelled this way, and the verb **plow**, still the US spelling for both noun and verb. **The ploughman's lunch**, bread and cheese usually served with pickle and salad is not the traditional rural snack it might seem, but can be traced back only to 1960, although over a century earlier we find this curious pre-echo: 'The surprised poet swung forth to join them, with an extemporized sandwich, that looked like a ploughman's luncheon, in his hand' (John Lockhart, *Memoirs of the Life of Sir Walter Scott*, 1837).

Pain

ache

The word ache illustrates how English spelling and pronunciation have developed and in many cases diverged from each other. The noun comes from Old English and used to be pronounced 'aitch' (like the letter H), whereas the verb was originally spelled *ake* and pronounced the way ache is today. Around 1700, people started pronouncing the noun like the verb. The spelling of the noun has survived, but the word is said in the way the verb (*ake*) used to be. The modern spelling is largely due to Dr Johnson, who mistakenly assumed the word came from Greek *akhos* 'pain'. Other pairs of words that have survived into modern English with k-for-the-verb and ch-for-the-noun spellings include **speak** and **speech**, and **break** and **breach**.

agony

Agony referred originally only to mental anguish. It comes via late Latin from Greek *agōnia*, from *agōn* 'contest' (the base, too, of **agonize**). The Greek sense development moved from struggle for victory in the games, to any struggle, to mental struggle specifically (such as Christ's agony in the Garden of Gethsemane). It was in English the sense was extended to include physical suffering. Greek *agōn* is also the source of the dramatic **protagonist** from Greek *proto-* 'first' and *agōnistes* 'actor, contestant' and at the root of **antagonist** from *anti-* 'against' and *agōnizesthai* 'struggle'.

anodyne

Introduced via Latin from Greek *anōdunos* 'painless', the base elements of anodyne are *an-* 'without' and *odunē* 'pain'.

excruciating

Excruciate is from Latin *excruciare* 'to torment or torture' based on *crux*. This meant 'a cross', of the kind used to **crucify** someone, and also gives us **crucial**, and **crux**. In English to excruciate someone was originally to torture them.

masochism

Sexual pleasure derived from pain features in several stories by the 19th-century Austrian writer Leopold von Sacher-Masoch. The German term *Masochismus* was used in 1890, and by 1892 English had adopted it as masochism.

pain

This goes back to Latin *poena* originally meaning 'penalty' but later meaning 'pain', which is also the source of **pine** 'to long for', but originally meaning 'to suffer'; **penal**; and **penalty**. **Punish** comes from the related verb *punire*. **Pain in the neck** dates from the 1920s; from this, a pain for an annoying person developed in the 1930s.

Pain

Although the phrase **no pain**, **no gain** is associated with exercise classes from the 1980s, the two words have been associated since the 16th century and 'No Pains, No Gains' is the title of a 1648 poem by Robert Herrick.

sadism

During several periods of imprisonment in the later 18th and early 19th centuries, French writer and soldier the Marquis de Sade (1740–1814) wrote pornographic books. One sexual perversion in particular fascinated him: arousal from inflicting pain on others. The French named it *sadisme* after him, and English adopted the word as sadism in the 1880s.

smart

The first English use of smart was as a verb meaning 'be painful', which survives in the verb meaning 'to feel a sharp, stinging pain in a part of the body'—its root is probably related to Latin *mordere* 'to bite'. The original meaning of the adjective was 'causing sharp pain', which led to 'keen or brisk' and developed into the current senses of 'mentally sharp, clever' and 'neat, well turned out'. We probably call an irritating person who always has a clever answer a **smart alec** after Alex Hoag, a notorious thief and conman in New York in the 1840s, who earned the nickname Smart Alex from his reputation for not getting caught. In the late 17th century **smart money** was money paid to sailors and soldiers to compensate them for wounds. Smart here meant 'physical pain'. Modern usage, from around 1900, refers to money bet by people with expert knowledge, with smart meaning 'quick-witted'. The sugar-coated chocolate sweets called **Smarties** were launched in 1937. Because of their similar appearance to pills, doctors are sometimes accused of handing out drugs 'like Smarties'.

Peoples

aborigine
This is a shortening of the 16th-century plural **aborigines** 'original inhabitants', used in classical times for the early people of Italy and Greece. It comes from the Latin phrase *ab origine* 'from the beginning'. Now both Aborigines and **Aboriginals** are standard plural forms for Australian Aboriginal people, a specialized use which dates from the 1820s.

Amazon
In Greek legend the Amazons were female warriors who were supposed to exist in the unexplored north. The word is Greek for 'without a breast', from the story that these women cut off their right breasts in order to draw their bows more easily. Nowadays an Amazon is any tall, strong, or athletic woman. The River Amazon got its name from European explorers who believed a race of female warriors lived on its banks.

Peoples

barbarian

The ancient Greeks thought well of themselves and poorly of other peoples. Everyone who did not speak Greek was *barbaros* or 'foreign', giving us barbarian, **barbaric**, **barbarity**, and **barbarous**. *Barbaros* originally imitated the unintelligible language of foreigners, which to the Greeks just sounded like *ba, ba*.

Eskimo

This traditional word for the indigenous people inhabiting northern Canada, Alaska, Greenland, and eastern Siberia is from the Native American language Algonquian, and may have originally meant 'people speaking a different language'. It was formerly thought the original meaning was 'person who eats raw meat'. Because this was seen as insulting, the word is now avoided by many. The peoples from the Canadian Arctic to western Greenland prefer to call themselves **Inuit**, the plural of *inuk* 'person'. Other words from the Inuit language are **kayak**, and **igloo** from *iglu* 'house'.

Gypsy

When Gypsies first appeared in Britain in the 16th century no one knew where they had come from. Their dark skin and hair led people to believe they were from Egypt, and they were called *Gipcyans*, short for Egyptians. In fact Gypsies probably originated in the Indian subcontinent. Their language, Romany, is related to Hindi.

pariah

This comes from the southern Indian languages Tamil and Malayalam, and literally means 'hereditary drummer' from the word meaning 'large drum'. The original pariahs were a people in southern India who acted as sorcerers and ceremonial drummers and also as labourers and servants. They were a tribal people outside the traditional Hindu caste system, and came to be regarded as 'untouchables' who did all the insanitary jobs. From there the sense 'a social outcast' developed in the early 19th century.

Scouse

The success of the Beatles and other Liverpool groups in the 1960s focused attention on their city, and Scouse and **Scouser** became familiar in Britain. They represent shortenings of **lobscouse**, a stew made with meat, vegetables, and ship's biscuit formerly eaten by sailors and so a staple food in the port of Liverpool. Its origin is unknown. Before the 1960s Scouse meaning 'Liverpudlian' appeared in print only in a 1945 report of a trial, where a witness used the word and a puzzled judge asked for an explanation. It was recorded 100 years earlier for the food.

spartan

Something spartan is lacking comfort or luxury. The word come from the Spartans of ancient Greece who left weak or sickly babies on mountain slopes to die and forced all children to live in military 'boarding schools' from the age of about seven. Their terse speech also gave us **laconic** (see under LANGUAGE).

vandal

In the 4th and 5th centuries AD the Vandals were a Teutonic people who ravaged Gaul, Spain, and North Africa, and sacked Rome in 455. The Latin for a Vandal was *Vandalus*, which is also behind Andalusia, the southernmost region of Spain. The Romans overthrew the Vandals in 533. Like most victors they discredited their opponents, resulting in the Vandals being branded as destroyers of anything beautiful or worth preserving. Our modern sense evolved in the 17th century, and **vandalism** in the 18th. The **Goths**, another Germanic tribe who invaded in the same period, suffered the opposite fate. **Gothic** was applied to medieval architecture in the mid 17th century often disparagingly, but once the style came back into fashion it became approving.

Viking

The Vikings were seafaring pirates and traders from Scandinavia who raided and settled many parts of north-western Europe from the 8th to the 11th centuries. Scholars formerly assumed the name came from Scandinavian *vík* 'creek, inlet', referring to their setting out from coastal inlets, but it may derive from Old English *wīc* 'camp', since their temporary encampments were a prominent feature of Viking raids. It is not an old word in English, being borrowed from Icelandic in the early 19th century, although there was an equivalent Old English word *wicing*.

Person to Word
SEE ALSO FICTION TO WORD

derrick
Derrick was first used to mean either the gallows or a hangman, and comes from the name of a London hangman who worked around 1600. This was then transferred to a tackle on a ship's mast, and from there extended to any hoisting device.

doily
This ornamental mat made of lace or paper with a lace pattern, is from Mr Doiley or Doyley, a 17th-century London draper, and was originally a term for a summer-weight woollen material said to have been introduced him. The current sense was originally *doily napkin* and dates from the early 18th century.

galvanize
Galvanize originally meant 'to stimulate a muscle or nerve by electricity'. It was based on the name of the Italian scientist Luigi Galvani (1737–98), who discovered

that frogs' legs twitched violently when he ran electricity through them. Galvani believed this was caused by 'animal electricity' in the body, an idea that inspired Mary Shelley to write *Frankenstein* in 1818. **Galvanized iron** or steel, coated with zinc to prevent rusting, was originally produced using electrical current.

gun

Gun in English may have originally meant a kind of catapult used to hurl rocks or arrows at enemies. The term may come from a pet form of the Scandinavian name **Gunnhildr** (from *gunnr* and *hildr*, both meaning 'war'). Giving female names to weapons has been a common practice over the centuries. Examples include Mons Meg, a 15th-century cannon in Edinburgh Castle; Brown Bess, for a musket used by the British army in the 18th century; and Big Bertha, a large German gun in the First World War. **Sticking to your guns** comes from the battlefield, where it meant remaining at your post under constant bombardment. **Gunning for** someone is looking for a chance to attack them. In the 17th century, though, to go gunning meant hunting. **Gunboat diplomacy**, foreign policy supported by the use or threat of military force, is first mentioned in the 1920s, about US policy in China.

lynch

During the War of American Independence (1775–83) Captain William Lynch of Pittsville, Virginia, headed a self-constituted court without legal authority which persecuted 'Tories', people who supported the British side. People called this illegal punishment Lynch's law or **lynch law**. The penalties handed out were beatings or tarring and feathering, but by the mid 19th century to lynch was generally to hang someone.

maverick

In the middle of the 19th century Samuel Augustus Maverick owned such a large herd of cattle in Texas that he left the calves unbranded. People noted this unusual practice and began to use maverick for any unbranded calf. From the 1880s maverick came to signify 'individualistic, unorthodox, or independent-minded'.

nachos

A Mexican chef called Ignacio 'Nacho' Anaya is thought to have invented nachos, small pieces of tortilla topped with melted cheese and spices, in the 1940s. An alternative origin could be the Spanish word *nacho*, which means 'flat-nosed'.

nanny

Both for a person taking care of young children and for nanny-goat, this is a pet form of Ann. The **nanny state** is found from the 1960s. **Nan** both is an abbreviation of nanny and a child's pronunciation of **gran**.

Person to Word

philistine

In biblical times, during the 11th and 12th centuries BC, Philistines were a people occupying the southern coast of Palestine. They frequently came into conflict with the Israelites. The first book of Samuel tells the story of David and Goliath, a Philistine giant, and Judges relates Delilah's betrayal of Samson to the Philistines. In the late 17th century students at the university of Jena in Germany, started using *Philister* (German for 'Philistine') as an insulting name for townspeople or non-students. By the 1820s English travellers had made this German slang familiar, and people began to use philistine for 'an uncultured person'. Philistine goes back to the same root as **Palestine**.

silhouette

Étienne de Silhouette (1709–67) was a French author and politician. Why he gave his name to the dark outline of something against a brighter background remains obscure. One account says that the word ridiculed the petty economies Silhouette introduced while Controller General, while another refers to the shortness of his occupancy of that post. A scholarly French dictionary suggested Silhouette himself made outline portraits with which he decorated the walls of his château at Bry-sur-Marne. We shall probably never know the truth.

Pets

see also HORSES, ON THE FARM

bunny

The first recorded example of bunny, in 1606, reads, 'Sweet Peg... my honey, my bunny, my duck, my dear'. Bunny was originally a term of endearment, and not found used for a rabbit until the late 17th century. It is a pet form of *bun*, dialect for 'squirrel' or 'rabbit'. Its origin is not known, but it is unlikely to be connected with **bun** 'small cake', also of obscure origin. The 1987 film *Fatal Attraction*, where Glenn Close's character, rejected by Michael Douglas, boils his child's pet rabbit, gave us **bunny boiler** for a woman acting vengefully after being spurned by her lover.

cat

The original Latin word for cat was *feles*, literally 'she who bears young' (also used of other animals, such as polecats, domesticated to keep down mice) the source of **feline**. In the early centuries AD *cattus* appears in Latin. It is generally thought to come from Egypt where cats were first domesticated, but may be Slavic. Most modern European languages use a form of this. It is typical of the different roles played in English by words from Latin and Germanic sources that while feline is generally linked with positive words like 'grace', **catty** is an insult. **Catgut** is typically made from sheep not cats,

and may come from a joke about the **caterwauling**,
from cat and a word related to 'wail', that can be
produced from the strings. **No room to swing a cat**
probably refers to a **cat-o'-nine-tails**, a whip with nine
knotted cords formerly used to flog wrongdoers,
especially at sea.

corgi

Not many English words derive from Welsh, but corgi,
literally 'dwarf dog' from Welsh *cor* 'dwarf' and *ci* 'dog',
does. Others include **coracle**, **flummery** originally in the
food sense from Welsh *llymru*, and **penguin**, from *pen
gwyn* 'white head'.

cur

A cur is now disparaging, whether used of dog or man,
but was initially used generally for 'dog'. It probably
comes from **cur-dog**, perhaps from Old Norse *kurr*
'grumbling', but used to mean 'house dog'.

dog

Dog appears only once in surviving Old English
literature, and until the Middle Ages **hound** was the
usual word for a dog. The past low status of dogs is
shown by phrases like **a dog's life**, **not have a dog's
chance**, and to **treat** someone **like a dog**. **A dog in the
manger**, 'someone inclined to prevent others having
things that they do not need themselves', derives from a

fable in which a dog lies in a manger to prevent the ox and horse from eating hay. A change in the status of dogs is found in the **man's best friend**, which is Victorian, and **love me**, **love my dog**.

guinea pig

The guinea pig comes from South America—not Guinea in Africa, or New Guinea in the South Pacific. Guinea pigs are chubby and can squeal like pigs, but why guinea was chosen nobody is really sure. It could have been confused with Guyana, South America, or used as a far-off, exotic country that no one knew much about. Guinea pigs have been bred by humans for some 3,000 years, and are no longer found in the wild. Their use in animal testing led to the word's acquiring the sense 'a person or thing used as a subject for experiment' in the 1920s.

husky

Husky for a hoarse-sounding person (a husky voice) and the term husky for an Arctic dog are unconnected. The first comes from **husk** 'the dry outer covering of a seed', a medieval word from Dutch *hūskjin* 'a little house' containing the seed. The dog used for pulling sledges probably comes from a Native American language. Our use is from the shortening of **husky dog** or 'Eskimo dog' from Newfoundland dialect *Huskemaw*, a form of **Eskimo** (see PEOPLES), first used in English in around 1830.

Pets

moggie

This informal word for a cat is a variant of Maggie, a pet form of the name Margaret.

pet

Pet was first used for 'a hand-reared lamb' in Scotland and northern England, where it also meant 'spoilt or favourite child'. It came from Scottish Gaelic *peata* 'tame animal'. By the early 18th century it had spread south applied to any domestic or tamed animal. The verb, 'to stroke or pat affectionately', is found in the early 17th century, although the sense 'to engage in sexually stimulating caressing', as in **heavy petting**, is first found in the USA in the 1920s.

rabbit

Rabbits were introduced to Britain by the Normans in the 12th century to provide meat and fur. The name is only recorded in the late 14th century, for a young rabbit. Before that, rabbits were **conies**. In 16th-century slang a coney was what we might call a mark—someone to cheat or rob, an activity known as 'coney-catching'. We are not sure where rabbit comes from, but it is most likely Old French, related to French dialect *rabotte* 'young rabbit'. It may be of Dutch origin and be linked to Flemish *robbei* 'rabbit'. Someone who chatters incessantly '**rabbits on**', from modern rhyming slang **rabbit and pork** meaning 'talk'.

Philosophy see also RELIGION

category

First used in philosophy, this comes via French or late
Latin, from Greek *katēgoria* 'statement, accusation', from
katēgoros 'accuser'.

conundrum

The origin of conundrum is itself a conundrum. In 1596
the English political writer Thomas Nashe used it as a
term of abuse for a crank or pedant: 'So will I . . . drive
him to confess himself a Conundrum, who now thinks
he hath learning enough to prove the salvation of
Lucifer.' The word later came to refer both to a whim
and a pun. The current sense of 'a riddle or puzzle' dates
from the late 17th century.

cynic

The original Cynics were members of a school of
ancient Greek philosophers who displayed a contempt
for wealth, luxury, and pleasure, believing that such
things distracted from the quest for self-knowledge. The
word comes from Greek *kunikos*. The Greek word
probably derives from *Kunosarges*, the name of the
school where one of their founders, Antisthenes, taught.
This is more likely than the traditional story that the
word comes from the Greek for dog, *kuōn*, and so means
'doglike or churlish'.

Philosophy

ethic

At first this term referred to ethics or moral philosophy. It comes via Old French from Latin *ethice*, from Greek *(hē)ēthikē (tekhnē)* '(the science of) morals'. The base is Greek *ēthos* 'nature, disposition', source of **ethos**.

eureka

In the 3rd century BC the Greek mathematician and inventor Archimedes of Syracuse in Sicily was asked by the king Hiero to test a crown to find out whether it was solid gold as the maker claimed, or an alloy made up to the same weight. The solution eluded Archimedes until he overfilled his bath, which overflowed as he got in. The solution to the problem hit him. He realized that he could test if the crown was pure gold by putting it in water and seeing whether it made the water overflow as much as a similar volume of genuine gold did. He is said to have run through the streets shouting 'Eureka!', or rather *heurēka*, 'I have found it' in Greek. The name **Archimedes' principle** is given to the law stating that a body immersed in a liquid is subject to an upward force equal to the weight of liquid it displaces.

guru

This is from Hindi and Punjabi, from Sanskrit *guru* 'weighty, grave, dignified' (comparable with Latin *gravis* 'heavy' source of **gravity**) which led to 'elder, teacher'.

paradox

Originally a paradox was a statement contrary to accepted opinion. It comes via late Latin from Greek *paradoxon* 'contrary (opinion)', formed from elements *para-* 'distinct from' and *doxa* 'opinion', found also in **orthodox**, where it combines with *orthos* 'straight, right'.

sceptic

Sceptic comes from Greek *skeptikos*, from *skepsis* 'inquiry, doubt' and was first used to refer to a philosopher denying the possibility of knowledge in a certain sphere; the leading ancient sceptic was Pyrrho (*c.*360–270 BC) whose followers at the Academy vigorously opposed Stoicism.

stoic

Today a child who falls over but does not cry might be described as stoic—a long way from the original Stoics (3rd century BC) of Athens. They were the followers of a school of philosophy teaching that wise men should live in harmony with Fate or Providence, indifferent to the ups and downs of life and to pleasure and pain. From there stoic or **stoical** came to mean 'enduring pain and hardship without complaint'. Stoic is from the *Stoa Poikilē*, or 'Painted Porch', where the school's founder, Zeno, taught.

sublime

Originally sublime meant 'dignified or aloof', from Latin *sublimis* 'in a high position, lofty', probably from *sub-* 'up to' and *limen* 'threshold or lintel'. The modern sense 'outstandingly beautiful or grand' arose in the 17th century. **Sublimate**, from the same source, was used by medieval alchemists as a chemical term. **From the sublime to the ridiculous** is a shortening of the saying **from the sublime to the ridiculous is only a step**, a remark attributed to Napoleon Bonaparte following the retreat from Moscow in 1812. Napoleon was not the first to express such an idea. The English political writer Thomas Paine wrote in *The Age of Reason* (1794): 'The sublime and the ridiculous are often so nearly related, that it is difficult to class them separately. One step above the sublime, makes the ridiculous; and one step above the ridiculous, makes the sublime again.'

Place to Word

Bristol

The city in south-west England, whose name means 'assembly place by the bridge', has been a leading port since the 12th century. This is the background to **shipshape and Bristol fashion**, 'in good order, neat and clean'. Something pleasing or well-ordered was described as Bristol fashion because sailors thought Bristol a model of prosperity and success. The port's importance for the wine trade gives us sherries such as

Bristol Cream. One of the city's two soccer teams,
Bristol City, is the reason that a woman's breasts are
sometimes called **bristols**. This is rhyming slang, from
Bristol City = titty.

Burton

To **go for a Burton** first appeared in RAF slang in the
1940s, when it was used to mean 'be killed in a crash'.
The most plausible explanation is that it was a reference
to going for a pint of Burton's beer. Burton upon
Trent in Staffordshire, England, was a well-known
centre of the brewing industry. Another suggestion is
that it referred to a suit from the British men's clothing
firm Burton's, but there is no known record of 'go
for a Burton's suit', as you might expect if this were
the origin of the phrase, and 'gone for a pint' is a much
more likely euphemism for a young man's sudden
death.

Coventry

The phrase **send someone to Coventry**, meaning to
refuse to speak to them, may be connected with the
English Civil War (1642–9), although it is not recorded
until the 1760s. The garrison of Parliamentarian soldiers
stationed in Coventry was apparently deeply unpopular
with the city's inhabitants, who refused to associate with
them socially. Another theory is that this staunchly
Parliamentarian city was where many Royalist prisoners
were sent to be held in secure captivity.

Place to Word

cravat

Cravat comes from the French word *Cravate*, meaning 'Croat'. Croatian mercenaries in the French army during the 17th century wore a linen scarf round their necks, which subsequently became fashionable among the French population at large.

currant

This comes from the phrase 'raisons of Corauntz', translating Anglo-Norman French *raisins de Corauntz* 'grapes of Corinth', which was their original source.

Derby

The 12th Earl of Derby founded the Epsom Derby, an annual race for three-year-old horses, in 1780. The simple form **Derby** as the name of the race is not recorded until the mid 19th century; fifty or so years later horse races in other countries, such as the Kentucky Derby in the USA, acquired the title. The significance of the event meant that in the early 20th century different sporting events appropriated the name. Derby is also used in the USA for a bowler hat, and people attribute this to American demand for a hat of the type worn at the English Derby. The name first appeared in the late 19th century.

magenta

This colour owes its name to Magenta in northern Italy, the site of a battle in 1859 fought shortly before the dye was discovered.

marzipan

The sugary paste used on cakes has taken an exotic journey starting at the port of Martaban on the coast of south-east Burma (Myanmar), once famous for the glazed jars it exported, containing preserves and sweets. In the course of a long trek through Persian and Arabic into European languages, the name Martaban transmuted into Italian *marzapane*, with a shift of meaning from the container to its contents. From the 16th to the 19th centuries the usual form in English was **marchpane**. It was not until the 19th century, when English reborrowed the Italian word, that marzipan became established.

muslin

Muslin means 'cloth made in Mosul' in Iraq. The place was called Mussolo in Italian and the cloth was called *mussolina*. This was adopted into French as *mousseline* (also used for a light sauce since the early 20th century) which in turn gave the English form.

oasis

In the classical world Oasis was the name of a particular fertile spot in the Libyan desert. It came ultimately from an ancient Egyptian word for 'dwelling place'. By the early 19th century the word was being used for a place of calm in the midst of trouble or bustle. In Sir Arthur Conan Doyle's *The Sign of Four* (1890), a character describes his richly furnished house as being 'an oasis of art in the howling desert of South London'.

Plants see also FRUIT

acorn

An Old English word, related to **acre**, meaning 'fruit of the open land or forest'. It was later applied to any fruit, then the most important fruit produced by the forest, the acorn. The spelling, originally *æcern*, was changed because people thought the word must have something to do with oak and corn.

aloe

Old English *alewe* was used for the fragrant resin or heartwood of certain oriental trees; it came via Latin from Greek *aloē*. The emollient **aloe vera** is early 20th century and modern Latin, literally 'true aloe', probably in contrast to the American agave, which resembles aloe vera.

banyan

The Indian fig tree known as a banyan comes via Portuguese, from a Gujarati word for 'a man of the trading caste'. Originally meaning a Hindu merchant, in the mid 17th century it was applied by Europeans to one particular tree, the Banyans' Tree, under which traders had built a pagoda.

catkin

This is from obsolete Dutch *katteken* 'kitten'.

daisy

Daisies close at night and open again in the morning, revealing their central yellow disc. This gives them their name, as daisy is a contraction of *day's eye*. Being dead and buried loses some of its fear when you are **under the daisies** or **pushing up daisies**. This is early 20th century, and the First World War poet Wilfred Owen (1893–1918) alludes to its use by soldiers in the trenches. **Fresh as a daisy** refers to the daisy opening in the morning. It was in use by the 14th century, appearing in the poetry of Geoffrey Chaucer (*c.*1343–1400).

dandelion

French *dent-de-lion* means 'lion's tooth', from its toothed leaves, and came into English in the late Middle Ages. Its usual name in French is now *pissenlit*, which has a parallel in English **pissabed**, another name for the dandelion. Dandelions were formerly well known for their diuretic properties.

onion

Onions have been cultivated since medieval times. The name comes ultimately from Latin where it meant 'a large pearl', but was used in non-standard speech for onion. **Know your onions**, to be very knowledgeable about

Plants

something, was first used in the USA in the 1920s, when
there were several similar phrases that involved knowing
a lot about foodstuffs. Onions may simply have been
chosen as a widely used vegetable. Another theory links
it with the lexicographer C. T. Onions, an early editor
of the *Oxford English Dictionary*. Despite his eminence as
a scholar it seems unlikely he would have been widely
known on both sides of the Atlantic.

petal

This comes via modern Latin from Greek *petalon* 'leaf',
from *petalos* 'outspread'. Since a petal is technically a
modified leaf the origin is appropriate.

rhododendron

Rhododendron means 'rose tree' from Greek *rhodos*
'rose', also found in the name Rhoda, and *dendron*
'tree' found in many plant names as well as in
dendrochronology, dating things through tree rings.
Rhododendron was originally used of the rose-flowered
oleander, and only transferred to the modern plant in
the mid 17th century.

spruce

Prussia was a kingdom that covered much of modern
north-east Germany and Poland. From the 14th to the
17th centuries it was also known in English as **Pruce** or
Spruce, which could also mean 'Prussian'. Spruce then

became the name of a type of fir tree grown in Prussia.
Spruce leather was a fashionable type of leather
imported in the 16th century from Prussia. The sense
'neat or smart' probably developed from this.

Politics see also RANK

aristocracy

This originally meant the government of a state by
its best citizens, later by the rich and well born, which
led to the sense 'nobility', regardless of the form of
government. The origin is Old French *aristocratie*,
from Greek *aristokratia*, from *aristos* 'best' and *-kratia*
'power'.

congress

A congress once meant an encounter during battle: it is
from Latin *congressus*, from *congredi* 'meet', literally 'walk
together'. Use for any 'coming together' is reflected in
obsolete or archaic uses such as **social congress**, **sexual
congress**.

crony

This derives from Greek *khronios* 'long-lasting', based on
khronos 'time', source also of **chronic**. Crony was
originally Cambridge University slang for 'an old friend,

Politics

a contemporary'. **Chum** is the Oxford equivalent. The
first record of crony is from the diary of Samuel Pepys
(1633–1703), a former Cambridge man, for 30 May 1665:
'Jack Cole, my old school-fellow ... who was a great
chrony of mine.' His spelling reflects the original Greek.
The political sense of **cronyism**, 'appointing your friends
and associates to positions of authority', originated in
the US during the 19th century.

democracy

The word democracy came directly from French in the
mid 16th century, but goes back to Greek *dēmokratia*,
from *dēmos* 'the people' and *kratia* 'power, rule'. *Demos* is
also the source of **demagogue**, combined with *agōgos*
'leading', and **epidemic** from *epidēmia* 'the prevalence of
disease' which goes back to *epi* 'upon' and *dēmos* 'the
people'.

despot

This comes, via French and medieval Latin, from Greek
despotēs 'master, lord, absolute ruler' (in modern Greek
used for a bishop). Originally, after the Turkish conquest
of Constantinople, the term denoted a petty Christian
ruler under the Turkish empire. The current sense dates
from the late 18th century.

dynasty

Dynasty comes via late Latin from Greek *dunasteia*
'lordship, power'.

fascism

The term fascism was first used of the right-wing
nationalist regime of Mussolini in Italy (1922–43), the
Partito Nazionale Fascista ('National Fascist Party'), and later
applied to the regimes of Franco in Spain and the Nazis in
Germany. It comes from Latin *fascis* 'bundle'. In ancient
Rome the fasces were bundles of rods, with an axe through
them, carried in front of a magistrate to symbolize his
power to punish people.

filibuster

A filibuster was an 18th-century pirate of the Caribbean.
The word links a number of languages, reaching back
through Spanish and French to *vrijbuiter*, from *vrij* 'free',
and *buit* 'booty', a Dutch word which also gives us
freebooter. In the 19th century the Spanish *filibustero*
was used of American adventurers stirring up revolution
in Central and South America, and filibuster came to be
used in the USA to describe behaviour in congressional
debates intended to sabotage proceedings. This became,
'a very long speech made in Parliament to prevent the
passing of a new law', linking the long-ago pirates with
politicians of today.

parliament

A parliament is historically a talking shop. It originates
from French *parler* 'to talk', from Latin *parabola* 'word',
also the root of **parable** and **parlour**, originally a place
for speaking.

rostrum

A rostrum, now a raised platform on which a person makes a speech, was originally part of a ship. It is from a Latin word meaning 'beak', which came from *rodere* 'to gnaw', also source of **rodent**. The Forum in ancient Rome had a platform for public speakers decorated with the 'beaks' or pointed prows of captured enemy warships.

 # Punishment see also CRIME, LAW

confiscate

This comes from Latin *confiscare* 'to store in a chest' or 'to take something for the public treasury', the original meaning in English. *Confiscare* was based on *con-* 'together' and *fiscus* 'chest or treasury', also the root of **fiscal**.

dungeon

The word dungeon had two main senses when it was first used in the 14th century: 'the great tower or keep of a castle' and 'an underground prison cell'. The first is now usually spelled **donjon** and regarded as a separate word. The core meaning was 'lord's tower', and the word goes back to Latin *dominus* 'lord, master'.

harass

This came from French in the early 17th century and is probably from *harer* 'to set a dog on'. The notion of intimidation arose during the 19th century, with **sexual harassment** acquiring particular prominence in the 1970s. The sound and sense of harass are similar to **harry**, but the two are unrelated: harry goes back to an ancient root meaning 'army, host', which also gave us the bird called a **harrier**, but not the dogs, which got their name from the **hares** they hunted.

jail

The words jail and **cage** both go back to Latin *cavea* 'hollow, cave, cell', from *cavus* 'hollow' the source of **cave**. In late Latin the *-ea* at the end of *cavea* softened to a 'ya' or 'ja' sound, which explains the sound changes between the source and the forms we use. Jail arrived in medieval English in two forms, from Old French *jaiole* and Anglo-Norman *gaole*, which survives in the old-fashioned British spelling **gaol**.

jury

This comes from the Latin word *jurare* 'to swear'. Early juries had to swear to give true answers to questions asked about their personal knowledge of an event they had witnessed. If you did not do this you committed **perjury** from the Latin for 'false oath'.

Punishment

magistrate

Magistrate is from Latin *magistratus* 'administrator', from *magister* 'master'. This also gives us **master** and its weakened forms **mister** and **miss**.

pillory

This is from Old French *pilori*, probably from Provençal *espilori*, possibly from a Catalan word meaning 'peephole'. A pillory was made up of two boards brought together leaving holes for the head and hands; in Great Britain this punishment was abolished except for perjury in 1815 and totally in 1837. Use continued in the States until 1905.

prison

This comes via Old French from Latin *prehendere* 'to seize'. *Prehendere* is a rich source of English words, giving amongst others **apprehend**, **comprehend**, **prehensile**, and **reprehensible**. A shortening of *prehendere* lies behind *praedari* 'plunder' and *praeda* 'booty', which give **depredation**, **predatory**, and **prey**.

scourge

Scourge is a shortening of Old French *escorgier*, from Latin *ex-* 'thoroughly' and *corrigia* 'thong, whip'. It is mostly used figuratively as in the **Scourge of God** for an instrument of divine chastisement, the title given to Attila the Hun in the 5th century.

verdict

After the Norman Conquest, French became the language of the law in England and many French legal terms passed into English. French *verdict* goes back to Latin *verus* 'true', source also of **verify**, **veritable**, and **very**; and *dicere* 'to say', from which **addict** originally 'assigned by decree' and so bound to something, **contradiction** 'speaking against', **dictate**, **predict** 'speaking in advance', and numerous other words derive.

Rank see also POLITICS

duke

Duke goes back to Latin *dux* 'leader', which is related to *ducere* 'to lead' also source of **duct**. The earliest meaning of duke was 'the ruler of a duchy' and referred to sovereign princes in continental Europe. It did not describe a member of the British nobility until the end of the 14th century.

earl

In Saxon times an earl was a man of noble rank, as opposed to a **churl** (source of **churlish**) or ordinary peasant, or **thane**, a man granted land by the king. In King Canute's rule in the early 11th century, an earl was the governor of a large division of England such as Wessex. Under the Normans earl meant any nobleman who held the continental title of **count**, from Latin *comes* 'companion, attendant'.

emperor

The root of emperor is the Latin word *imperare* 'to command', also the ultimate source of **empire**, **imperative**, **imperial**, and **imperious**. Latin *imperator* meant 'military commander', a title given to Julius Caesar and to Augustus, the first Roman emperor, and adopted by subsequent rulers of the empire. In English, emperor first referred to these Roman rulers, and then to the head of the Holy Roman Empire.

esquire

An esquire was originally a young man of gentle birth who attended a knight. Esquire comes from an Old French word meaning 'shield bearer' from Latin *scutum* 'shield'. **Squire** is the same word. Esquire later came to mean a man belonging to the order of English gentry below a knight, and then became a polite title added to the name of a man, initially only one regarded as a 'gentleman'.

monarch

Monarch comes via late Latin from Greek *monarkhēs*, from *monos* 'alone' and *arkhein* 'to rule'. *Monos* also lies behind **monastery** which comes from *monazein* 'to live alone', while **monk** comes from *monakos* 'solitary'.

pharaoh

Pharaoh goes back to Egyptian *pr-'o* 'great house'. Early English spellings included *Pharaon* and *Pharaoe*; the final h in later English spellings was influenced by the Hebrew spelling in the Bible.

plebeian

This is based on Latin *plebeius*, from *plebs*, 'the common people', as opposed to the more aristocratic **patricians** who were the 'fathers of their country', getting their name from Latin *pater* 'father' (source of other words such as **paternal**).

Rank

queen

The Old English spelling of queen was *cwēn*. This originally meant 'a wife', specifically of a king or other important man. Related to *cwēn* was Old English *cwene* 'woman', which became the archaic **quean**, 'a bold or impudent woman', sometimes encountered in Shakespeare. In his day it was also a term for a prostitute. Because the two words came to be pronounced identically the derogatory sense dropped out of use as too confusing. The sense of queen 'an effeminate gay man' dates from the beginning of the 20th century.

slave

Our word slave was shortened from early French *esclave* in the Middle Ages. Its medieval Latin equivalent, *sclavus*, is identical with *Sclavus*, the source of **Slav**. The Slavic peoples of Europe were conquered and reduced to a servile state during the 9th century. **Wage slaves** comes from the English translation of the *Communist Manifesto* by Karl Marx and Friedrich Engels.

sovereign

Old French *soverain* was formed from Latin *super* 'above'. In English the ending was later altered to look as if the word was associated with **reign**. It was a term for a gold coin minted in England from the time of Henry VII to Charles I originally worth 22s. 6d. Sovereigns were revived in 1817 with a value of one pound.

Religion

see also CHRISTIANITY, HEAVEN AND HELL,
PHILOSOPHY

auspicious

Romans tried to predict future events by watching the
behaviour of animals and birds. An *auspex* was a person
who observed the flight of birds for omens. The related
auspicium, the source of **auspice**, meant 'taking omens
from birds'. Both words came from *avis* 'bird' and *specere*
'to look'. Auspice was originally used for the Roman
concept, but later became 'a premonition or forecast,
especially of a happy future'. Auspicious accordingly
meant 'fortunate or favourable'. If the *auspex's* omens
were favourable, he was seen as the protector of an
enterprise, hence **under the auspices of**, 'with the
help, support, or protection of'. An *auspex* was also
called an *augur* (from, *avis* 'bird' together with *garrire* 'to
talk'). If something **augurs well**, it is a sign of a good
outcome.

dogma

Dogma comes via late Latin from Greek *dogma*
'opinion', from *dokein* 'seem good, think'.

exorcize

This comes from Greek *exorkizein* 'exorcise', from *ex-* 'out'
and *horkos* 'oath'. It originally meant 'conjure up or

273

command (an evil spirit)'; the sense 'drive out an evil spirit' is 16th century.

faith

Both faith and **fidelity** come from the Latin *fides*. **Fido**, a traditional name for a dog, is also related; from the Latin for 'I trust'. Other words from the same source include **confident**, and **diffident**, which originally meant 'lacking in trust'. **Fiancée**, the French for 'promised', is related.

idol

Both **idyll** and idol go back to Greek *eidos* 'form, shape, picture'. Idol's earliest use in English was for false gods, images revered as objects of worship, condemned by Jewish and Christian tradition. Non-religious objects of excessive devotion have been idols since the mid 16th century. The 'picture' element is prominent in idyll—a picture in words. The word meant 'description of a picturesque scene or incident', the sense in the title of Tennyson's series of poems based on Arthurian legend, *The Idylls of the King*. His popularization of the term in the mid 19th century led to the word **idyllic** and the development of the modern sense, 'an extremely happy, peaceful, or picturesque period or situation'.

lama

This honorific title applied to a spiritual leader in Tibetan Buddhism is from Tibetan *bla-ma* (the b is silent); the literal meaning is 'superior one'.

pagan

In Latin *paganus* originally meant 'of the country, rustic', and also 'civilian, non-military'. Around the 4th century AD, it developed the sense 'non-Christian, heathen'. One theory is that belief in the ancient gods lingered in the rural villages after Christianity had been accepted in the towns of the Roman Empire; another focuses on the 'civilian' sense, and points out that early Christians called themselves 'soldiers of Christ', making non-Christians into 'civilians'. A third compares heathens to people outside the civilized world of towns, belonging to the countryside. Curiously, Pagan was used as a given name, a custom recently revived. The Latin root *paganus* came from *pagus* 'country district', also the source of **peasant**. **Heathen** developed similarly, coming from a word meaning 'inhabiting open country' related to **heath**.

shrine

Old English *scrīn* was a 'cabinet, chest, reliquary'. Its ultimate source is Latin *scrinium* 'chest for books'.

synagogue

Despite its strong Jewish associations, this came via Old French and late Latin from Greek *sunagōgē* 'meeting', from *sun-* 'together' and *agein* 'bring'.

taboo

Not many English words come from the Polynesian language of Tongan, but taboo is one. It was introduced into English by the explorer Captain James Cook in 1777. He wrote: 'Not one of them would sit down, or eat a bit of any thing…they were all taboo.' He went on to explain that the word was generally used to mean 'forbidden'.

Reptiles and Amphibians

adder

One of the words Anglo-Saxons used for a snake was *naedre*, which became *nadder* in medieval times. Sometime during the 14th or 15th century the word managed to lose its initial *n*, as people heard 'a nadder' and misinterpreted this as 'an adder'. A northern dialect form **nedder** still exists. A similar process of 'wrong division' took place with words such as **apron** and **umpire** and the opposite can happen too, as with, for example, **newt** (see below) and **nickname** (originally an *eke* 'extra' name). In time adder became a specific poisonous snake, also known as the **viper**.

alligator

Alligator comes from two Spanish words *el lagarto*, 'the lizard'. The first record of its use is from an account of his travels written by 16th-century English adventurer Job Hortop. He was press-ganged to sail to the Americas on a slaving voyage when only a teenager, and wrote vividly of the strange animals he encountered, among them the alligator.

Reptiles and Amphibians

chameleon

A lion and a giraffe feature in the history of the lizard's name. Chameleon is derived via Latin from Greek *khamaileōn*, from *khamai* 'on the ground' and *leōn* 'lion'. So a chameleon was a 'ground lion'. It was often spelled *camelion*, which sometimes got mixed up with **camelopard**, an old word for a **giraffe** (see ON SAFARI). So for a time, in the 14th and 15th centuries, a **camelion** was also a name for the giraffe.

crocodile

The name of the crocodile comes from Greek *krokodilos* 'worm of the stones', from *krokē* 'pebble' and *drilos* 'worm', a reference to the crocodile's habit of basking in the sun on river banks. In medieval English the spellings *cocodrille* and *cokadrill* were common. Shedding **crocodile tears**, putting on a display of insincere sorrow, dates from the mid 16th century and comes from the ancient belief that crocodiles wept while luring or devouring their prey. A 16th-century account of the sailor John Hawkins's voyages says the crocodile's nature 'is ever when he would have his prey, to cry and sob like a Christian body, to provoke them to come to him, and then he snatcheth at them'.

frog

In the Middle Ages frog was a term of abuse. In the 17th century it was used particularly for a Dutchman, but by the late 18th century it was being applied to the

Reptiles and Amphibians

French, probably partly due to alliteration, and partly to the reputation of the French for eating frogs' legs. Someone who is hoarse is said to have a **frog in the throat**. This dates from the late 19th century, but 'frog' here goes back to an earlier meaning of soreness or swelling in the mouth or throat. Frog, a decorative fastening, does not seem to be the same word and its origin is unknown.

newt
Like adder (above), newt is an example of the phenomenon known as 'wrong division' or 'metanalysis', whereby people attach the last letter of one word to the beginning of the next. In Old English the animal was an *ewt*.

python
A python's name comes from Greek *Puthōn*, a monstrous serpent killed by Apollo in Greek legend. Poets in the 17th and 18th centuries sometimes described any monster or plague as a python. Python was only used as a generic term for a snake that crushes its prey from the early 19th century. The BBC comedy series *Monty Python's Flying Circus* was first shown on 5 October 1969. The name was deliberately chosen to have no real meaning—it was the winning candidate from a list of absurd titles such as *Gwen Dibley's Flying Circus*, *Vaseline Review*, and *Owl-Stretching Time*. The programme became so popular and influential that in 1975 it gave the

language a new word, **Pythonesque**, to describe surreal humour.

reptile

Today reptile conjures up a picture of snakes and lizards, but in the 14th century the word included other creatures. It comes from Latin *repere* 'to crawl' and was originally used for any crawling animal. The first use of reptile as an insulting term is in Henry Fielding's *Tom Jones* (1749) 'For a little reptile of a critic to presume to find fault with any of its parts . . . is a most presumptuous absurdity.'

snake

The ancestor of snake is an ancient Germanic word that meant 'to crawl or creep'. Serpent has a similar origin— it comes from Latin *serpere*, with the same meaning. Yet another word with this original sense was Old English **slink**. You can describe a treacherous person as a **snake in the grass**, with the idea of a lurking danger. Snakes are associated with treachery not only in Genesis but in the 6th century BC fables of the Greek storyteller Aesop. In one of his stories a man finding a snake frozen with cold puts it close to his chest to warm. As soon as the snake revives it bites him. Before the 17th century a treacherous person was called a **pad in the straw** (pad is an old dialect word for a toad). The children's game **Snakes and Ladders**, (in the USA **Chutes and Ladders**), is late 19th century. It may be based on an ancient Indian

Reptiles and Amphibians

game called *Moksha Patamu*, which was used to teach children about the Hindu religion—the good squares allowed a player to go to a higher level of life, whereas the evil 'snakes' sent them back through reincarnation to lower tiers of life.

Sadness

see also EMOTION, HAPPY, MIND AND MENTAL ILLNESS

alas

This comes from Old French *a las*, *a lasse*, from *a* 'ah'
and *las(se)*, from Latin *lassus* 'weary'. Late Middle
English **alack** is a comparable exclamation, from 'ah!'
and *lak* 'lack'. It originally expressed dissatisfaction and
the notion 'shame that it should be the case'; this came
to convey regret or surprise, as in **alack-a-day**.

deplore

To deplore something was originally to weep over it,
then regret deeply. It weakened over time until in the
mid 19th century it was merely to disapprove strongly.
Deplore comes from Latin *deplorare*, from *de-* 'away,
thoroughly' and *plorare* 'bewail'.

dismal

This originally referred to 24 days each year, two in each
month, that medieval people believed were unlucky. It
comes from Latin *dies mali* 'evil days', and appeared in
English in the early Middle Ages as *the dismal*, and then
the dismal days. Soon dismal days could be any time of
disaster, gloom, or depression, or old age. In 1849 the
Scottish historian and political philosopher Thomas
Carlyle (1795–1881) nicknamed economics (then known
as 'political economy') **the dismal science**.

Sadness

forlorn

In Old English forlorn meant 'morally corrupted', but
the core idea was 'lost', from the verb *forlese* 'to lose'.
In the 16th century the current sense of 'pitifully sad'
developed. A **forlorn hope**, a desperate hope that is
unlikely to be fulfilled, came into the language as a
mistranslation of Dutch *verloren hoop* 'lost troop'. It was
originally a band of soldiers picked to begin an attack,
many of whom would not survive.

misery

Misery comes via French from Latin *miser* 'wretched',
which also gives us **miser**.

poignant

A keen sense of sadness or regret can be described as
poignant. This comes from an Old French word that
meant 'pricking' derived from Latin *pungere*, 'to prick'.
In the Middle Ages you could describe a weapon as
poignant, meaning that it had a sharp point. It could also
be applied to sharp tastes or smells, as in 'a poignant
sauce' or 'a poignant scent'. This sense is now covered
by the related word **pungent**, which originally meant
'very painful or distressing' and at one time could also
mean 'telling, convincing', as in Samuel Pepys's 'a very
good and pungent sermon'. The slim dagger called a
poinard looks as if it should be related. However, this
illustrates the danger of jumping to conclusions in
etymologies. It gets its name from the fact that it is held

in the fist, from Latin *pugnus* 'fist', also the source, via *pugnare* 'to fight', of **pugnacious**.

sad

The original meaning of sad in Old English was 'having no more appetite, weary'. The word comes from the same root as Latin *satis* 'enough', the source of **satiated**, **satisfactory**, and **satisfy**. The idea was similar to our expression **fed up**—of being unhappy through being too 'full' of something. Sad then developed through 'firm, constant' and 'dignified, sober' to our modern sense of 'unhappy' in the medieval period. In the 1990s '**You're so sad**!' became slang. This use of sad, to mean 'pathetically inadequate or unfashionable', was not completely new, and had been around since the 1930s.

sorry

In the Anglo-Saxon period to be sorry was to be pained or distressed, full of grief or sorrow—the meaning gradually weakened to become 'sad through sympathy with someone else's misfortune', 'full of regret', and then simply an expression of apology. The source was **sore**, which originally had the meaning 'causing intense pain, grievous'. **Sorrow** is also Old English, but is not closely related to the other two words. The expression **more in sorrow than in anger** is taken from Shakespeare's Hamlet. When Hamlet asks Horatio to describe the expression on the face of his father's ghost, Horatio replies, 'a countenance more in sorrow than in anger'.

weep

A Germanic word in origin, Old English *wēpan* is
probably imitative of the sound of moaning and
sobbing, although in modern use the verb indicates the
more or less silent shedding of tears. Weep is now
normally restricted to literary use.

woe

Many ancient languages, including Old English, Latin,
and Greek, had woe or a similar word—a natural
exclamation made by someone unhappy or in distress.
The medieval word betide, meaning 'to happen', comes
from the same source as **tide** 'time' from Old English,
and these days is mainly found in the phrase **woe betide**,
a light-hearted warning that someone will be in trouble
if they do a particular thing.

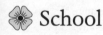 School

academy

An academy today is a place of learning or culture.
Appropriately, the word originated with one of the most
influential scholars who ever lived, the Greek
philosopher Plato. In 4th century BC he taught in an
Athenian garden called the *Akadēmeia*, which was named
after an ancient hero *Akadēmos*. It gave its name to the
school Plato founded, the Academy.

bully

People originally liked bullies. It came into the English language in the 16th century, probably from an old Dutch word *boele* 'lover', as a term of endearment, much like 'sweetheart' or 'darling'. At the end of the 17th century it was used to mean 'admirable or jolly', and finally a general sense of 'first-rate' developed, which survives in **bully for you**!, 'well done! good for you!'. The usual modern sense is late 17th century, probably from its use as an informal way of addressing a male friend, or as 'lad' or 'one of the boys'. The bully of **bully beef** is a mid 18th-century alteration of French *bouilli* 'boiled'.

degree

The source of degree is a French word based on Latin *de-* 'down' and *gradus* 'step' source of **grade** (see below). Early senses of degree include 'step, tier', 'rank', and 'relative state'. Degree for an academic qualification came from the medieval Mastership or Doctorate, which was attained in stages or degrees. The 'step' sense is found in the geometrical use, measurement of heat, and in **by degrees** or step by step.

essay

Essay is a variant of **assay** 'try, test', going back to Latin *exigere* 'ascertain, weigh'. In writing contexts, it meant initially 'a first draft' but came to mean 'a composition'. This seems to have come from the French philosopher and essayist Montaigne (1533–92) whose *Essais* were first published in 1580.

grade

A grade is literally a step from Latin *gradus* 'step', and was originally used in English as a unit of measurement, a use largely replaced by **degree** (see above). *Gradus* is also found in **graduate** 'take a degree', **gradient**, **gradual** 'by degrees', and **degrade**.

pupil

The two words spelled pupil have entered English by different routes and have different meanings, but share a root, Latin *pupa*, meaning both 'doll' and 'girl'. The first pupil was originally an orphan or ward under the care of a guardian, from which emerged the idea of someone taught by another. It came into English via Old French from Latin *pupus* 'boy' and *pupa* 'girl'. The other pupil, in the centre of your eye, comes from the 'doll' meaning of *pupa*. People noticed the tiny images of themselves reflected in another person's eyes and thought they resembled little dolls (a similar idea is behind an old use of baby). In the 18th century **pupa** was borrowed directly from Latin for an insect in its inactive immature form, between larva and adult.

school

The school that children go to derives from Greek *skholē* 'leisure, philosophy, place for lectures', the source also of

scholar. Many ancient Greeks clearly spent their leisure time in intellectual pursuits rather than physical recreation. This is not the same school that large groups of fish or sea mammals congregate in. Here the word comes from early German and Dutch *schōle*, 'a troop, multitude', from the same root as **shoal** and related to **shallow**.

swot

A variation of **sweat** that started life as army slang. Swot was first 'studying, school, or college work', and referred especially to mathematics. This led to its use to describe someone who studies hard or excessively.

syllabus

An early syllabus was a 'concise table of headings of a text'. From modern Latin, it was originally a misreading of Latin *sittybas*, from Greek *sittuba* 'title slip, label'. Use in educational contexts for a programme of study is recorded from the late 19th century.

truant

In the 13th century a truant was someone who begged out of choice rather than necessity, what the Elizabethans called 'a sturdy beggar'. The idea of voluntary idleness led to its application in the later medieval period to children staying away from school without permission. The word came from Old French, but is probably ultimately of Celtic origin, related to Welsh *truan* and Scottish Gaelic *truaghan* 'wretched'.

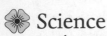

Science

see also CHEMISTRY, COMPUTERS, MATHEMATICS, UNIVERSE

clone

The word clone, from Greek *klōn* 'twig, cutting from a plant', is first recorded in 1903, when it referred to a group of plants produced by taking cuttings or grafts from an original. It has been used of genetic duplication of mammals since the early 1970s. Nowadays it is also used for someone who slavishly imitates someone else and for a computer that simulates another more expensive model. In gay culture a clone is a gay man who adopts an exaggeratedly macho appearance and style of dress.

ecology

The word ecology is thought to have been invented in 1869 by the German biologist Ernst Haeckel. Originally spelled *oecology*, it is based on the Greek word *oikos* 'house'—the natural environment is seen as the home of all the plants and animals that live within it.

electricity

The word **electric** seems to have come before electricity, having been first used by the scientist William Gilbert in a Latin treatise called *De Magnete* (1600). Gilbert, who discovered how to make magnets and coined the term **magnetic pole**, spelled it *electricus*. Electricity is first recorded in 1646, in the writings of the physician Sir Thomas Browne. Both were based on the Latin word *electrum* 'amber', because rubbing amber produces an electric charge which will attract light objects.

evolve

The word evolve was first used in the general sense 'make more complex, develop'. It comes from Latin *evolvere*, from *e-* (a variant of *ex-*) 'out of' and *volvere* 'to roll', also the source of **evolution**. Early senses related to the tactical 'wheeling' manoeuvre in the realignment of troops or ships. Current senses stem from a notion of 'opening out' and 'unfolding', giving rise to a general sense of 'development'.

gene

The word gene is from German *Gen*, from *Pangen* (from Greek *pan-* 'all' and *genos* 'race, kind, offspring'), a supposed ultimate unit of heredity. **Genetic** first meant 'arising from a common origin': from **genesis** 'creation', on the pattern of pairs such as antithesis and antithetic.

microbe

Microbe is from French based on the Greek elements *mikros* 'small' and *bios* 'life'. The word was coined by C. Sédillot in March 1878.

Science

nucleus

The nucleus of something is literally its 'little nut'. Latin *nucleus* meant 'kernel, inner part', and was a diminutive of *nux* 'nut'. Nucleus originally referred to the bright core at the centre of a comet's head, and then to the central part of the earth. Today its main meaning is 'the positively charged central core of an atom'. This was identified by Sir Ernest Rutherford (1871–1937), regarded as the founder of nuclear physics, in 1911.

quantum

Although you will often come across a sentence like 'This product represents a quantum leap forward in telecommunications technology', the curious thing about **quantum leap** is that, strictly speaking, it does not describe a large change at all, but a tiny one. Quantum comes from Latin *quantus*, 'how big?' or 'how much?', and originally meant 'a quantity or amount'. In physics a quantum (a term introduced by the physicist Max Planck around 1900) is a very small amount of energy, the minimum amount that can exist in a given situation, and a **quantum jump** is the abrupt change of an electron or atom from one energy state to another. Although this is tiny in terms of size, it is instantaneous and dramatic, which explains why the term came into general usage from around 1970 to describe a sudden large increase or major advance. **Quantity** comes from the same root as quantum.

quark

In physics a quark is a subatomic particle believed to be one of the basic constituents of matter. The name was coined in the 1960s by the American physicist Murray Gell-Mann, who initially spelt it *quork* but changed this to quark after he came across the line 'Three quarks for Muster Mark' in James Joyce's *Finnegans Wake* (1939). Joyce's word is meant to suggest the cawing sound seagulls make. It appealed to Gell-Mann, as at the time only three varieties of quark (known as up, down, and strange quarks) were believed to exist.

science

Originally science was knowledge in general—any branch of knowledge, including the arts. It is from Latin *scire* 'to know' (also found in **conscience** 'inner knowledge'). The modern sense, concentrating on the physical and natural world, dates from the 18th century. **Science fiction** was first mentioned in 1851, but the term did not become common until the end of the 1920s, when US 'pulp' magazines (so called because of the cheap paper they were printed on) carried tales of space adventure. Before science fiction was coined the stories of writers such as Jules Verne were called **scientific fiction** or **scientifiction**.

Sea see also SHIPS

barnacle

A barnacle was originally what we would now call a
barnacle goose. The name appeared in English in the
early Middle Ages, but its ultimate origin is unknown.
The barnacle goose breeds in the Arctic tundra of
Greenland and similar places, but for a long time its
place of origin was something of a mystery. People
thought it hatched from a type of barnacle that attaches
itself to objects floating in the water and has long
feathery filaments protruding from its shell, which
suggested the notion of plumage. The shellfish started
to be called a barnacle in the 16th century.

clam

It is not easy to prise apart a clam, and this tight grip lies
behind the origin of the word. Clam originally meant
'clamp', and probably had the same source. There is also
an English dialect word **clam**, meaning 'to be sticky or
to stick to something', which is related to **clay**. It is
where **clammy**—originally spelled *claymy*—comes from.

iceberg

The earliest meaning of iceberg in English was for a
glacier which is seen from the sea as a hill. It comes from
Dutch *ijsberg*, from *ijs* 'ice' and berg '*hill*'. The expression
the tip of the iceberg, 'the small visible part of a larger

problem that remains hidden', is surprisingly recent,
being recorded only from the 1950s.

lobster

Lobsters and **locusts** are linguistically the same. Latin
locusta had both meanings. A close-up view of the two
clearly shows the similarity. Lobster was used as a
contemptuous name for British soldiers from the mid
17th century. Originally applied to a regiment of
Roundhead cuirassiers who wore complete suits of
armour, the term was later associated with the red
military coats worn by British soldiers.

pirate

The key idea behind pirates is that they are people who
attack you. It comes from Latin *pirata*, which went back
to Greek *peirein* 'to attempt, attack'.

shark

We do not know where the name for the fish comes
from, but the shark as in **loan shark** may be from
German *Schurke* 'worthless rogue', influenced by the
fish. **Shirk**, originally meaning a scrounger, may be from
the same German word. The sense 'avoid work' dates
from the late 18th century.

tide

In Old English a tide was a period or season, a sense
surviving in Eastertide and Shrovetide. It was not used in

connection with the sea until the later medieval period.
The saying **time and tide wait for no man** originally
referred just to time, with tide used as a repetition to add
emphasis. Despite the difference in their contemporary
meanings, **tidy** is from tide. Until the early 18th century
it meant 'timely, seasonable, opportune'. Its current
sense developed via 'attractive, good-looking' and 'good,
pleasing'. Perhaps based on tidy is **titivate** which in the
early 19th century was also spelt *tidivate*.

trout

Late Old English *truht* is from late Latin *tructa*, based on
Greek *trōgein* 'gnaw'. Use of the derogatory **old trout**
for an elderly woman is found from the late 19th century.

turtle

English sailors gave the turtle its name in the 1650s. They
probably based it on *tortue*, an early form of **tortoise**,
from French *tortue* and Spanish *tortuga* 'tortoise' of
uncertain origin. A boat is said to **turn turtle** when it
turns upside down, either because it looks like the shell
of a turtle, or because it is as helpless as a turtle on its
back. **Mock turtle** soup, inspiration for the Mock Turtle
in Lewis Carroll's *Alice in Wonderland*, is made with a
calf's head, in imitation of turtle soup, once an
important part of grand banquets. The turtle in **turtle
dove** is a different word whose ultimate source is Latin
turtur, imitating the bird's cooing.

walrus

The Anglo-Saxons seem to have thought the walrus looked a bit like a horse, for they called it the *horschwæl*, 'horse-whale'. We owe our name for the creature to the Dutch, who took the same idea but reversed it: the *wal-* bit is 'whale' and *-rus* is probably 'horse'.

Sensations see also ANGER, EMOTIONS, PAIN

bitter

Like **bit**, bitter shares a Germanic root with **bite**. In the phrase **to the bitter end** 'until something is finished, no matter what', is probably not from this word. It derives instead from a nautical term **bitter**, meaning the last part of a cable, that goes around the 'bitts' or fastening points for ropes on board ship. The biblical quotation 'her end is bitter as wormwood' may have helped popularize the phrase. Many Englishmen love their pint of **bitter**. This use seems to have started life as Oxford University slang in the 1850s, when students would talk of 'doing bitters'.

bland

In early use bland was 'gentle in manner', from Latin *blandus* 'soft, smooth'. This Latin adjective also forms the base of the Middle English noun **blandishment**.

Sensations

cool

As early as the 1880s, cool, an Old English word related to **cold**, was being used by black Americans to mean 'excellent, pleasing', and 'stylish'. It only became more widely known when people started associating it with a style of jazz in the 1940s. It then declined in popularity for a decade or two before regaining its popularity. **Cool as a cucumber** is older than might be expected, going back to the mid 18th century.

damp

We do not think of something damp as being dangerous, but it originally meant a noxious gas. This survives in **firedamp** for methane, especially when it forms an explosive mixture with air in coal mines. Damp did not refer to wetness until the 18th century. The **damp squib** which failed to go off comes from firework displays—a squib is a small firework that burns with a hissing sound before exploding. From the mid 19th century the phrase was used of events that were less impressive than expected. Nowadays, it is sometimes heard as '**damp squid**', people substituting a more familiarly damp word for the rarer squib. Both damp and **dank** are Germanic in origin, but were not originally connected.

delicious

This comes from late Latin *deliciosus*, from Latin *deliciae* 'delight, pleasure'. **Luscious** may be an alteration of delicious.

enthusiasm

Enthusiasm is from Greek *enthous* 'possessed by a god, inspired', from *theos* 'god', also the root of words including **atheist**, **pantheon**, and **theology**. Until relatively recently enthusiasm, **enthusiast**, and **enthusiastic** had less favourable meanings than nowadays. Enthusiasm was originally religious mania or divine inspiration, often involving 'speaking in tongues' and wild, uncontrollable behaviour. An enthusiast was a religious fanatic or fundamentalist, or a hypocrite pretending to be one. Subsequently the force of enthusiasm and related words weakened so that they arrived at our modern meanings.

frenetic

This comes via French and Latin from Greek *phrenitikos*, from *phrenitis* 'delirium', and was initially used to mean 'insane'. Originally **frantic** was merely an alternative form of the word. **Frenzy** is from the same root.

goo

This word for 'a sticky substance' was originally US and is perhaps from **burgoo**, originally a nautical slang term for porridge, but now a thick soup or stew particularly associated with Kentucky. It is based on Persian *bulġūr* 'bruised grain', a word found in **bulgar wheat**.

numb

Old English used to have a verb *nim* meaning 'take'. It was one of those verbs, like sing, that show the past form by changing the vowel. In this case the past was *nome* 'taken'. This then evolved into numb for sensation that had been taken away.

tacky

The origin of tacky in the sense 'sticky' is from **tack** 'to fasten lightly'. The origin of this word is obscure. The sense meaning 'in poor taste, cheap' is different, but equally obscure. It was first found in the early 19th century in the USA meaning a weedy horse. By the late 19th century it was applied to poor whites in some southern states, and had also acquired its modern sense. The shortening **tack** did not happen until the 1980s. The sense **tack** for horse equipment is a shortening of **tackle**.

 Sex see also PAIN

bonk

Bonk is an imitation of the sound of a solid object striking a hard surface. It first appeared as a verb, meaning 'to shell', in the First World War. The sexual sense does not seem to have been used before the mid 1970s, but has become established, perhaps because people feel it is an acceptable term that is not too rude. The link with **bonkers**, 'mad', probably comes from the idea of a mad person having been 'bonked' on the head one too many times.

bugger

A bugger was originally a heretic—this was the meaning of Old French *bougre*. The word ultimately comes from *Bulgarus*, which was the Latin term for a Bulgarian, in particular one who belonged to the Orthodox Church, which was regarded by the Roman Catholic Church as heretical. Bugger was first used in English in reference to members of a heretical Christian sect based in Albi in southern France in the 12th and 13th centuries, the Albigensians. The sexual use of the term arose in the 16th century from an association of heresy with forbidden sexual practices.

condom

This is often said to be named after a physician who invented it, but no such person has been traced, and its origin is unknown.

fornication

Latin *fornix*, the source of this word, originally meant a vault or arch. In Rome prostitutes would ply their trade under certain arches such as those around the Colosseum. From this *fornix* acquired the sense 'brothel' and then passed into late Latin as a term for extra-marital sex.

harem

This is from Arabic *harīm* which is literally 'prohibited, prohibited place', thus 'sanctuary, women's quarters' and, by extension, 'women'.

Sex

hussy

'You brazen hussy!' is now the sort of thing someone might call a female friend as a joke, but until the mid 20th century hussy was a serious term for an immoral woman. The original hussy was far more respectable, though—she was a housewife. Hussy developed in the mid 16th century from **housewife**, which was the word's first meaning. Some hundred years later it became a rude or playful way of addressing a woman, and also a derogatory term implying a lack of morals.

orgy

The word orgy goes back to Greek *orgia* 'secret rites or revels'. In the classical world these were part of the worship of Bacchus, the god of fertility and wine, in the annual festivals held in his honour, which were celebrated with extravagant dancing, singing, and drinking.

ribald

This was first used as a noun for a 'lowly retainer' or a 'licentious or irreverent person'. It comes from Old French *ribauld*, from *riber* 'indulge in licentious pleasures', from a Germanic base meaning 'prostitute'. It became an adjective in the early 16th century.

titillate

Titillate is from Latin *titillare* 'to tickle'. The parallel, but not directly related **tickle your fancy** is 18th century.

voluptuous

Voluptuous is from Latin *voluptas* 'pleasure'. The word became associated with fullness of form suggesting sensuous pleasure from the early 19th century.

Ships see also SEA

barge

A barge was originally a small seagoing vessel rather than a flat-bottomed boat for carrying freight. The word is French and probably comes ultimately from Greek *baris*, for a kind of Egyptian boat used on the Nile. The sense 'move forcefully or roughly' refers to the way a heavily laden, unwieldy barge might collide with the bank or other traffic.

berth

Originally berth meant 'sea room', or space to turn or manoeuvre, hence **give someone a wide berth**. This developed the sense 'a ship's allotted place at a wharf or dock', but could also mean the place where seamen stowed their chests, then later, the space where the sailors themselves slept.

catamaran

This boat with twin hulls in parallel is from Tamil *kattumaram*, which means literally 'tied wood'.

Ships

cox

The cox or **coxswain** steers a boat. The cox part is from the old word **cock** 'small boat', which is not related to the bird but to Latin *caudex* or *codex* 'block of wood'. The second half of the word, **swain**, now means 'a country youth or peasant' but was originally 'a young man attending a knight' and 'a male servant'. It is also the second half of **boatswain** (often abbreviated to **bo'sun**), a ship's officer in charge of equipment and the crew.

doldrums

To most people the doldrums are a period of stagnation or depression, but to sailors it is an equatorial region of the Atlantic Ocean with calms, sudden storms, and unpredictable winds. For sailing ships, being becalmed in the doldrums was a serious occupational hazard. The earliest form of the word, in the late 18th century, was singular *doldrum*, and it meant 'a dull, sluggish, or stupid person'. It may come from **dull**, which originally meant 'stupid'.

flotsam

This legal term for wreckage found floating on the sea or washed up on the beach comes ultimately from French, from the verb *floter* 'to float'. **Flotsam and jetsam** is useless or discarded objects. Jetsam came originally from **jettison**, a term for deliberately throwing goods overboard to lighten a ship in distress, which came ultimately from the Latin *jactare* 'to throw'. In the 16th century it was shortened giving first *jetson* and then the modern jetsam. There are strict legal distinctions made between what you can do with flotsam and with jetsam.

hulk

A hulk was originally a large cargo or transport ship. It is probably of Mediterranean origin and related to Greek *holkas* 'cargo ship'. In the late 17th century hulk came to apply to an old ship stripped of fittings and permanently moored, especially one used for storage or as a prison. Large, clumsy people began to be described as hulks in the late Middle Ages.

pilot

The aerial pilot first appears in the 1830s for the person flying a balloon. The ultimate root is Greek *pēdon* 'oar, rudder'. '**Dropping the pilot**', now 'abandoning a trustworthy adviser', was the caption of a famous cartoon by John Tenniel, published in *Punch* on 20 March 1890. It depicted Kaiser Wilhelm II's dismissal of Otto von Bismarck as German Chancellor. Bismark had guided the country for many years.

quay

One of those words that seems designed to trip up poor spellers, this was originally spelt as it is pronounced, key. It comes from Old French *kay*, of Celtic origin. The change of spelling occurred in the late 17th century, influenced by the modern French spelling *quai*. **Cay** or **key** for a sand bar is the same word.

titanic

In Greek mythology the **Titans** were gigantic gods, the children of Uranus (Heaven) and Gaia (Earth). They were the source of titanic, 'of exceptional strength, size, or power'. The main association of the word nowadays is with the *Titanic*, the British passenger liner that was the largest ship in the world at her launch and supposedly unsinkable. She struck an iceberg in the North Atlantic on her maiden voyage in April 1912 and sank with the loss of 1,490 lives. In 1976 Rogers Morton, President Ford's campaign manager said, after losing five of the last six primaries 'I'm not going to rearrange the furniture on the deck of the *Titanic*'. Although references similar to **rearranging the deckchairs on the *Titanic*** have been recorded earlier than this, this comment popularized the concept.

 Shopping see also FASHION

afford

Old English *forthian* 'to further' lies behind afford. The original sense was 'accomplish', later coming to mean 'be in a position to do'. The association with wealth is recorded from late Middle English.

bazaar

A Persian word for 'market' is the ultimate source of bazaar, which came into English from Italian *bazarro* that was in turn borrowed from Turkish.

catalogue

Catalogue came via Old French and late Latin from Greek *katalogos*, from *katalegein* 'pick out or enrol'.

cheap

Nowadays something that is cheap is inexpensive or of low value. In Old English, though, *ceap* (derived from Latin *caupo* 'small trader, innkeeper') meant 'bargaining or trade'. The obsolete phrase *good cheap* meant 'a good bargain', and from this the modern sense developed. In place names such as **Cheapside** and **Eastcheap**, cheap means 'market'. Something **cheap at the price** is well worth having regardless of the cost. A stronger alternative is **cheap at twice the price**, and you will also hear the confusing inversion **cheap at half the price**.

emporium

An emporium is unconnected with **emperor** (see under RANK), but comes via Latin from Greek *emporion*, from *emporos* 'merchant', based on the word for 'journey'.

Shopping

gazump

Since the 1970s we have associate gazumping with the buying and selling of houses to mean 'to raise the price of a house after accepting an offer for it', but in the early 20th century it simply meant 'to swindle', coming from Yiddish *gezumph* 'to overcharge'. In the late 1980s the opposite **gazunder** (a combination of gazump and under) was coined to describe lowering the amount of an offer that the seller has accepted, threatening to withdraw if the new offer is not accepted.

mall

The game **pall-mall** was popular in the 17th century. Players used a mallet to drive a boxwood ball through an iron ring suspended at the end of a long alley, also called a pall-mall. The game got its name, via French, from the Italian for 'ball' and 'mallet'. Pall Mall, a street in central London formerly a fashionable place to promenade, was originally a pall-mall for the game. From the 18th century other sheltered places for walking came to be called malls—the first reference to a mall for shopping dates from 1950 in the USA. **Malleable** got its name from the same source as mall, for it originally meant 'able to be hammered' and goes back, like **mallet** and **maul**, to Latin *malleus* 'hammer'.

price

The medieval word *pris*, which was from Old French, meant not only 'price' but also '**prize**' and '**praise**'. Over

time these three meanings split into three different
words. *Pris* became price, and the meaning 'praise'
started to be spelled *preise* and then praise. Originally
simply an alternative way of spelling price, **prize** too
became a separate word. The Latin original of the
French was *pretiem* 'price' which also lies behind
appreciate, and the related **appraise** and **apprize**, all
with the basic sense of 'set a price to'; **depreciate**;
and **precious**.

retail

Retail is from an Anglo-Norman French use of Old
French *retaille* 'a piece cut off', from *tailler* 'to cut', from
selling in small quantities, as opposed to the large
quantities of **wholesale**.

shop

The earliest shops were small stalls or booths, like the
ones you might see today in a market. Shop came into
English as a medieval shortening of early French
eschoppe 'lean-to booth'. The activity of **shopping** dates
from the 1760s. The slang sense 'to inform on' is earlier,
dating from 1583—the original implication was of
causing someone to be locked up. A slang dictionary of
1874 first recorded **all over the shop** as 'pugilistic
[boxing] slang'—to inflict severe punishment on an
opponent was 'to knock him all over the shop'.
Nowadays it means 'everywhere, in all directions', or
'wildly or erratically'.

Slang see also FOOLS, INSULTS

bling

This term, probably suggested either by the idea of light reflecting off a diamond or by the sound of jewellery clashing together, first appeared in a song by the US rapper B.G. ('Baby Gangsta') in 1999. From there it moved quickly into the mainstream to describe ostentatious jewellery and flashy clothes. Such has been the impact of the word that black slang has been dubbed **Blinglish**.

chav

Baseball cap, fake designer sportswear, cheap jewellery—that is the uniform of the chav, a loutish, obnoxious youth who barged his way into the British consciousness in 2004. Popularized by websites and the tabloid press, the term caught on quickly, and soon women and older people too were being described as chavs. New words appear all the time, but chav caused great excitement to word scholars when it came on the scene. It seems to have been popular around Chatham in Kent during the late 1990s, and some people think that it is an abbreviation of the town's name, while others suggest it comes from the initial letters of 'Council House And Violent'. The most plausible suggestion is that it is from the Romany word *chavi* or *chavo*, 'boy, youth'. The related dialect word *chavvy* 'boy, child' was used in the

19th century and is still occasionally in use. The north-east variant of chav, **charver**, has been around since at least the 1960s, and chav can mean 'mate, pal' in Scots dialect. Chav was probably knocking around as an underground expression for a long time before it was taken up as a new way of insulting people.

codswallop

Meaning 'nonsense or drivel', codswallop seems to be a fairly recent addition to English, with the earliest recorded use appearing in a 1959 script for the radio and TV comedy *Hancock's Half Hour*. It is sometimes said that the word comes from the name of Hiram Codd, who in the 1870s invented a bottle for fizzy drinks, although the evidence for this is sketchy. The **wallop** part may relate to the word's use as a 1930s slang term for beer or other alcoholic drink.

dingus

There are many words for something one cannot name or remember such as **thingamabob** or more simply **thingy**. Dingus is made on the same pattern, being a South African adoption from Afrikaans *ding* 'thing'.

doolally

This British term for 'temporarily insane' originated in India in the military sanatorium at Deolali, which also doubled as a transit camp where soldiers would await their boat home at the end of their duty tour. As boats

only left between November and March, some soldiers
were there for many months, during which boredom set
in and behaviour began to deteriorate. Men could go
doolally, the Englishman's pronunciation of 'Deolali'.

geek

This is originally US slang from the related English
dialect word **geck** 'fool', from a Germanic source. It is
related to Dutch *gek* 'mad, silly'. In *Webster's New
International Dictionary of the English Language* of 1954,
the definition read: 'Geek: a carnival "wild man" whose
act usually includes biting off the head of a live chicken
or snake'.

geezer

An informal word for a 'man', geezer represents a dialect
pronunciation of the earlier form **guiser** (related to
disguise) meaning 'mummer, someone who dresses up'.
In recent use it sometimes has a connotation of shady
dealing.

manky

This word meaning 'inferior, worthless, off-colour' is
probably from obsolete *mank* 'mutilated, defective', from
Old French *manque* 'lack', from Latin *mancus* 'maimed'.

nark

The original meaning of nark was 'an annoying or
troublesome person', a sense which survives in Australia

and New Zealand, and in the verb nark, 'to annoy'. The word is from Romany *nok* or *nak*, 'nose'. **Snout** and **snitch** (of unknown origin) are other words that mean both 'nose' and 'informer', and the word **nosy** itself implies an inappropriate interest in other people's business.

scarper

This is probably from Italian *scappare* 'to escape', influenced by the rhyming slang **Scapa Flow** 'go'.

 # Song see also ENTERTAINMENT, MUSIC

baritone

Italian has given us the names for different ranges of singing voice, including **alto** 'high', **soprano**, from *sopra* 'above', and baritone, which is ultimately from Greek *barus* 'heavy' and *tonos* 'tone'.

choir

The early spellings with a 'q' are from Old French *quer*, from Latin *chorus* (which entered English in the mid 16th century). The spelling change in the 17th century was due to association with the Latin. The spelling variant **quire** has never been altered in the English Prayer Book ('In Quires and Places where they sing, here followeth the Anthem').

Song

croon

Originally Scots and northern English, croon is from Middle Low German and Middle Dutch *krōnen* 'groan, lament'. The use of croon in standard English was probably popularized by poet Robert Burns (1759–96).

mellifluous

Latin *mel* 'honey' and the verb *fluere* 'to flow' are the base elements of mellifluous. **Mellow** may look as if it should be related, but it is not. It first meant 'ripe, soft, sweet and juicy' and may be a development of Old English *melu* 'meal'.

minstrel

Originally a minstrel would be employed to provide a variety of entertainment. Minstrels sang, played music, told stories, juggled—whatever their employer demanded. A minstrel could be closer to a jester or buffoon than the singer of heroic and lyrical poetry that later writers romantically portrayed. Sir Walter Scott's poem *The Lay of the Last Minstrel*, published in 1805, was instrumental in developing this view. It is a romance based on an old Border ballad, put into the mouth of an ancient minstrel, the last of his race. The Irish poet Thomas Moore, who died in 1852, also played his part: in the song 'The Minstrel Boy' he wrote of 'the warrior bard' with 'his wild harp slung behind him'. The original meaning of minstrel was simply 'a servant'. It goes back to Latin *minister* 'servant', the source also of **minister**.

opera

An adoption from Italian which goes back to Latin *opus*, meaning literally 'labour, work'. In mid-1970s America the saying the **opera isn't over till the fat lady sings** became a way of warning that something had not been finally settled, and that an outcome could still change. The reference is probably to the final solo of an operatic heroine, often played by a large woman.

serenade

A serenade conjures up an image of a young man singing or playing to his beloved under her window or balcony at night. The word's origins imply none of these things, requiring only that the performance be 'serene'. It goes back through French and Italian to Latin *serenus* 'calm, clear, fair'. The idea of serenading by night may derive from association with *sera*, the Italian word for 'night'. *Serenus* is also the source of **serene** and **serenity**.

shanty

The sea shanty, the song to which sailors hauled ropes, probably comes from French *chantez*!, an order to 'sing!'. It is recorded from the mid 19th century. A slightly earlier shanty appeared in North America for a small, crudely built shack and may come from Canadian French *chantier* 'lumberjack's cabin, logging camp', a specialized used of the word which usually means 'building site' in France. This shanty gave the world the **shanty town**, such as the **favela** in Rio de Janeiro and other Brazilian cities. This word, from the Portuguese equivalent of shanty is first recorded in English in 1961.

siren

In classical mythology the Sirens were bird-women whose beautiful singing lured sailors to their doom on submerged rocks. People hear a **siren song** or **siren call** when they are attracted to something that is both alluring and potentially harmful or dangerous. In 1819 the French engineer and physicist Charles Cagniard de la Tour used siren as the name for his invention of an acoustic instrument for producing musical tones. Later in the century steamships began to use a much larger instrument on the same lines as a foghorn or warning device, and in the Second World War sirens sent people scurrying to bomb-shelters for protection from air raids. **Siren suit**, dating from the 1930s, came from its use as a one-piece garment for women in air-raid shelters.

tenor

In medieval music the tenor part was given the melody, and therefore 'held' it, reflecting its root, Latin *tenere* 'to hold'. The tenor of something, as in 'the general tenor of the debate', also goes back to Latin *tenere*, via *tenor* 'course, substance, meaning of a law'.

Sport see also ENTERTAINMENT, GAMES

athlete

In Greek *athlon* meant 'prize', and the word *athlētēs*, from which we get athlete, literally meant 'someone who competes for a prize'. It originally referred to one of the competitors in the physical exercises—such as running, leaping, boxing, and wrestling—that formed part of the public games in ancient Greece and Rome.

champion

Title-deciding boxing matches are often contested between the challenger and the defending champion, the holder of the title. But, historically, both boxers would have been described as champions, as the word originally meant 'a fighting man'. It came from medieval Latin *campio* 'fighter or gladiator', from Latin *campus* 'a field, place of combat'.

cricket

Cricket is first recorded in an document of 1598 in which a man of 59 swears that when he was a schoolboy he used to play cricket on a particular bit of land in Guildford, Surrey. This takes the game back to the reign of Henry VIII. Cricket would have been very different then: the bats were more like hockey sticks, the wicket two stumps with one long bail and the ball was trundled along the ground rather than bowled. The word appears to be closely related to French *criquet* 'a stick', although whether this originally referred to the wicket or the bat is not entirely clear. The idea of cricket being the epitome of honourable behaviour, as in '**It's just not cricket**!', dates from the mid 19th century. In 1867 *The Cricketer's Companion* told its readers: 'Do not ask the umpire unless you think the batsman is out; it is not cricket to keep asking the umpire questions.' The other cricket, the grasshopper-like insect, is a completely different word. It comes from Old French *criquet* 'a cricket', based on *criquer* 'to crackle, click, or creak', probably suggesting the chirping sound the insect makes.

golf

The first recorded mention of golf is in 1457, in a Scottish edict that banned certain games (including football) because King James II thought they distracted people from archery practice. It seems to have been a Scottish game originally, although the word may be related to Dutch *kolf* 'a club or bat'. It is now popular around the world, but according to the American writer Mark Twain, golf is 'A good walk spoiled'.

gymnasium

Ancient Greek men exercised naked. This fact is preserved in the origin of the word gymnasium, which came into English from Latin but is ultimately from Greek *gumnazein* 'to exercise or train naked', *gumnos*

being the Greek word for 'naked'. The shortened form
gym first appeared in the late 19th century.

marathon

In 490 BC the Athenians won a victory over an invading
Persian army at Marathon on the coast of Attica in
eastern Greece. The Greek historian Herodotus
described how the herald Pheidippides ran the 150 miles
from Athens to Sparta to get help before the battle. In a
later tradition a messenger ran from Marathon to
Athens, a distance of 22 miles, with news of the victory,
but fell dead on arrival. The first modern Olympic
games in 1896 instituted the marathon as a long-distance
race—fortunately for competitors, based on the shorter
version of the story.

soccer

This is a shortening of **Association football**, the official
name given in the late 19th century to the game, to
distinguish it from rugby football. The word was formed
by the same process that gave us **rugger** for **rugby**.

sport

Sport comes from a shortening of **disport**, formed, via
French, from Latin *dis* 'away' and *portare* 'carry' used
in much the same way as the expression 'to take
someone out of themselves'. Sport meant any kind of
entertainment, and only started to be used in the modern
sense of activities with set rules in the late 18th century.

Sport

The **sport of kings** once referred to war-making but was later applied to hunting and horse-racing.

tennis

Around 1400 tennis was the name for what is now **real tennis**, played on an enclosed court, but since the 1870s it has meant the outdoor game of **lawn tennis**. It probably comes from Old French *tenez* meaning 'take!'—presumably the server's call to an opponent. **Anyone for tennis**? is supposedly a typical line spoken by a young man in the drawing-room comedies popular in the 1920s or 1930s, although no actual example has been traced—the closest is 'Anybody on for a game of tennis?', from *Misalliance* (1914) by George Bernard Shaw.

toboggan

The origin of this word is Canadian French *tabaganne*, from the Micmac *topaĝan* 'sled'.

Theatre see also ENTERTAINMENT, SONG

dialogue

This comes via Old French and Latin from Greek *dialogos*, from *dialegesthai* 'converse with, speak alternately': the formative elements are *dia-* 'through, across' and *legein* 'speak'. The tendency in English is to confine the sense to a conversation between two people, perhaps by associating the prefix *dia-* with *di-*. *Dia-* is also found in **diameter** 'the measure across'; **diaphanous** 'shows through'; **diaphragm** a barrier that is literally a 'fence through', and **diaspora** a 'scattering across'.

drama

This came via late Latin from Greek *drama*, from *dran* 'do, act' source also of **drastic**. The Latin **dramatis personae** has been used since the mid 18th century for a list of the characters in a play.

farce

In 1796 the cookery writer Hannah Glasse wrote, 'Make a farce with the livers minced small.' Farce was an adoption of a French word meaning 'stuffing', its first sense in English. It took on its modern English meaning when applied to comic interludes which were 'stuffed' into the texts of religious plays. From this the term was used for a complete comic play, these days one that involves a lot of slapstick.

Theatre

interlude

Performances of medieval miracle plays could last all day, so to provide variety and relieve tension, performers would introduce short and often humorous dramatic pieces between the acts, which were the original interludes. The word derives from Latin *inter* 'between, among' and *ludus* 'a play'. By the 17th century people were using interlude for the interval of time between the acts of a play, and by the 18th for any intervening time, space, or event.

interval

The word interval is from Old French *entrevalle*, based on Latin *intervallum* 'space between ramparts, interval', from *inter-* 'between' and *vallum* 'rampart'.

pantomime

This word comes from Greek *pantomimos* 'imitator of all'. In Latin *pantomimus* was used for an actor using mime. This later developed into a comic dramatization with the stock characters of Clown, Pantaloon (whose costume gave us the type of trousers called **pantaloons**), Harlequin, and Columbine. The familiar **panto** based on fairy tales such as Mother Goose or Cinderella and involving music, topical jokes, and slapstick comedy developed in the 19th century, with a new set of conventional characters including the dame, the principal boy, and the pantomime horse. **Mime** and **mimic** come from the same root.

scene

The scenes in **behind the scenes**, 'in private', are the pieces of scenery on a theatre stage. This reflects the origin of scene, which is ultimately from Greek *skēnē* 'tent, stage', source also of **scenario**, **scenery**, and **scenic**. The theatrical associations of scene gave us the meaning 'a public display of emotion or anger'.

theatre

The earliest theatres were the open-air theatres of the classical world, first mentioned in English in the writings of Geoffrey Chaucer. People go to the theatre to watch a play, and the word itself goes back to the Greek *theasthai* 'to look at'. A theatre for surgical operations, or **operating theatre**, gets its name, recorded from the 1660s, because early rooms of this type were arranged like theatres, with banks of seats for observers.

thespian

The dramatic poet Thespis, who lived in the 6th century BC and is traditionally regarded as the founder of Greek tragedy, gave us this word for an actor.

vaudeville

Olivier Basselin was a 15th-century Frenchman from Vau de Vire, Normandy, who composed songs reputedly given the name *chansons du Vau de Vire*, or 'songs of the valley of Vire'. This was adapted to French *ville* 'town' and became *vau de ville* and later vaudeville, applied to a

light popular song sung on the stage, the first meaning
of vaudeville in English in the mid 18th century.

 # Time

century

Latin *centuria* (from *centum* 'hundred') referred to a
group of 100, particularly a company of 100 men in the
Roman army. Early English usage carried the meaning 'a
hundred', as in a batsman's century of a hundred runs in
cricket. The '100 years' sense is 17th century, initially as a
shortened form of 'century of years'.

chronic

Words beginning *chron-* concern time, coming from
Greek *khronos* 'time'. A chronic illness persists for a long
time. In informal British English it also means 'of very
poor quality', as in 'the film was chronic', a sense
developing from the idea of unending tedium.

clock

Clock comes from medieval Latin *clocca* 'bell'. The
English word originally meant 'bell', then 'the striking
mechanism of a clock'. Gradually clock came to mean
the instrument itself. Clock 'to hit in the face' is
originally 1920s Australian slang from the sense 'a
person's face'. The meaning 'to notice or watch',

from the 1930s, refers to a person checking the time on a clock.

minute

English words spelled minute have two different pronunciations and entered English by different routes, but share an origin in Latin *minutus* 'small', the source also of **mince** and **menu**. Closest to the original Latin sense is minute 'small'. The minute referring to 60 seconds comes through medieval Latin *pars minuta prima* 'first minute part' (see **second** below). The **minutes** of a meeting come from when a scribe would make a draft record in 'small writing' (Latin *scriptura minuta*) before the fair copy.

noon

Noon originally meant 'the ninth hour from sunrise', approximately 3pm, from Latin *nona hora* 'ninth hour'. The time change appears to be medieval: noon meaning 'midday' is found from around 1225, and was the usual sense by the 14th century. The Church service of **nones** suggests why it shifted. Nones—from the same root— are prayers generally said at 3pm, but Italian Benedictine monks held the service closer to midday.

second

This comes from Latin *secundus* 'following, second', from *sequi* 'to follow'. The time sense is from medieval Latin *secunda (minuta)* 'second (minute)', referring to the

323

Time

'second' division of an hour by 60 (see **minute** above).
Second a motion comes from French *en second* 'in the
second rank (of officers)'. This was originally military,
involving the removal of an officer temporarily from his
regiment to an extra-regimental appointment. **Sect**,
originally 'a following' is also from *sequi*, as are
persecute 'to follow with hostility', and **sequel**.

time

To the Anglo-Saxons time and **tide** (see under SEA)
meant the same thing. Both **time immemorial** and **time
out of mind** were originally legal formulas. They meant
'a time beyond legal memory', fixed by statute in 1276 as
1 July 1189, the beginning of Richard I's reign. If you
could prove possession of land or rights from that date
there was no need to establish when or how it was
originally acquired. Everyone but the lawyers soon
forgot the specific meaning and both phrases developed
the general sense of 'long ago'. **Time is money** has a
modern ring to it, but seems to have been coined in 1748
by Benjamin Franklin, in 'Advice to Young Tradesmen'.
However, 'the most costly outlay is time' is attributed to
the ancient Athenian Antiphon.

Tuesday

The ancient Germanic god Tiw is the source of Tuesday.
When Germanic peoples came into contact with the

Romans they realized their god Tiw was similar to Mars, Roman god of war, whose day was the third of the week (hence forms such as French *mardi*), and started to call that day 'Tiw's day'. Other days of the week were formed similarly: **Wednesday** was Woden's day, **Thursday** Thor's day, and **Friday** Freya's day; Woden or Odin was ther supreme god, Thor the thunder god, and Freya or Frigga the goddess of love and fertility.

week

An Old English word that is probably from a root meaning 'sequence, series'. The seven-day week of the Hebrew and Christian calendar corresponds to the biblical creation story, where God created the universe in six days then rested on the seventh. The Romans, who adopted it in AD 321, brought this week to Britain. '**A week is a long time in politics**' was coined by British prime minister Harold Wilson during the 1964 sterling crisis.

winter

Winter is probably related to **wet**, with the basic idea 'the wet season'. *Richard III*: 'Now is the winter of our discontent / Made glorious summer by this sun of York' gave us the **winter of discontent** of 1978–9 in Britain, when widespread strikes forced the Labour government out of power.

Tools

anvil

An anvil is something to strike on. In Old English the spelling was *anfilte*, from the Germanic base of *on* and a verb meaning 'beat'.

apparatus

This is a Latin word, from *apparare* 'make ready for', from *parare* 'make ready'. Other words going back to *parare* include **disparate**, 'prepared apart'; **pare**; **prepare** 'prepare in advance'; and **separate** from *se-* 'apart' and *parare*.

hammer

Old English *hamor* has a Germanic origin, related to German *Hammer*, and Old Norse *hamarr* 'rock, crag'. The original sense was probably 'stone tool or weapon'. **Hammer and tongs**, 'with energy and speed', comes from the blacksmith showering blows on the iron taken by tongs from the fire.

nail

When the word nail emerged in Old English it already had its main modern meanings of 'small metal spike' and 'fingernail'. **To nail a lie**, to expose a falsehood, known from the early 19th century, probably refers to shopkeepers nailing forged coins to shop counters to put them out of circulation. Money paid **on the nail** is paid without delay. It may come from the *Satires* of the Roman poet Horace, who used *ad ungulum*, 'on the nail', to mean 'to perfection, to the utmost'. This referred either to Roman sculptors making the finishing touches to their work with a fingernail, or to carpenters using a fingernail to test the accuracy of a joint.

pin

Pin was adopted from Latin by the Anglo-Saxons before they invaded Britain. Its source is Latin *pinna* 'feather', which also meant 'point, tip, edge', and then developed the sense 'peg', pin's earliest sense in English and still found in mechanics. The sense 'thin metal fastener' had developed by 1250. A **pinafore** was originally an apron with a bib pinned afore or on the front of a dress. The pin in **pin money** was the decorative kind used to fasten hair or clothing. The phrase, dating from the late 17th century, was originally an allowance made to a woman by her husband for personal expenses such as clothing.

scissors

Scissors is from Old French *cisoires*, from late Latin *cisoria*, 'cutting instruments'. *Cis-* here is a variant of *caes-*, from *caedere* 'to cut', a variant also found in **chisel**. The spelling with *sc-* occurred in the 16th century by association with Latin *sciss-* from *scinder* also 'to cut'.

Tools

screw

Pigs have curly tails like corkscrews, and the ultimate source of screw is Latin *scrofa* 'a sow', source also of **scrofula**, a disease people thought sows were susceptible to. Scrofula was also called the King's Evil, because kings were traditionally thought to be able to cure it. *Scrofa* changed its meaning to 'screw' in Latin, and then altered its form as it passed through French to English. The slang sense 'to have sex', found from the 18th century, is probably the source of **screw up** meaning 'to mess up', which appeared in the Second World War as a US euphemism for f— up.

spanner

The word spanner is based on German *spannen* 'draw tight'.

trowel

The word trowel is from Old French *truele*, an alteration of Latin *trulla* 'scoop'.

tweezers

In the 17th century a **tweeze** was a case of surgical instruments. It appears to be a shortening of *etweese*, plural of *etui*, a term for a small ornamental case for holding needles, cosmetics, and other articles, that came from French. In the 17th century tweeze was extended to **tweezer**, while the plural tweezes became tweezers.

In the 1930s tweeze was re-formed from tweezers to mean 'to pluck with tweezers'.

 # Toys see also CHILDHOOD

ball

The spherical ball dates from the early Middle Ages, and comes from an old Scandinavian word that was the ultimate root of Italian *ballotta*, from which English took **ballot** and is also via French or Italian of **balloon**. The ball where people dance came from French, and goes back to Latin *ballare* 'to dance', also the source of **ballad** and **ballet**. In America a **ball game** is a baseball match played in a **ballpark**. These give a **whole new ball game**, 'a completely new set of circumstances', **in the right ballpark**, 'a particular area or range', and a **ballpark** (approximate) **figure**. Testicles have been **balls** since the Middle Ages, but the sense 'nonsense' is Victorian. The meaning 'courage, determination' is more recent still, dating only from the 1950s. People often claim that the phrase **cold enough to freeze the balls off a brass monkey** comes from a naval custom of storing cannonballs on a brass rack or 'monkey'. When the weather was cold the rack could contract and eject the cannonballs. However, cannonballs were stored on a wooden rack, and only extreme cold would cause sufficient contraction for this to happen. Moreover, the earliest recorded versions of the phrase (from the 19th century) feature noses and tails rather than balls, suggesting that the reference is to a brass statue of a monkey, and that the 'balls' are testicles.

crayon

Crayon was adopted from French *craie* 'chalk', from Latin *creta*, source also of **cretaceous**, mainly used to describe the geological period when chalk was laid down.

doll

Doll started as a pet form of the name Dorothy, and a doll was originally a man's lover. The toy sense is 17th century—previously people used **poppet** or **puppet**. The sense 'attractive girl' is US slang from the 1840s.

kite

In Old English this word was used for the bird of prey, remarkable for its ability to hang effortlessly in the air. The bird's name was transferred to the toy that floats in the air in the same way.

marble

Marble goes back to Greek *marmaros* 'shining stone', limestone used for building and sculpture. The small balls of the children's game have been called marbles since the late 17th century, though they are now mostly made of glass. In the game players take turns at shooting their marble inside a ring, trying to knock others' marbles out of it to win them. Some players **lose their marbles**—the idea behind marbles for someone's mental faculties.

teddy

Theodore 'Teddy' Roosevelt, US president 1901–9, was a keen bear-hunter, a fact celebrated in a comic poem published in the *New York Times* of 7 January 1906, about two bears called 'Teddy B' and 'Teddy G'. These names were then given to two bears presented to the Bronx Zoo later that year, and toy manufacturers saw an opening. Toy 'teddy bears' or 'Roosevelt bears' were imported from Germany, and became an instant success in America. **Teddy boys** or **Teds** owe their name to Teddy as a pet form of Edward. In the mid 1950s some youths began to favour a style based on the fashions which had been current in the early 20th century in Britain, during the reign of Edward VII.

top

The child's toy was being played with by the eleventh century although we do not know where the word came from. The other top came from Old Norse into Middle English. **Go over the top** originated in the First World War, describing troops in the trenches charging over the parapets to attack the enemy. It developed the meaning 'to do something to an excessive degree', possibly in

Toys

reference to the number of soldiers who died. It was soon shortened to **over the top**, and since the early 1980s reduced even further to **OTT**, particularly referring to acting.

toy

A toy was originally a funny story or remark, and later a prank or frivolous entertainment. The sense 'an object for a child to play with' is 16th century. The origin of toy is medieval but otherwise unknown.

Wendy house

The name for a toy house large enough to play in comes from J. M. Barrie's play *Peter Pan* (1904). In the play, which Barrie novelized in 1911, Peter and the Lost Boys build a small structure for Wendy to live in in Neverland, where she keeps house for them.

yo-yo

Although toys resembling yo-yos were known in ancient China and Greece, the name probably comes from the Philippines, where the yo-yo had been popular for hundreds of years. It entered English in 1915, and became a verb meaning 'to move up and down, fluctuate' in the 1960s.

Travel

aeroplane

An aeroplane is literally an 'air wanderer'. Coined in the late 19th century, the word is from French *aéro-* 'air' and Greek *-planos* 'wandering', so the short form **plane** has the less-than-reassuring meaning of 'wanderer'.

caravan

Caravan first meant a group of people travelling across a desert in Asia or North Africa. It comes via French *caravane*, from Persian *kārwān*. The sense 'covered horse-drawn wagon' dates from the early 19th century when it also described a third-class 'covered carriage' on a railway. A **caravanserai** is from Persian *kārwānsarāy*, literally a 'caravan palace': it describes an inn with a central courtyard for travellers. **Van** is a shortening of caravan. The workman's white van is such a familiar sight that **white van man** entered the language to mean an aggressive van driver, or an ordinary working man with forthright views.

juggernaut

If you are stuck behind an articulated lorry or juggernaut on the motorway, a resort on the Bay of Bengal is probably not what springs to mind. But Juggernaut (Sanskrit *Jagannātha*, 'Lord of the World') is the local name given the Hindu god Krishna worshipped in Puri, eastern India. Each year his huge image is dragged through the streets in a heavy chariot. The sense 'large, heavy vehicle' came into English, along with many other Hindi words, in the 19th century.

limousine

In French a *limousine* was a cloak with a cape, of a type worn in the Limousin region of central France. People saw a resemblance between this and early forms of motor car where the driver's seat was outside in a separate compartment covered with a canopy. The name passed to large, luxurious cars driven by a chauffeur separated from the passengers by a partition. The word was abbreviated to **limo** in the 1960s, while in the 1980s the **stretch limo** appeared.

moped

This is made up of syllables from the Swedish phrase *(trampcykel med) mo(tor och) ped(aler)* 'pedal cycle with motor and pedals'.

tram

This is from the Dutch word for a shaft or beam, and was first used for the shafts of a cart or barrow; then for barrow-like devices used in coal mines. In the early 19th century trams were the parallel wheel tracks in a mine, on which the public tramway was modelled; hence the word's use for the passenger vehicle.

travel

Travel comes from Middle English **travail** 'painful or laborious effort'. The two forms were interchangeable, and originated in an instrument of torture, called *trepalium* 'three stakes' in Latin. Robert Louis Stevenson, a keen traveller, first expressed the view that **it is better to travel hopefully than to arrive**, in 1881. **Travel broadens the mind** appeared first in 1900.

trek

Boers, Dutch settlers in South Africa, got their name from the Dutch for 'countryman, farmer'. Between 1835 and 1837 large numbers of Boers, discontented with British rule in the Cape area of South Africa, migrated north and founded the Transvaal Republic and the Orange Free State. This was the **Great Trek**, which largely introduced the Dutch word trek to the English-speaking world. It came from *trekken* 'to pull, travel', from which **track** may also derive. During the 20th century trek migrated into international English for any long, arduous journey. The US science-fiction television programme *Star Trek* was first shown in 1966 and has given us **Trekkie** for a *Star Trek* fan. The 'pull' sense of *trekken* lies behind the thing you pull on a gun, the **trigger**.

voyage

Voyage was first used for a journey by sea or by land. It is from Old French *voiage*, from Latin *viaticum* initially meaning 'provisions for a journey' and, in late Latin, 'journey'.

 Trouble see also ADVENTURE

accident

An accident was originally 'an event, something that happens', not necessarily a mishap. It came into English via Old French, from Latin *cadere*, meaning 'to fall', source of words such as **cadaver** 'someone fallen', **decay** 'fall away', **incident** 'fall upon' so 'happen', and **occasion**. The idea of an event 'falling' remains in the English word **befall**. Later accident evolved into 'something that happens by chance', as in a **happy accident**. By the 17th century the modern meaning was established.

aspersion

To engage in **casting aspersions** is almost literally mud-slinging. Aspersion originally meant 'sprinkling water or other liquid on someone', especially in baptism, and came from Latin *spargere* 'to sprinkle' (the root of **disperse** 'scatter widely', and **intersperse** 'sprinkle between'). Sprinkling a person with water developed into the idea of spattering them with something less pleasant, such as mud or dung. This then led to soiling a person's reputation by making false and damaging insinuations.

bother

The origins of bother are in Ireland. It is probably related to Irish *bodhaire* 'deafness' and *bodhraim* 'to deafen, annoy', and it is first recorded meaning 'noise, chatter'. In the 18th century emphasis moves to worry, annoyance, and trouble. The word quickly spread out of its Anglo-Irish confines, and in the 19th century appears as a common mild oath. The late 1960s gave us **bovver**, 'deliberate troublemaking', from the cockney pronunciation of the word. The **bovver boy** (a hooligan or skinhead) wore **bovver boots**, heavy boots with toe caps and laces.

doubt

In English doubt goes back to Latin *dubitare* 'to hesitate, waver', from *dubium* 'doubt' (from which **dubious** also derives). The immediate sources were French forms in which the 'b' had been lost, and people never pronounced the 'b'—it was a learned spelling to show the writer knew the Latin origin. The first **doubting Thomas** was the apostle Thomas, who refused to believe that Christ was risen again until he could see and touch the wounds inflicted during the Crucifixion.

enemy

An enemy is obviously not your friend, which is, in fact, the derivation of the word. It came from Old French *enemi*, from Latin *inimicus*, based on *in-* meaning 'not' and *amicus* 'friend'. *Inimicus* is the source of **inimical** or 'hostile', and *amicus* of **amicable** or 'friendly'.

Trouble

insult

An insult was originally an attack or assault, especially a military one. Sir Walter Scott (1771–1832) in his poem *Marmion* wrote: 'Many a rude tower and rampart there / Repelled the insult of the air.' Insult goes back to Latin *insultare* 'to jump or leap upon'. **To add insult to injury** comes from the 1748 play *The Foundling* by Edmund Moore.

trouble

Our word trouble comes, via Old French *truble*, from Latin *turbidus* 'disturbed, turbid', source of **turbid**, and related to **disturb**, **perturb**, and **turbulent**. '**Man is born unto trouble, as the sparks fly upward**' is from the biblical book of Job, a virtuous man that God tested by sending him many troubles. Most people think of **the Troubles** in Northern Ireland as beginning in the early 1970s, but the same term was applied to the unrest around the partition of Ireland in 1921, and in an 1880 glossary of Irish words the Troubles are defined as 'the Irish rebellion of 1641'.

upbraid

Late Old English *upbrēdan* meant 'allege (something) as a basis for censure', based on *braid* in the obsolete sense 'brandish' thus giving a notion of holding something up for disapproval. The current sense 'find fault with' is Middle English.

victim

Latin *victima*, the source of this word, originally meant an animal killed as a religious sacrifice. Use for a person who is harmed by another is mid 17th century.

vulnerable

This comes from late Latin *vulnerabilis*, from *vulnus* 'wound'. The word appeared later than its opposite **invulnerable** which is late 16th century.

Universe see also SCIENCE

comet

We get comet from Greek *komētēs* 'long-haired'. The ancient Greeks gazed into the night sky and observed a comet's long tail. To their eyes it resembled streaming hair, hence their name for 'the long-haired star'.

cosmos

That both cosmos and **cosmetic** go back to Greek *kosmos* gives an interesting insight into ancient Greeks' thought. *Kosmos* had a central meaning 'order', but also meant 'world' and the putting of oneself in order that involved 'adornment'.

crater

The Greeks and Romans drank their wine mixed with water, and thought it uncivilized to drink it neat. They mixed their wine in a large wide-mouthed bowl called in Greek *kratēr* and in Latin *crater*. English adopted this word for the bowl-shaped hollow that forms the mouth of a volcano.

eclipse

Eclipse comes via Old French and Latin from Greek *ekleipsis* formed from *ekleipein* 'fail to appear, forsake its accustomed place'.

galaxy

Looking into the sky on a dark moonless night, you can see a band of pale light crossing the sky—vast numbers of stars that appear to be packed together. This is the **Milky Way**, a direct translation of what the Romans called *via lactea*. The Greeks were also reminded of milk and named it *galaxias kuklos* the 'milky vault', from *gala* 'milk', the origin of galaxy. In medieval English it referred specifically to the Milky Way, though later it applied to any system of millions of stars.

planet

Early Greek astronomers observed certain heavenly bodies moving around the night sky while the stars stayed in a fixed position. This is why they are called planets, from Greek *planētēs* 'wanderer'. The Sun and the Moon were once thought of as planets too. **Plankton**, the term for small and microscopic organisms floating in the sea, comes via German from the related Greek word *planktos*, 'wandering or drifting'.

satellite

In 1611 the German astronomer Johannes Kepler, writing in Latin, gave the name *satellites* to the moons of Jupiter, which Galileo had recently discovered. In Latin *satelles*, of which satellites is the plural, meant 'attendant or guard', a use occasionally found in 16th-century English, usually with overtones of subservience. In 1936 satellite was first applied to a man-made object (at that point just a theoretical one) put into orbit around the earth. The first artificial satellite was the Russian Sputnik 1, in 1957, and in 1962 the Telstar satellite relayed the first satellite television signal. **Sputnik** means 'fellow traveller' in Russian, while **Telstar** got its name because it was built by Bell Telephone Laboratories and used for telecommunications.

star

The Latin word *stella* 'star', which gave us star, **constellation**, and **stellar**, was related to the two Greek equivalents, *astēr* and *astron*, the source of words such as **asterisk** and **astrology**. Astrology gives us **thank your lucky stars**. Star was used for famous entertainers from the early 19th century. **Superstar** was coined around 1925, followed by **megastar** in 1976.

vacuum

This modern Latin word is from Latin *vacuus* 'empty', as was **vacuous** meaning, in early examples, 'empty of matter'. 'Unintelligent' became one of the word's meanings in the mid 19th century.

zenith

Zenith was originally an astronomical term from Arabic, from *samt ar-ra's*, 'path over the head'. In astronomy the zenith is the point in the sky immediately above the

observer, and also the highest point reached by a
particular celestial object, when it is **at its zenith**. Its
opposite, the **nadir**, is the point in the sky immediately
below the observer, from Arabic *nazīr*, meaning
'opposite [to the zenith]'. Its general sense, 'the lowest
or most unsuccessful point', developed in the early
17th century.

Wealth

bonanza

Bonanza first referred in the US to success when mining. It is a Spanish word meaning 'fair weather, prosperity', from Latin *bonus* 'good'.

bonus

This was probably originally Stock Exchange slang, coming from Latin *bonus* 'good'. Recently, the word **malus** has been recorded for a fine or penalty, based on Latin *malus* 'bad' on the pattern of bonus. The French form of *bonus, bon* may lie behind the mainly Scottish **bonny** 'good, fair'. **Bounty** goes back to the same source.

budget

When the British Chancellor of the Exchequer holds up the red case containing details of his budget speech, he may not know he is making a gesture towards the origin of the word. A budget was originally a pouch or wallet. It came from French in the Middle Ages, and goes back to Latin *bulga* 'leather sack, bag', from which English also gets **bulge**.

capital

Capital first meant 'concerning the head or top of something'. From this evolved such modern meanings as

'the large form of a letter' and 'chief city'. It goes back to
Latin *caput* 'head'. Financial capital was originally the
capital stock of a company or trader, their main or
original funds. The use as an adjective meaning 'excellent',
now old-fashioned, is 18th century. The capital of a column
comes via French from Latin *capitellum* 'a little head'. Latin
caput 'head', is source also of **cap**, **chief** and **captain**, both
the 'head' of a group of people, and **decapitate**.

exchequer

Around 1300 an exchequer was 'a chessboard'. It came
into English from Old French *eschequier*, based on
medieval Latin *scaccus* 'check'—the origin of our word
check. Its current sense came from the department of
state that dealt with the revenues of the Norman kings
of England which kept accounts by placing counters on
a chequered tablecloth, which was called the Exchequer.

finance

Finance is from Old French, from *finer* 'make an end;
settle a debt', from *fin* 'end'. The original sense was
'payment of a debt, compensation, or ransom', which
later developed into 'taxation, revenue'. Current senses
date from the 18th century. **Fine** in the sense money you
pay, comes from the same source and was originally a
sum paid to settle a lawsuit, while the other sense of
fine, 'high quality' leading to 'thin', goes back to the
earlier sense 'thoroughly finished', and lies behind

refine, **define**, **finery**, and **finesse**. **Finish** goes back to the same root.

money

In ancient Rome money was coined in a temple to the goddess Juno, where she was identified with a pre-Roman goddess called Moneta and known as Juno Moneta. Latin *moneta* has come down to English as money, and also as **mint**. **Money is the root of all evil** comes from the biblical Book of Timothy, where it is stated more carefully 'the love of money is the root of all evil'. People down the ages have agreed that **money can't buy happiness**, though this exact form appeared only in the 19th century. In Britain money gained with little effort is **money for jam**. Dating back to the early 20th century, this probably originated in military slang. In 1919 *The Athenaeum* stated it came from the 'great use of jam in the Army'.

revenue

The word revenue is from Old French *revenu(e)* meaning 'returned', from Latin *revenire* 'return', from *re-* 'back' and *venire* 'come'. A rare, obsolete use was 'return to a place'; it was more commonly 'yield from lands and property', what would today be called a return on your investment. **Venue** is an obvious relative, first used as a term for an 'attack' or 'thrust' in fencing and as a legal term meaning 'the county or district within which a criminal or civil case must be heard'. The sense 'a place for entertainment' only dates from the 1960s. **Avenue** which first meant 'way of approaching a problem' is another relative. It then developed a mainly military sense of a way to access a place, and from that a formal approach to a country house. Only in the middle of the 19th century did it become a term for a wide street.

treasure

This came through Old French from Greek *thēsauros* 'treasure, store, storehouse', also the source of **thesaurus**. A **treasure trove**, now a collection of valuable or pleasing things found unexpectedly, originally referred to valuables of unknown ownership found hidden, which were the property of the Crown. The term came from Anglo-Norman French *tresor trové* meaning literally 'found treasure'.

tycoon

A tycoon is now a powerful businessman, but was originally a Japanese ruler. It comes from Japanese *taikun* 'great lord'. Foreigners applied the title to the shogun, or military commander of Japan, in power between 1857 and 1868, and in the same period Americans nicknamed President Abraham Lincoln 'the Tycoon'. The word then extended to any important or dominant person, from the 1920s especially to a business magnate.

Weather see also GEOGRAPHY

breeze

A breeze was originally a north or north-east wind, especially a trade wind on the Atlantic seaboard of the West Indies and the Caribbean coast of South America. This is the meaning of the Spanish and Portuguese word *briza* from which breeze probably derived.

calm

Calm can be traced back to the idea of the heat of the midday sun in a hot climate, when people are indoors and everything is quiet and still. It came into English via Italian, Spanish, or Portuguese from Greek *kauma* 'heat of the day', perhaps also influenced by Latin *calere* 'to be warm'.

cloud

Old English cloud was first used for a mass of rock or earth, and is probably related to **clot**. Only around the end of the 13th century did the meaning 'visible mass of condensed watery vapour' develop, presumably because people could see a resemblance in shape between a cloud and rocks. A possible source of the expression **cloud nine** is the classification of clouds in a meteorological guide published in 1896 called the *International Cloud Atlas*. According to this there are ten

basic types of cloud, fluffy **cumulonimbus** (from Latin
cumulus 'a heap') being number nine. 'Cloud nine' is said
to have been popularized by the Johnny Dollar radio
show in the USA during the 1950s about a fictional
insurance investigator who got into a lot of scrapes.
Every time he was knocked unconscious he was taken to
'cloud nine', where he recovered. **Cloud cuckoo land**
translates Greek *Nephelokokkugia* (from *nephelē* 'cloud'
and *kokkux* 'cuckoo'), the name the ancient Greek
dramatist Aristophanes gave to the city built by the birds
in his comedy *The Birds*.

hurricane

When Christopher Columbus arrived in the Caribbean
in 1492 he encountered the Arawak. These peaceful
people did not long survive the coming of the Spanish,
and are thought to have died out from the diseases
carried by the Europeans and attacks by their aggressive
neighbours, the Carib. Hurricane came into English via
Spanish *huracán* from the name of the Arawak god of
the storm, *Hurakan*.

icicle

An icicle was originally an *ickle*. In the early Middle
Ages people put ice and *ickle* together to form a
compound; writers spelled the term as two words into
the 17th century, after which icicle emerged as the
standard term.

Weather

meteor

In early use the term was used for any atmospheric phenomenon: it comes via modern Latin from Greek *meteōron* 'of the atmosphere', from *meteōros* 'lofty'. The same source gave us **meteorology**.

ozone

Ozone is a strong-smelling, poisonous form of oxygen, whose name goes back to Greek *ozein* 'to smell', and was originally believed to have had a tonic effect and to have been present in fresh air, especially at the seaside. Today the usual association is with the **ozone layer**, a layer in the Earth's stratosphere that absorbs most of the harmful ultraviolet radiation from the sun, which is under threat from atmospheric pollutants.

tornado

A tornado was originally a violent thunderstorm over the tropical Atlantic Ocean. The word may be an alteration of Spanish *tronada* 'thunderstorm', influenced by *tornar* 'to turn', a reference to the shape of a 'twister'.

tsunami

The tsunami of Boxing Day 2004 made this Japanese word for a huge sea wave caused by an underwater earthquake known to everyone, replacing the misleading term tidal wave. It is formed from *tsu* 'harbour' and *nami* 'wave'.

typhoon

The fierce tropical storm brings together two sources,
Arabic *tūfān*, which may be from Greek *tuphōn* 'whirlwind',
and Chinese dialect *tai fung* 'big wind'. The Portuguese
picked up the first in the Indian oceans, while sailors in the
China seas would have encountered the Chinese
expression. A wide variety of spellings appeared before the
word finally settled down into typhoon in the 19th century.

 # Writing see also BOOKS

ampersand

A corruption of 'and per se and', an old phrase that used
to be chanted by schoolchildren as a way of learning the
character &. *Per se* is Latin for 'by itself', so the phrase
can be translated '& by itself is and'. It is based on a
Roman shorthand symbol for Latin *et* 'and'.

apostrophe

Now a punctuation mark, apostrophe originally referred
to the omission of one or more letters; it comes via late
Latin from Greek *apostrophos* 'accent of elision', from
apostrephein 'turn away'.

asterisk

The Greeks had two words for 'star', *astēr* and *astron*.
They go back to an ancient root that is also the source

of the Latin word *stella*, which gave us **star** itself and
also **stellar**. An asterisk is a little star, the meaning of its
source, Greek *asteriskos*. *Astēr*, source of the plant **aster**,
is also the root of *asteroeidēs* 'star-like', source of
asteroid, a term coined by the astronomer William
Herschel. Words beginning with *astro-* come from
astron such as **astronomy**. The Greek word it
descends from meant 'star-arranging'. An **astronaut**
is a 'star sailor' from Greek *astron* 'star' and *nautēs*
'sailor'.

brochure

Although now associated particularly with holidays,
brochure is a French word meaning 'stitching' or
'stitched work', for the first brochures were little
booklets that were roughly stitched together rather than
properly bound. The root, Latin *brocchus* or *broccus*
'projecting [tooth], something that pierces', connects
brochure with **broach** 'to pierce (a cask)' and **brooch**.
This was originally a variant of broach and meant a
skewer (as in **brochette**) and then an ornamental pin.
Broccoli is from the same source, which became *brocco*
'sprout, shoot, projecting tooth' in Italian, and then
broccoli 'little sprouts'.

calligraphy

This is from Greek *kalligraphia*, from *kallos* 'beauty' and
graphein 'write'. In **callisthenics** (US **calisthenics**) *kallos*
is combined with *sthenos* 'strength'.

ditto

A Tuscan dialect form of Italian *detto* 'said', from Latin *dictus*, is the root of ditto. In the 17th century it meant in Italian '(in) the aforesaid month'. English merchants began to use it in accounts and lists, where the word is usually represented by double apostrophes (ditto marks). In the later 18th century clothiers and tailors used it as shorthand for 'the same material', and a **suit of dittos** was a suit of the same material and colour throughout.

hyphen

This word came into English via late Latin from Greek *huphen* 'together'.

jot

Greek iōta (ι), the smallest letter of the Greek alphabet, gave us jot for a very small amount—'i' and 'j' being interchangeable in medieval writing. **Not one jot** or **not one iota** for none at all, reflects the warning given by Jesus in St Matthew's Gospel: 'Till heaven and earth pass, one jot or tittle shall in no wise pass from the law' (a tittle is a small stroke or accent). **To jot something down** appeared in the early 18th century and seems to have developed from the idea of a short sharp action as in writing a jot.

pen

The earliest type of pen was a feather with its quill sharpened and split to form a nib, and pen reflects this,

Writing

going back to Latin *penna* 'feather'. **The pen is mightier than the sword** appeared in the works of the Latin author Cicero in the 1st century BC. The origin of Old English pen in the sense of an animal enclosure is not known.

write

The idea behind write in the ancient Germanic languages was 'to score or carve'—people in northern Europe would have written first by inscribing letters on wood. The original meaning in Old English was 'to draw the shape of something'. If you say that something is **written all over someone's face**, you are echoing Shakespeare. In *Measure for Measure* Duke Vincentio says: 'There is written in your brow, Provost, honesty and constancy.'

Index

Index

357

Index

Index

Index

Index

Index

Index

Index

Index

Index

Index

Index

Index